PROVEN WOMEN WORKBOOK

A discipleship guide with an emphasis on sexual integrity

The battle for sexual integrity is fierce. You must be constantly on guard.
This study provides you with the tools necessary to be victorious.

The name for Proven Men Ministries, Ltd., was derived from our acrostic PROVEN WOMEN™ and stands for women who are stamped "proven" by the Lord because they are striving to be:

Passionate for God,

Repentant in spirit,

Open and honest,

Victorious in living,

Eternal in perspective, and

Networking with other *PROVEN Women.*

Those who have used this study and experienced lasting victory over addiction to pornography or related sexual issues have two things in common: They have developed the attitude that:

(1) pornography—or other sexual sin—is no longer an option, and

(2) they are willing to do whatever it takes—God's way this time.

You're invited to become connected with us and join our team. Plan to use this study to gain the necessary tools to stand firm yourself, while at the same time encouraging and being encouraged by other PROVEN WOMEN.

Published and printed in the United States of America by Proven Men Ministries, Ltd., Lynchburg, Virginia

First Edition

ISBN: 978-1-940011-23-3

Proven Women, Proven Woman, Proven Men, Proven Man, Proven Path, Proven Life, and the PROVEN term and acrostic are protected trademarks and service marks of Joel Hesch.

Scripture quotations marked (NIV) are taken from the NEW INTERNATIONAL VERSION (NIV): Scripture taken from THE HOLY BIBLE, NEW INTERNATIONAL VERSION ®. Copyright© 1973, 1978, 1984, 2011 by Biblica, Inc.™ Used by permission of Zondervan.

Scripture quotations marked (ESV) are from The ESV® Bible (The Holy Bible, English Standard Version®), copyright © 2001 by Crossway, a publishing ministry of Good News Publishers. Used by permission. All rights reserved.

Scripture taken from the New King James Version®. Copyright © 1982 by Thomas Nelson. Used by permission. All rights reserved.

Italics in Scripture quotations have been added by the author for emphasis.

Interior and Cover Design: 1106 Design

Proven Women Workbook / Joel Hesch.

1. Sex—Religious aspects—Christianity. 2. Temptation. 3. Christian women—Religious life. 4. Sexual Health Recovery.

PROVEN WOMEN WORKBOOK STUDY

A discipleship guide with an emphasis on sexual integrity

TABLE OF CONTENTS

Endorsement 4

Acknowledgments 5

Orientation to the Study 7

Foreword 11

Introduction...13

Week One Study 15

Week Two Study 45

Week Three Study 79

Week Four Study 111

Week Five Study 145

Week Six Study 173

Week Seven Study 205

Week Eight Study 235

Week Nine Study....................................269

Week Ten Study 299

Week Eleven Study.................................327

Week Twelve Study 353

Appendix A: Names of God 377

Appendix B: Attributes of God.............379

Appendix C: Book Recommendations...............382

Appendix D: Developing a Heart of Worship......383

Appendix E: The Armor of God............387

Appendix F: How Do I Feel?.................388

Appendix G: The Purpose, Practice, and Power
of Prayer of Proven Women 389

Appendix H: Network Partnerships,
a Key to Breaking Free from the
Grip of Pornography 381

Endnotes 395

ENDORSEMENT

"If you are one of the many women today who privately struggle with some form of sexual addiction, *Proven Women* is a much-needed, direct, and no-nonsense journey to freedom."

—Shaunti Feldhahn,
groundbreaking social researcher, and best-selling author of *For Women Only*

ACKNOWLEDGMENTS

Joel Hesch for his commitment to the Lord, allowing Him to work through his story to impact the lives of many.

Angela Hanson and Nicholas Liberto for their dedication to editing this workbook and leader's guide.

Allie Kapus for her writer-mind and support.

Amanda Richmer and 1106 Design for their genius in design.

Shane O'Neill for his careful collaboration in co-authoring this workbook.

The Lord for putting the right people together to make this happen. It is an honor to work for Him and with Him.

 # ORIENTATION TO THE STUDY

1. This study is based upon a five-day format, so begin on a Monday. Schedule a specific time each day to do the study. Most find that the first thing in the morning is best, even though it means getting up early. It sets a good tone for the rest of the day and prepares you to battle temptations. In addition, it can be hard to find blocks of time later in the day. However, if you simply cannot do it in the morning, be diligent in protecting whatever time you set. It may mean that you must cut out television, internet, or other entertainment or recreation.

2. The study is very intense because it addresses an intense problem. Plan on devoting forty-five minutes each day. The time it takes to cover everything varies greatly from person to person. Even if you spend forty-five minutes a day, you may find that you cannot complete all of the daily items. This is especially true if you are meditating upon verses and searching your heart. If you have time, you can review some of those items on the weekend. If not, that's okay. Don't beat yourself up. First, guilt and shame are already nooses around your neck that make throwing in the towel or escaping into fantasy appealing. Second, meeting with God is what changes you, not finishing all the work in this study. Therefore, guard against merely checking off homework instead of openly meeting with the Lord. The key point to remember is that you should seek quality and quantity of time meeting with the Lord. Again, don't be consumed with whether you finish the material. If you open your heart to meeting with the Lord each day for the time set, even completing one-half of the material each day is excellent.

3. It's best to use the study in a small group or with another woman. Healing will be thwarted if you use these materials just like reading another book or following the latest self-help program. In fact, one of the roots that keep you in bondage to sexually immoral practices is a lack of real intimacy with the Lord and other women. A Proven life depends upon developing close relationships and putting into practice what you are learning. Don't try to go it alone. It's crucial to seek out an accountability partner before starting the study. You should talk to her once a week, sharing your temptations, failures, and victories. Give her permission to ask you what your mind dwelt upon and how you struggled. Regardless of the level of her compulsion, ask her to do the study with you. She'll be glad she did.

4. Share daily with someone (your spouse if you're married, or a friend if you're single) the exciting things you are learning. Sharing spiritual truths wisely opens your heart to the healing power of God, and it strengthens and encourages others. The Bible says, "Confess your sins to each other and pray for each other so that you may be healed" (James 5:16).

5. Seek a broken spirit (soft heart). Feeling guilty is not the same as being repentant (Hebrews 12:16–17; 2 Corinthians 7:10). God only changes a willing heart that seeks after Him. Therefore, purpose to meet with the Lord to get to know Him. Yield your entire life to God, asking Him to conform your will to His. Commit to doing "whatever it takes" to be free from bondage to sin and enter into a new relationship with God. Accept that healing is a lifelong process, but one in which you'll experience victories along the way. Be committed to staying the course even as setbacks occur. Dedicate the next year to seeking the Lord and pursuing sexual integrity.

Many women struggle with sexual impurity—pornography, masturbation, lust, or fantasy—and many are trapped in bondage to it. Breaking free requires more than self-will. You need God's strength. Fortunately, He provides a path to lasting freedom. This material not only teaches you how to be on guard, but to trust in and rely upon God's power to live out sexual integrity. You'll learn how to embrace and apply the following six essential components of a **PROVEN** life:

P*assionate for God.* By taking the focus off yourself (including your rights and circumstances) and putting it onto the Lord, you'll discover the perfection and goodness of God, who deserves to be praised. Your newfound passion for the Lord replaces the lust for selfish desires and practices. During times of intimate worship, you'll experience God's very nature and receive His healing in all areas of your life.

R*epentant in Spirit.* Until seeing your conduct as wrong because it separates you from closeness to God, you won't truly want to change. Repentance is not self-manufactured, and it means more than merely having feelings of guilt or shame. Rather, it's a gift from God, granted to those who humbly seek Him with all of their hearts. True repentance includes both confessing sins and submitting to God, which leads to a changed life.

O*pen and Honest in communication with God and others.* One inward reason people turn to false forms of intimacy (like pornography, masturbation, or fantasy) is that it seems safer or easier than the work required in real, *open and honest* relationships. But your heart and soul inwardly long for true intimacy. Fortunately, God will enable you to fully trust. He will also teach you how to be open and to permit feelings to surface so you can engage in fulfilling and real relationships, instead of escaping into the false forms of intimacy that have ensnared you.

V*ictorious living in God's strength.* You cannot overcome temptation or defeat lust in your own strength. Yet, by daily guarding your heart and turning to Christ, you'll lead a victorious life. Each moment you yield to the Lord and rely upon His power, your actions become pure and holy, as He is pure and holy. He won't lead you into, but through temptation while in charge of your life!

Eternal in your perspective. Dwelling on the temporary (your present circumstances) leads to acting according to immediate thoughts and desires. Taking on an eternal perspective, however, brings hope and perseverance during temptations and trials. By looking to God's promises and allowing Him to be your guide, you'll live out integrity in all circumstances. You'll no longer be worn out from chasing temporary pleasures or defeated from the constant battle of trying to control life.

Networking with other PROVEN WOMEN. Christ always sent His disciples out two-by-two. Victory over an addictive behavior is not won alone. Other **PROVEN WOMEN** become great sources of encouragement and act as iron sharpening iron (Proverbs 27:17). Become part of the team.

Each of these six "letters" is vital for breaking and remaining free. This study helps you put them into place. If undertaken with humility and purposefulness, it will position you to have the Lord renew your mind, transform your heart, spark your soul, and change your desires. The work is challenging. It requires commitment, perseverance, and a willingness to do "whatever it takes" to meet with the Lord and receive His healing. Therefore, make a permanent and irrevocable decision to seek the Lord with all of your heart, mind, and body.

In the past, you have probably tried using your own strength. This is self-reformation, and it doesn't work. Now it's time to turn to and rely upon God. The study is sometimes referred to as *"Heartwork"* because it is designed to position you to meet with the Lord daily and be changed by Him. A person's sinful conduct changes only when her heart toward God changes. You'll be shown how to stop striving in your own power and how to give up control to the Lord. To be set free, you must really want to turn from sin and live out a **PROVEN** life of holiness in dependence upon the Lord. This is the beginning of a fulfilling relationship with the one True God who loves you and the start of lasting freedom from the bondage of sin.

We highly recommend that this study be used by a small group or two women working through it at the same time. Although each woman works independently through the study every day, the two should gather on a weekly basis to share their struggles and victories while discussing what they are learning. *Networking* is a vital component to getting the most out of the study.

You should note that *networking* with other women means more than surface relationships, which is the same style of relating that has led you to false forms of intimacy. That's why you must avoid the temptation to go without true accountability. Otherwise, you'll simply move on to the next book or program and continue relying on your own strength. There is something powerful about regularly confessing sins and sharing your trials that helps free you from guilt, shame, and other traps that keep you from meeting with the Lord and experiencing His healing. In other words, there are two important parts of guarding your heart. The first is turning to the Lord in devotion and dependence, and the second is linking up with other women with whom you are being vulnerable, open, and honest about your feelings, challenges, and direction in life. Also, keep this eternal perspective: Healing is a lifelong process. Undoing years of habits and backward thinking (following the ways of the world instead of the Lord) won't just happen overnight, and it shouldn't end in twelve weeks. It takes time and effort to implement into your life the characteristics associated with being stamped Proven. Don't treat the study as a 12-week program or expect a quick fix. Those who want the easy way out or a list of things to avoid will not persevere or stand up under the trials of life that surely will follow. Instead, consider the study as a blueprint for daily guarding your heart. Before a builder starts construction, she carefully examines the blueprint, and during the building process she keeps referring to the plans. You should return to this study and continue doing other Bible-based studies for the rest of your life.

Won't you join with us by purposing to become God's friend and be transformed by Him each day? Leading a Proven life is all about humbly seeking and relying upon the Lord and developing the spiritual disciplines leading to newness of life. When you strive for sexual integrity, God will give you His power and strength to live out your commitment to purity, love, and devotion.

Our supporters made this resource possible.

As you begin this journey and start experiencing breakthroughs and victory, we want you to know that the generous support of faithful men and women like you made this study a reality. It is our vision to provide life-transforming resources to every man and woman who wants to experience lasting victory from the strongholds of pornography and sexual addictions by partnering with local churches to offer our studies combined with accountability and ongoing discipleship. As a non-profit organization, our work is not possible without donations from like-minded individuals, companies, and foundations. Therefore, if this study proves to be a blessing to you, we ask that you prayerfully consider blessing others by becoming a ministry partner through your financial support. You can learn more and make your gift at our website: *www.ProvenWomen.org.*

 **FOREWORD**

I was in the adult film industry for seven years of my life. Like many people, I was searching for love and acceptance. I was searching for the right things, but I was searching for them in all the wrong places. For many years, I believed the lie that sex and promiscuity were empowering, that I was somehow more loved if a man would sleep with me. This very lie is what led me into the porn industry; this lie is also what is leading the secular world today and sadly much of the church. The truth is, we are not empowered through sex, nor how desirable we are to the opposite sex. We are empowered because of who we are in Christ. It took me nearly twenty-six years of my life to discover this truth.

I thought I would find what I was looking for in sex, fame, and money; but after seven years in the porn industry I was left more broken than before. I had become a full-blown drug addict, doing whatever drug I could get my hands on. My life was a mess. In December 2012, I was on an airplane flying to film a porn scene in Las Vegas when I decided to open up a Bible I had been given three years prior at a church service I had attended with my grandparents. I turned to Revelation 2:20–24 (NIV). It said, "Nevertheless, I have this against you: You tolerate that woman Jezebel, who calls herself a prophet. By her teaching she misleads my servants into sexual immorality and the eating of food sacrificed to idols. I have given her time to repent of her immorality, but she is unwilling. So I will cast her on a bed of suffering, and I will make those who commit adultery with her suffer intensely, unless they repent of her ways. I will strike her children dead. Then all the churches will know that I am he who searches hearts and minds, and I will repay each of you according to your deeds."

Wow! What a scripture to digest just hours before I had to shoot a sex scene. I began to cry on the airplane and I asked God for forgiveness. Out of deep conviction, I quit the porn industry that day. I knew if this wasn't the lifestyle God wanted me to lead, then He must have something far greater for me in store. So, I began to search for God daily through the Bible, prayer, worship, fasting, and church. When I sought God, I found Him, and in Him I found everything my heart had been longing for. God has set me free! In fact, I am now married, and my husband and I travel the world preaching on purity because this was something we lived out. The day I fully gave my life to the Lord is the day I committed my purity to Him. My husband

and I waited for marriage and didn't dabble in porn or masturbation. This is good news, friends, because if I can do it then so can you. Remember, with God nothing shall be impossible.

Jeremiah 29:13 (ESV) says, "You will seek me and find me, when you seek me with all your heart." This is why I love Proven Women! Proven Women is a 12-week study guide that will guide you directly to the heart of God. This book will inspire you to seek God for what only He can provide you with, lasting fulfillment and complete deliverance. You can't do this on your own, you need Jesus just as much as all of us. *Proven Women* gives you a powerful blueprint to follow that has the breath of God all over it. I believe over the next twelve weeks you will become a brand-new woman! You will find healing, the strength to forgive, and as you grow closer to God He will empower you to conquer the sin that has been conquering you. Are you ready for freedom? Because freedom is what you have to look forward to through the work God will do in you through *Proven Women*.

Evangelist & Public Speaker
www.BrittniDeLaMora.com

Brittni is a wife, young adults ministry leader, and passionate advocate for women involved in the sex industry.

At the pinnacle of her career in the adult entertainment industry, she had acquired fame, money and success by having landed over 250+ roles in film. However, the prominent memories she recalls during this time were the deepest, darkest days of despair leading her to survive by way of drugs, alcohol, and ultimately, failed suicide attempts.

It was through a divine series of events, she began to encounter the love of God and that became substantial enough for her to make a dramatic, unexpected decision by all who knew her to leave the industry overnight once and for all.

Now she travels around the world with her husband, Richard, preaching the gospel, and sharing the love of God that set her free and is a firm believer if He did it for her He can do it for anyone else who would just believe in Him.

 # INTRODUCTION

D o you ever feel a stirring? A restlessness? Like you are searching for something and it is just a little beyond your fingertips? Perhaps you can't even figure out what it is you are searching for, but if you could just get a glimpse of it, then you could identify it and run after it and grasp it or achieve it or master it or receive it, or whatever it is you are trying to do. Maybe you will gain "it" through a person, or a relationship. Maybe a new status or title like mother, wife, employer, minister, leader. Maybe it will be through an achievement. Maybe... just maybe someday you will feel settled, content, arrived, enough, done. We will do whatever it takes to settle this restlessness. Whatever it takes to become... to be... to achieve... It is hard to come across the right word, because the goal is fleeting, beyond my reach, even to identify.

Each of us longs for a perfection that will not be reached in this lifetime. A perfection that existed before time began. God took this perfection and crafted it into a beautiful, magnificent world full of harmony, joy, peace, and—well, there are just no words, which is why it is hard to articulate this longing in my soul. I long for something for which I can only hope and not yet know.

Sin destroyed this perfection, and it has been destroying this world and each one of our hearts since that time. There is a war raging inside each and every one of us. We long for this perfection. We long for holiness. We long for Jesus. But anytime our eyes get off of Christ, there is a glorified mirage that will do anything to get our attention. Each of our mirages may look different, but they still are all mirages, a false image which promises something it will not deliver. I know I am not the only one who feels this way, because whether or not we realize it, desire is the very thing that drives us.

If you are reading this book, it is probably because the mirage that has drawn you is some sort of sexual sin. My heart aches for you, that you have been struggling, but I am so grateful that you are seeking freedom. God longs to help you find this freedom, and my prayer is that this book will be a journey for you, God, and others that you invite to come along. Please do not be afraid to invite others. Contrary to popular opinion, you are not the only lady who is struggling with porn, masturbation, one-night stands, sexual relationships or what have you. There are women all around you who feel as trapped as you do. This journey with God is much better alongside others.

For many years, we have heard lust addressed as a male issue, but that simply is not true. It is not a male issue. It is a human issue. Women all over the globe struggle with lust. Symptoms include pornography, masturbation, premarital sex, adulterous affairs, fantasies, same-sex attraction, and unhealthy relationships. The problem is, when a woman hears that this is a man issue, yet knows that she struggles with it, she feels like she is the only one. Oftentimes, she will not seek out help due to shame and embarrassment. I believe this is a tactic of Satan. When he uses shame to keep a sin hidden, there is a much better chance that person will remain enslaved to that sin. So many women struggle in isolation, completely unaware that some of their closest friends would not only listen to them and understand, but have their own confession to give as well.

Women get into this sin in different ways and for different reasons. Some were introduced to porn at a young age and quickly became addicted. Some were introduced to sexual practices through sexual abuse. Others are single and feel helpless in finding intimate love. Starved for affection, they seek pleasure through their own means. Others may be married and the marriage is not living up to their expectations, so they escape into fantasy, porn, and masturbation. Others have no idea why. There really isn't an explanation, just somewhere along the way they got tripped up with temptation, and here we are. First, I want to say, "Welcome. You are not alone. And there is hope."

PW

WEEK ONE

TESTIMONY

"I remember once a year at church there would be a weekend where the girls all went into one room and the boys in another. The girls would talk about modesty, body image, and self-esteem issues; the boys, sexual immorality and pornography. The first time I saw pornography I was eight years old. I just happened to stumble upon it one night when I was up way too late watching television. From then on, all the way through college I struggled with lust and pornography. I hated myself for it. I would go to that meeting once a year at church and think, why don't I have body image issues like the other girls, and WHY do I struggle with what the boys struggle with? What is wrong with me?

In my struggle, I chose not to talk to anyone. After all, I thought I was weird! Why am I, a girl, struggling and enslaved to this thing that is supposed to be a male issue? I felt so alone. In my junior year of college, I began praying that God would strip me of my desires. I would go to bed and wrap the bed sheets around my wrists and hold on to the bedpost to keep myself from giving in. This went on for months, and I can honestly say the only person that saved me from myself was Christ Jesus. No plot twist there. Once I broke from my addiction I felt free, free in Christ, and free to start talking about it. Once I did, the result was astounding, I wasn't alone, other girls struggled as well!

The enemy so desperately wants us to feel alone. He succeeds every day with girls that struggle with lust and are too ashamed to admit it. The majority of the girls that I have spoken to have said, 'I actually struggle with that too. Wow, I've never told anyone that.' It is so important that we know that we are not alone. Christ has designed us for community and he intends that we lean into it. I praise God every day for bringing me out of my enslavement, but I can't stress enough how much easier the journey would have been if I had fellow Christians alongside me to help and guide me through."

Passionate for God,
Repentant in spirit,
Open and honest,
Victorious in living,
Eternal in perspective, and
Networking with other *PROVEN Women.*

MEMORY VERSE

Romans 8:1 (NKJV) "'There is therefore now no condemnation for those who are in Christ Jesus.'"

WEEK 1 DAY 1 (MONDAY)

Begin this morning by memorizing the weekly memory verse. Read through it several times. Over the next twelve weeks you'll be asked to memorize twelve short passages of Scripture. At the end of this study, you should be familiar with and even able to recite each one. Here's a helpful suggestion: Write the verses on 3×5 cards and take them with you wherever you go.

DAILY READING

As you go over the Daily Reading, be sure to mark up your page and jot down notes. You should not just gain knowledge, but engage in a time of reflection and plan out how to incorporate these things into your life.

This study is not a self-help program. We believe that one becomes free through growing in an intimate relationship with God through our Lord Jesus Christ. We do not want to assume that everyone who has picked up this book already has a relationship with Jesus, so we want to take this first day to walk through the gospel. This may be new to some of you. For those who have already made Jesus Lord in their life, please do not skip this section. The gospel is never something we move beyond, only something we fall deeper in love with. We will walk through this in four parts: Creation, Fall, Redemption, and Completion.

CREATION

Many of you probably know the beginning of this story. In the beginning, God created the heavens and the earth. He created the beauty and majesty of the ocean, mountains, and sunsets. He made all of the animals, birds, and fish. Then He made man in His image. He said it was not good for man to be alone, therefore, he fashioned woman as a companion for man. This shows that He designed for all of mankind to be in community. He wanted

WEEK 1 · · · · WEEK 2 · · · · · · · WEEK 3 · · · · · · · · WEEK 4 · · · · · · · · WEEK 5 · · · · · · · WEEK 6 · · · · · · · WEEK 7 · · · · · · · WEEK 8 · · · · · · · · WEEK 9 · · · · · · · · WEEK 10 · · · · · · · WEEK 11 · · · · · · · WEEK 12

DAY 1

us to be in perfect harmony with Him and with each other. In Genesis, after he creates everything, including man, we are told that creation was very good. Within God's design, He also thought through and created relationships. God created husband/wife, father/daughter, brother/sister, friendship and so forth. These relationships were meant to be beautiful, fulfilling, and symbolic of His relationship with us. God made us to be intimate beings, able to fully trust God and each other. I wish I could have seen life back then. It was perfect, beautiful, and good.

FALL

Unfortunately, that is not what we experience today. In the midst of all of that perfection, God gave man free will. Adam and Eve, the first man and woman, sinned against God, and sin has been in the world ever since. We are born into a broken world and we ourselves are broken. Here are a few verses that show us our current condition.

"Therefore, just as sin came into the world through one man, and death through sin, and so death spread to all men because all sinned" (Romans 5:12, NIV).

"For all have sinned and fall short of the glory of God" (Romans 3:23, NIV).

"And you were dead in the trespasses and sins [2]in which you once walked, following the course of this world, following the prince of the power of the air, the spirit that is now at work in the sons of disobedience—[3]among whom we all once lived in the passions of our flesh, carrying out the desires of the body and the mind, and were by nature children of wrath, like the rest of mankind" (Ephesians 2:1–3, NIV).

Those are some very hard things to hear. We were dead in our sin walking through this world following after Satan. Because of that, God had wrath and anger stored up against us. Just as a loving father has very real anger toward someone when they hurt or threaten one of His kids, God has righteous anger when He sees us sin against one another. This is saying that our natural self turns us away from God and makes us His enemy. Because God is so holy and righteous, we were separated from knowing Him. Fortunately for us, this passage does not stop there. Ephesians 2:4 gives us two beautiful words, "but God."

"But God, being rich in mercy, because of the great love with which he loved us, [5]even when we were dead in our trespasses, made us alive together with Christ—by grace you have been saved—[6]and raised us up with him and seated us with him in the heavenly places in Christ Jesus, [7]so that in the coming ages he might show the immeasurable riches of his

WEEK 1

WEEK 2 ..... WEEK 3 ...... WEEK 4 ...... WEEK 5 ...... WEEK 6 ...... WEEK 7 ...... WEEK 8 ...... WEEK 9 ...... WEEK 10 ...... WEEK 11 ...... WEEK 12

DAY 1

grace in kindness toward us in Christ Jesus. [8]For by grace you have been saved through faith. And this is not your own doing; it is the gift of God, [9]not a result of works, so that no one may boast. [10]For we are his workmanship, created in Christ Jesus for good works, which God prepared beforehand, that we should walk in them" (Ephesians 2:5–10, NIV).

REDEMPTION

My sister, God has seen the sin in your life. He sees how broken you are. Because He is righteous and just, He cannot just look the other way when we sin. Sin has to be dealt with and justice granted. For each of us, that justice looks like eternal separation from God. He also knows that we cannot become good enough on our own, but God loved us too much to allow anything to separate us from Him. So, out of His love for us, He sent Jesus, His one and only son to earth. Jesus, fully God and fully man, lived a perfect life, then died on the cross. While on the cross, Jesus took all of our sin onto Himself. Jesus stood in the gap with us. He died and was buried, but three days later He conquered sin and death by rising from the dead. He then returned to heaven and is seated at the right hand of the throne of God. Jesus is no longer suffering on your behalf. He has already defeated your sin and empowers you to live in victory. But we cannot see the beauty of the resurrection until we sit with Jesus before His cross.

RESTORATION

Once you have become His child, God desires for you to become the person He created you to be. He wants to see you transformed into His image, into His character. He is patient and consistent as He works with you. This will be a lifelong process. Philippians 1:6 (ESV) "And I am sure of this, that he who began a good work in you will bring it to completion at the day of Jesus Christ." He is refining us and transforming us to live this life the way He designed it to be, in harmony with God and one another.

There will be a day in the future when all of those who have put their faith in Christ will be fully restored. Jesus has promised to return for those who are His. God will make a new heaven and new earth and we will live for eternity with God. All relationships will be as they are meant to be. We are called to place our hope in Jesus' restoration of all things. But we don't have to wait to start the restoration process. God is in the midst of restoring you now. We will learn a lot more about this process as we journey through this book together.

SALVATION

If you have not yet given your life to Christ, what do you need to do to ask Jesus to be your Savior? The Bible says, "If we confess our sins, He is faithful and just and will forgive us our sins and purify us from all unrighteousness" (1 John 1:9, ESV). Jesus will not reject you. You can know this because Jesus was rejected on the cross for you. Everyone who turns to Jesus and believes in Him becomes a child of God and therefore inherits eternal life in this age and in the age to come (John 1:12). This includes you and me, but you must personally ask for and accept the free gift of forgiveness. He died for you and He wants to know you.

If you turn to Jesus and accept His shed blood as the perfect sacrifice and substitute for your penalty, you're no longer considered impure, no matter what wrong things you've done or will do. God the Father will not reject you because His Son already paid the full penalty of death for all your sins.

Right now, go to God with a surrendered heart. You'll be asking Jesus, who paid the death penalty that you deserve, to forgive you and to enter your heart. Ask Him for His grace and mercy. He wants to give it to you.

To ask Jesus into your heart and accept God's righteousness, pray something like this:

> God, I know that I am a sinner and deserve death. I know that Jesus is God and that He died on the cross to rescue me from the penalty of my sin. Please forgive me. I receive the free gift of eternal life, which comes solely from the perfect sacrifice of Jesus Christ for my sin. I pray and ask You, Jesus, to come into my heart right now and to make it Your permanent home. Take total control of my life. I choose to follow You and to turn away from sin, including my former lifestyle. Thank You for loving me and forgiving me. I commit to following You forever. In Your precious name, Jesus, I pray these things. Amen.

These are not magic words that save you if repeated. The important part is to bow before God as the good, Holy Father and repent of your sin, accepting Christ as the sacrifice needed on your behalf. If you prayed this prayer with your heart, then congratulations! You're my eternal sister in Christ. You're free from the power of death. Jesus now permanently lives in you, and you're God's child.

Write out John 17:3.

_____

_____

JESUS AS LORD

It's now time to daily make Jesus the Lord of your life. That's the key to sexual integrity. You've taken a very important step. You've realized that you cannot win the battle on your own. You've probably tried many times and failed, but you're finally on the right track. You see, your battle is not about using more of your own power or even about overcoming bad influences. Instead, it's a spiritual battle. In fact, the Bible teaches that "our struggle is not against flesh and blood, but against the rulers, against the authorities, against the powers of this dark world and against the spiritual forces of evil in the heavenly realms" (Ephesians 6:12, NIV).

The only way to stop being a slave to sin is to rely on Jesus Christ. These are more than just words. When you need forgiveness, power, and strength, you go to the source of forgiveness, power, and strength: Jesus, His cross, and resurrection. His power is available to you through the Holy Spirit, so turn and yield your entire life to Him.

"But you will receive power when the Holy Spirit has come upon you, and you will be my witnesses in Jerusalem and in all Judea and Samaria, and to the end of the earth" (Acts 1:8, NIV).

Now the journey begins. You never travel alone! A wonderful by-product of having an intimate relationship with God is victory over sins, including sexual immorality. Jesus desires to take control of your life and lead you in His holy and pure ways. The power of the Holy Spirit is ready, willing, and more than able to lead you victoriously if you let Him; but you must want to love and serve God more than your former selfish and prideful ways. You need to start hating sin because it blocks your relationship with Jesus Christ.

Making Jesus Lord over your daily life is what being on the Proven Women team is all about. Each day you wake up, you give control to the Lord. Throughout the day, you test your thoughts and actions against the six PROVEN letters:

Passionate for God

Repentant in spirit

Open and honest

Victorious in living

Eternal in perspective

Networked with other PROVEN Women.

WEEK 1 ... WEEK 2 ..... WEEK 3 .... WEEK 4 .... WEEK 5 .... WEEK 6 .... WEEK 7 .... WEEK 8 .... WEEK 9 .... WEEK 10 .... WEEK 11 .... WEEK 12

DAY 1

Proven Women, in its most basic form, is a guide to being Jesus' disciples. Plan to link together with other Proven Women as you learn how to live out a Proven life. It's a journey you never have to face alone because you're part of the family of God and Proven Women. You've lived for yourself and that has left you empty. Today we hand our lives over. We commit to being His disciples—to knowing His cross and resurrection.

HEARTWORK

Every day, we will ask you to spend some time in prayer, talking with God. The entire purpose of this Bible study is to help you develop an intimate relationship with God. Prayer is simply talking openly and honestly with God. If you have placed your faith in Jesus, then He grants you access to God the Father. But just like any relationship, we need to spend time with Him. God is always with you, and seeking Him in this truth will help us know Him throughout the day. God is always listening to your prayers. Pray with humility and sincerity to deepen your relationship.

Hebrews 5:7 (ESV) says, "In the days of his flesh, Jesus offered up prayers and supplications, with loud cries and tears, to him who was able to save him from death, and he was heard because of his reverence."

Spend some time talking with God. If you just prayed to ask Jesus to be your Savior, then spend some time thanking Him for this new relationship. If you already have a relationship with Christ, thank Him for the years that you have known Him. Ask Him to help you get to know Him more and to love Him more

Write out the areas of your life that you haven't acknowledged Him in. Invite Him into those places.

_____

_____

_____

MEMORY VERSE

Romans 8:1 (NKJV): "'There is therefore now no condemnation for those who are in Christ Jesus.'"

WEEK 1 DAY 2 (TUESDAY)

KEY THOUGHT: God is always for us and will never stop pursuing us.

DAILY READING

Throughout this study, you are going to hear that you will need to rely on God in order to see victory in your life. This, however, is impossible if we do not have an accurate view of God. As we saw yesterday, we cannot earn our way to heaven and need Christ as our Savior. If you are a Christian, then hopefully you understand this. In my experience, however, even those of us who see our need for Christ as our Savior may still not understand how God's grace affects our current relationship with Him.

I want to be very clear that the view I am about to describe about God is a false view, and it's a very common false view. Although we rely on Jesus' death and resurrection to be able to go to heaven someday, many believe it is still up to us to maintain and keep God's favor in our life. Perhaps we picture God far away, watching from a distance. His eyes are constantly on us, he knows exactly what we are doing, and he is always judging. It's almost as if we live on a pedestal that goes up and down based on how well we are behaving. If we read our Bible and pray we go up a few notches. Help somebody out and we go up another notch. Lead someone to Christ and we go up several notches. On the contrary, if we are negligent in these spiritual disciplines, then our pedestal slowly sinks lower and lower. If it seems like it is getting too low, we try to jump back into reading our Bible and praying, hoping we didn't drift too far down.

If we do a "big sin" like premarital sex, going to a drunken party, or caving once again to the temptation of pornography and masturbation, then we crash and burn. At this point, we are still saved, but we feel like we have to start all over again in our relationship with the Lord. He looks on us with disgust and disappointment in His eyes. During these low times, we often feel like we are still expected to pray, but we do not expect God to listen to us. We are still expected to open our Bible and read, but we do not expect God to speak to us. We are still expected to go to church; however, we feel like a hypocrite if we raise our hands in worship. But if we keep doing these things—reading our Bible, praying, worshiping—then we feel like we are working our way back into God's good favor. Once we get our pedestal high enough that He likes us again, then He will be there to help us overcome temptation, but until then, we are not worthy of His help, so we are on our own. It is exhausting and discouraging to do it on our own, and we will just keep failing.

Praise the Lord this view is completely and utterly false. God's grace is not just a gift to get to heaven. It is also the gift of a relationship with Him that is based on Christ's righteousness and not our own. I've mentioned righteousness before. What is it? It's basically a fancy word for right-standing. Jesus is God's perfect child and because Jesus died for us, we don't have to earn that right-standing by proving ourselves worthy. He made us worthy. That's amazing news, because we *couldn't* earn right-standing with God if we had to on our own.

Hebrews 4:14–16 tells us that we can boldly come before the throne of grace to receive grace and mercy in our time of need. Many times in the past, when I read that verse I only felt confident to come to Him when I felt worthy. I reworded it in my mind, come boldly before the throne when you are at your best. Other times, when I knew I was struggling, I would cower in my shame and avoid Him. These verses, however, are calling us to come boldly to Him for grace and mercy in our time of need. We are always in need of grace and mercy, but especially in our time of sin and temptation.

We have more to battle than our own sin-nature. We'll talk more about him in week 4, but for now, you need to know that we have an adversary. Our adversary wants you to feel like you have to do this on your own in order to please God, but that is the complete opposite of the gospel. God stands before you with arms open wide begging you to run to Him in order to receive His strength, His mercy, His forgiveness, and His cleansing that you need in order to live in victory. Remember, this is not because sin is not a big deal, but because Christ took all of that shame on Himself on the cross. And He did this for you. He did this so that you would have the freedom to sprint to God in your moments of need. In victory, we run to be held by Him. In sin, we turn so that we can be held by Him. There is no losing. My sister, please do not buy into the lie that God is angry at you and holding you away at a distance. He will not give you the silent treatment or a cold shoulder. He will not ignore you. He absolutely loves you and longs for you to give Him your entire heart. He does this because he wants to be loved completely by you, and He also knows that this is best for you. This is both all for His glory as well as for you. God is that good!

HEARTWORK

Look at how you have been living the past few days. How have you been doing with lust?

_____

_____

_____

_____

Based on this, how do you think God views you? Don't just give the right answer. Give the honest answer that comes to mind. In order to embrace truth, we have to be aware of any lies that may be lurking in our minds. If you discussed this in your group this past week, hopefully your perspective of God's view of you is starting to be transformed. If so, how is your perspective changing?

_____

_____

Whether you are doing well or really struggling, if you have given your life to Christ, God bases His view of you on Christ's righteousness, not your own. Your status is not dependent on your actions. His love for you is consistent. But we must be careful that we do not allow this view of grace to give us the impression that we have the freedom to continue in sin.

Without using religious vocabulary, write out what you love most about Jesus.

_____

_____

WEEK 1 ...... WEEK 2 ...... WEEK 3 ...... WEEK 4 ...... WEEK 5 ...... WEEK 6 ...... WEEK 7 ...... WEEK 8 ...... WEEK 9 ...... WEEK 10 ...... WEEK 11 ...... WEEK 12

DAY 2

How freeing would it be if you knew that you could come clean about everything in your life, even the darkest corners of your heart, and that it would not change that person's view of you? That is what grace allows us to do with God.

READ THE BIBLE

Read Romans 5:18–6:14.

What does this say about grace?

_____

_____

What does this say about sin?

_____

_____

PRAY

Remember, if you have put your faith in Christ, Jesus gives you access to the Father. You don't have to fear whether God will accept you or not. You do not have to fear whether He is listening or not. Spend some time telling God about how you viewed Him in the past and spend time thanking Him for Jesus.

_____

_____

MEMORY VERSE

Romans 8:1 (NKJV): "'There is therefore now no condemnation for those who are in Christ Jesus.'"

WEEK 1 DAY 3 (WEDNESDAY)

KEY THOUGHT: God's design for our life is the best thing for us.

DAILY READING

God designed and perfectly created both male and female. A husband and wife complement each other. Marriage is a union, such a perfect fit that two become one (Ephesians 5:31). The master design was for a couple to permanently join together physically, mentally, emotionally, and spiritually. When entering into this lifelong commitment, the bride and groom make irrevocable vows that the union will never be broken, neither by divorce nor through the giving of oneself to any other.

How incredible is it that God designed such a perfect relationship as a representation of our permanent relationship with Christ? However, when we act outside of this union in ways such as premarital sex or wandering eyes, we reject God's gift in order to chase after temporary pleasure, which never really fully satisfies. All forms of lust, such as fantasy, porn, and masturbation, break down the bond of marriage and negatively affect our relationships with God and a spouse, even if it is a future spouse.

Why does God want you to live a sexually pure life according to His design? When the Lord tells you to be faithful to your spouse, you can be sure that it's for your own good as well as for His glory. God wants to protect you from harm. He knows that sexual immorality not only endangers your body, but also scars your soul and spirit. You pretend to know better and say, "No one is hurt" or "We both consented, so where is the harm?" But who knows the long-term spiritual damage better than God? Put an end to this by believing God and trusting in His Word. The Lord knows and desires what is best for you. Sexual misconduct

WEEK 1 ⬤ WEEK 2 ...... WEEK 3 .... WEEK 4 .... WEEK 5 .... WEEK 6 .... WEEK 7 .... WEEK 8 .... WEEK 9 .... WEEK 10 .... WEEK 11 .... WEEK 12

DAY 3

harms you in many ways. Surely guilt, shame, and shutting down your heart are among them. Other ways are more subtle. The pornographic images are stored in your mind and compete with your present real relationships. We also carry over perverted and adulterous thoughts and fantasies into marriage.

What real person could ever measure up to a fantasy? Your illicit lusts and fanciful expectations are self-centered and anti-relational. Over time you actually train yourself to be selfishly served and instantly gratified. You also discipline yourself to withhold love and feelings.

The evils you entertain also end up blocking your perfect union with God. When you chase after the idols of selfish pleasure, you build a dividing wall. The sign on your heart declares "Keep out!" or "Off limits." By walking in step with the world, you turn away from the One who created you and loves you most. Remember, God is still turned toward you and loves you. He has not distanced Himself from you because the cross has removed that barrier, but sin causes you to distance yourself from Him. You stop listening to God's voice, and you cannot discern His will. Your requests of God go unanswered because they are selfish and cold (James 4:3). You drift through life self-deceived, thinking that your ways can bring satisfaction.

Even though your soul cries out for divine union with God, you incorrectly interpret this yearning for self-gratification. You end up turning repeatedly to selfish and prideful indulgences which blind you to the beauty and perfection of God and His ways. Doubt about God's goodness creeps in. Like sheep we go astray, each to his own way (Isaiah 53:6). You deceive yourself into thinking that you know best and that all is well, but inside you rot.

What is the cure? Only by acknowledging and repenting from your sinful and selfish ways and running to God in an open and honest relationship do you allow God to repair the damage.

Fortunately, God is the Good Shepherd. He does not abandon the lost. Instead, He gently calls and encourages you to return to the safety and fulfillment of His green pastures. The Lord wants to supply every true need. As you respond and move toward Him, God cleanses you and heals your wounds. The Lord perfectly guides and protects His flock. He will renew and transform all who are willing. Will you respond to His call?

In what ways have you tried to design your life?

_____

WEEK 1   WEEK 2 ...... WEEK 3 ...... WEEK 4 ...... WEEK 5 ...... WEEK 6 ...... WEEK 7 ...... WEEK 8 ...... WEEK 9 ...... WEEK 10 ...... WEEK 11 ...... WEEK 12

DAY 3

HEARTWORK

Use your own words to explain why all sexual thoughts and activity that do not conform to God's intention grieve Him.

_____

_____

Will you agree with God that these things are wrong?

_____

_____

Read Ephesians 5:25–33. What strikes you and why?

_____

_____

God designed the union between husband and wife to be both emotional and spiritual. In God's perfect plan, marriage guides us to an understanding of how much Christ loves the Church. Just as Christ is faithful to, loves, and nurtures the Church, Christian men are to be totally faithful and devoted to loving and nurturing their wives. In the same way, as the Church is called to love Christ and be devoted and committed to Christ, wives in turn are to love and respect their husband with faithful devotion.

The "test" for purity is not whether it feels good or whether the other person consents, like premarital sex. In fact, all sexually impure thoughts or acts offend God and harm your spirit, regardless of your consent. Think about this for a moment. Write out how you feel Jesus is challenging you to live out sexual purity. How do you want to know purity in your life?

_____

_____

WEEK 1
WEEK 2 .... WEEK 3 .... WEEK 4 .... WEEK 5 .... WEEK 6 .... WEEK 7 .... WEEK 8 .... WEEK 9 .... WEEK 10 .... WEEK 11 .... WEEK 12

DAY 3

_____

_____

Because God is good and is loving, His design is always best for us. For example, His command that men and women have only one spouse (including in their hearts and thoughts) is not a burden, but a blessing. God knows that if you have a divided heart, you'll never have a trusting, safe, and fulfilling marriage. God also knows that your heart will not have true peace or contentment if you seek to serve two masters or are divided in your love and loyalty. Matthew 6:24 (ESV)—"No one can serve two masters, for either he will hate the one and love the other, or he will be devoted to the one and despise the other."

Will you decide today that you won't be divided between loving the world and loving God? God wants your heart devoted not just to good works or outward appearances, but to Him personally. He doesn't delight in sacrifices but in a broken and contrite heart (Psalm 51:16–17). Be fully devoted to pursuing intimacy with Christ. Keep drawing near to God, and He will draw near to you (James 4:8).

PRAY

"O" is for Open and Honest. Go to the Lord now in open communication. Tell Him about your struggle with pornography, masturbation, fantasies, or other sexual sins. Ask Him to show you how sin breaks His heart. Ask Him that it would break your heart too.

Are you being open with others when they ask you how you are feeling? Talk to God about it. Do you hide your feelings or pretend all is well?

- Ask the Lord to loosen your tongue to talk openly to Him and others. If you're afraid of doing this, tell Him why. He wants to hear from you.

- Ask God to reveal what walls you have built around your heart that block out God and others, and to show you how to tear them down. Be still and listen for a moment.

- If you are single, ask the Lord to help you understand purity in your singleness.

- If you are married, ask the Lord to make you a one-man woman who seeks purity (including thoughts) in your sexual relationship with your husband.

  o Pray for blessings and protection for your husband and for your family.

Keep praying for other Proven Women.

_____

_____

_____

_____

_____

READ THE BIBLE

Is God giving you new insights and revealing truth in your heart as you read the Bible? Ask Him to do so! Read Proverbs 5 slowly while asking God to meet with you. Don't worry about the role of the man versus the woman in this text. Ask God to bringing conviction wherever needed. As you read, consider not only on the temporary pleasures of fantasy or immorality, but on the high cost of dwelling on and chasing after the flesh (the world). Agree to listen to the Lord and allow other godly women to give you instruction as you strive to live out purity.

Special note to singles: Don't fall for the lie that you are incomplete if not married. In fact, the Bible says in 1 Corinthians 7:8 that it's good to be unmarried. Don't be deceived: Sexually impure thoughts and actions will not simply go away when you get married! Therefore, when reading about how married women should act in purity, don't shrug it off. Rather, be all the more committed to living in absolute purity right now by allowing the Lord to renew and transform your mind and by putting into place all six elements of a Proven life!

Some singles may have decided they will never marry, so they think they are justified in impure thoughts because they are not sinning against a future husband. Our top priority should be faithfulness to the Lord. For the forever single person, even though impure thoughts would not be sin against a husband, they would still be sin against God because He is the one calling us to purity. Jesus was pure in His singleness for us.

MEMORY VERSE

Romans 8:1 (NKJV): "'There is therefore now no condemnation for those who are in Christ Jesus.'"

WEEK 1 DAY 4 (THURSDAY)

KEY THOUGHT: We are made for community, but only intimacy with God will restore our broken soul.

DAILY READING

We live in a day and age that glorifies sex. People worship sex, are ruled by sex, rely on sex, and allow sex to define them. You cannot look anywhere without being bombarded by sexual images. Something that God designed as a sacred, intimate aspect of marriage has been distorted into a dark, sinful plague. Some may go to the other extreme, picturing sex as an evil to avoid at all cost. This view is also wrong. Sex is not evil; however, experiencing it outside of God's will and design is. What is sex? No, I am not going to give you an anatomy lesson, however, I will give you theology. Have you ever noticed that all relationships are symbolic of our relationship with God? God designed the father-daughter relationship and has adopted us as His daughters. He designed friendship and has called us friend. I think the most beautiful relationship is that of a husband and wife. Ephesians 5 tells us that husbands and wives represent Christ and the Church. Ephesians 5:31–32 (ESV) says, "'Therefore a man shall leave his father and mother and hold fast to his wife, and the two shall become one flesh.' This mystery is profound, and I am saying that it refers to Christ and the church.

God designed sex to express intimacy between a husband and wife. During sex, their bodies become one—completing one another in a unique way that allows them to reproduce. God also allows them to express their love to one another and to experience great joy and pleasure while accomplishing God's work of reproduction. In the same way, Christ loves the Church, and the Church hopefully loves Christ. We are unified as one as we express both love and intimacy while accomplishing God's work of bearing fruit. Sex is beautiful and it is symbolic. It is one of the most intimate and sacred things within God's creation. That is probably why Satan has worked so hard to twist, distort, and destroy it.

One question that single people need to ask is, what should be my current role with sex? I believe we are called to respect it and view it as sacred. It is not for our entertainment or humor. It is not for singles to experiment with or to see how much of it they can experience without crossing a line. We need to remember that this is symbolic of our intimacy with Christ. Jesus is not holding back from us.

At times, it can feel like something is missing in life. As Christians, we are whole and complete in Christ, yet there are times when in it still feels like there is a void. Singles often feel like a husband will fill this void. Those who are in relationships may be tempted to fill this void with their husband or boyfriend. When they fall short, there is a temptation to go elsewhere to fill it. This void, however, is meant to take us deeper and deeper in our relationship with God. It is not our place to fill it with false intimacy. If we take matters into our own hands and begin to feed this void with pornography, masturbation, romance novels, fantasies and unhealthy relationships, we have begun feeding a bottomless pit. The more it is fed, the hungrier it gets. The void becomes larger and becomes darker. It becomes a dungeon, a dark pit with chains and a slave master. We need to get out.

As a married woman, sex is meant to be a form of intimacy with our husband. We do not have the right to find sexual pleasure by any other means if it is not being currently fulfilled by our husband. Even sex within marriage is not about what you can get out of it. Both husband and wife are meant to give of themselves to each other. Sex is an expression of love to each other. When both are doing this, it obviously brings delight and pleasure to both husband and wife. This was never meant to be about our individuality but about the expression of intimacy within a relationship. However, our own selfishness and pride, along with influence of culture, have twisted sex into a personal endeavor. Because lust is about quenching a selfish desire for pleasure, it can bring a heightened sense of selfishness into marriage. Our husband becomes a means to bring us pleasure rather than someone we are devoted to loving and serving.

We need to be intentional about seeking our Creator's design and purpose for sex, since He is the one who created it for us. To go outside of His plan is destructive to self and to relationships, but it is also offensive to Him.

WEEK 1 · WEEK 2 ...... WEEK 3 ...... WEEK 4 ...... WEEK 5 ...... WEEK 6 ...... WEEK 7 ...... WEEK 8 ...... WEEK 9 ...... WEEK 10 ...... WEEK 11 ...... WEEK 12

DAY 4

How have you stepped outside of His plan?

HEARTWORK

Sexual sin is destructive and we need to get out. Here are some steps to freedom. Take some time to read through this and prayerfully ask yourself if you believe in and are living out each of these steps:

1. Trust that God's way is better.

    Remember, God is the One who designed life. We think we know what we want, but God understands our hearts so much better than we do. Isaiah 55:8–9 (ESV) says, "For my thoughts are not your thoughts, neither are your ways my ways, declares the Lord. ⁹For as the heavens are higher than the earth, so are my ways higher than your ways and my thoughts than your thoughts." He knows what will help us to heal and flourish. He wants to protect us from the destruction of sin. He also wants our hearts to be turned toward Him with love and trust. We were designed to worship Him and love Him with all of our heart, mind, soul, and strength. We will find that our heart is much more joyful and free when we do things His way. Confess how you have seen it wrong, ask God to redeem your imagination.

    _____

    _____

    _____

2. Repent and cry out to God for rescue.

    Trusting and following God is not natural for us, so where we have gone astray, we need to repent and call out to God. When we confess, He is faithful and just to cleanse and forgive us of our sin (1 John 1:9). Write specific hurts in your life.

    _____

    _____

    _____

3. Turn your heart toward Him with love and affection.

    We will talk about this more as we get into the study, but it is so important to find ways to stir our affection for the Lord. We are not meant to follow after God out of obligation, but because we love Him and want to follow Him. We love God more when we spend time with Him and get to know Him more. Which is why it is important to be in the Word frequently and to be open and honest with Him. This cultivates a deeper, more intimate relationship with our Creator. Ask God how He feels about you (Hebrews 12:2).

    _____

    _____

    _____

4. Cling to Him when your thoughts try to steer you back toward the darkness.

    Unfortunately, our minds and hearts are fickle. They often steer us back toward lustful thoughts, sometimes minute by minute. We need to remember that God is always there ready to embrace and empower us to overcome temptation and to forgive us if we have fallen into sin. Do not allow shame and fear to keep you from turning to God in those moments. List the ways God sees you and spend time delighting in what He says about you.

    _____

    _____

    _____

READ THE BIBLE

Read Psalm 40.

WEEK 1   WEEK 2 .... WEEK 3 .... WEEK 4 .... WEEK 5 .... WEEK 6 .... WEEK 7 .... WEEK 8 .... WEEK 9 .... WEEK 10 .... WEEK 11 .... WEEK 12

DAY 4

PRAY

Spend some time talking with God. Thank Him for how He has put such intentionality into the way He designed life and relationships. If you disagree with an aspect of His design, don't be afraid to admit that to Him. Ask Him to reveal to you how His design is good. Pray through each of the steps above. Spend some time praying for others as well.

If you are married, pray for your husband, that God will allow you to love Him and put His interests above your own. Ask God to help sex be an expression of your love rather than an expectation of what your husband can do for you.

If you are pursuing a dating relationship, ask God to shape your perspective and teach your heart to serve. Matthew 20:28 (ESV): "Even as the son of man came not to be served but to serve and to give His life as a ransom for many."

If you are single, ask God to help you be available to Him. Singleness is a gift because you are able to fully devote yourself to God, free of any obligation to a husband. Being single does not mean you are your own woman, free to revel in independence. 1 Corinthians 6:19–20 (ESV), "Do you not know that your body is a temple of the Holy Spirit within you? You are not your own, for you were bought with a price. So glorify God in your body."

_____

_____

_____

_____

_____

_____

WEEK 1

WEEK 2 ...... WEEK 3 ...... WEEK 4 ...... WEEK 5 ...... WEEK 6 ...... WEEK 7 ...... WEEK 8 ...... WEEK 9 ...... WEEK 10 ...... WEEK 11 ...... WEEK 12

DAY 4

MEMORY VERSE

Romans 8:1 (NKJV): "'There is therefore now no condemnation for those who are in Christ Jesus.'"

WEEK 1 **DAY 5 (FRIDAY)**

KEY THOUGHT: God is more intimate than your fantasy.

DAILY READING

Yesterday we talked through steps to overcoming sexual temptation.

- Trust that God's way is better.

- Repent and cry out to God for rescue.

- Turn your heart toward Him with love and affection.

- Cling to Him when your thoughts try to steer you back toward enslavement.

We have to believe that God's way is best and God created sex for marriage. Stimulating your sexual drive by outside sources (other than unselfish intimacy with your spouse) is improper and fuels a lust that cannot be quenched. Setting expectations of how often you must have some form of sexual release is living for self-gratification, which only sets your heart on a continuous pursuit to satisfy a nature that will always want more. What changes will you make as a result of these truths? Will these changes include considering others more important than yourself? Will they include taking on an eternal perspective? Write out your commitments.

_____

_____

_____

WEEK 1 WEEK 2.....WEEK 3.......WEEK 4.......WEEK 5.......WEEK 6.......WEEK 7.......WEEK 8.......WEEK 9.......WEEK 10.......WEEK 11.......WEEK 12

DAY 5

As women, sometimes we struggle with lust because we have such a deep desire to be loved and appreciated. Some people reading this may not be in a current relationship, and waiting is so difficult. Others may be in a marriage that feels loveless, and they feel like they have a right to give themselves pleasure since they are not finding it from their husband. The truth is, we are called to find the deepest part of our hearts touched by the love of Christ. I have had many girls tell me, "Emily, I know God loves me, and that's great, but I want 'someone' to love me. I am glad God loves me and is there for me in the spiritual world, but I want someone physical. I want real arms wrapped around me. God cannot hug me." During the time of waiting, it becomes tempting to take matters into our own hands and fulfill these desires through sexual sins such as pornography and fantasies.

It is true that God cannot give us a hug—but neither can pornography, a romance novel, a fantasy, or your own hands. Let me share with you my favorite definition of lust: "Desire becomes so easily twisted. I like it becomes I want it. I want it becomes I need it. I need it becomes 'God, you owe it to me,' which becomes 'never mind, I will just take it.'"[1] Satan would love nothing more than to make you distrust God and His design, so that he can lead you to destruction. That is exactly what Satan did with Eve in the garden. "Did God really say...? ... You won't die. God knows that when you eat it you will be like Him, knowing good and evil." Satan made Eve think God was holding out on her, and then he pointed her eyes to the very thing he knew would destroy her. But in that moment, he made her think it was the most desirous thing. How true is that in the struggle with lust? God gives us an amazing relationship with Him and the gift of sex and intimacy within marriage. Yet if we are asked to wait, Satan is close by and ready to suggest:

- God is holding out on you (even though He is protecting you).

- His love is not tangible (although it is more real than anything else you have experienced).

- Then he points your eyes toward the very thing he knows will destroy you—pornography, romance novels, masturbation, fantasies, one-night stands and unhealthy relationships.

To choose one of those things in the moment is to slap God in the face. It is as if to say, "Because You have not delivered, I am deciding that this momentary pleasure is more rewarding than Your love for me which You expressed by giving your all and laying your life down for me on the cross."

I know my words are extreme and paint a harsh picture, but they are true. Our sin destroys us while spitting in Jesus's face. That is why Satan loves sin so much and is relentless in His

WEEK 1 WEEK 2 ... WEEK 3 ... WEEK 4 ... WEEK 5 ... WEEK 6 ... WEEK 7 ... WEEK 8 ... WEEK 9 ... WEEK 10 ... WEEK 11 ... WEEK 12

DAY 5

pursuit of us. He absolutely hates God and he hates us. Why not kill two birds with one stone? He watches with bliss while our choices throw us into the pit and turn us away from the One who loves us and can rescue us. Then, while we are down, Satan accuses and showers shame on us, telling us we cannot turn to God in that moment because we are unworthy.

It is important for us to be aware of Satan's tactics and to also have an accurate view of God. One of Satan's tactics is to accuse. Many times, as we start toward sin, we begin to feel unworthy and distant from God and think we cannot go to Him for help. In times like this, we turn away from God and strive. We strive to overcome the sin and clean ourselves up so that we can return to God and to our relationship with Him. But the moment we turn away from God—game over—we just guaranteed failure. As we turn from God we are turning from the power that we receive from God to say "no" to sin and to be cleansed. We cannot clean ourselves up for God. We have to run to God who is the living water and He will cleanse us. We cannot save our own lives.

HEARTWORK

"[10]The thief comes only to steal and kill and destroy. I came that they may have life and have it abundantly. [11]I am the good shepherd. The good shepherd lays down His life for the sheep" (John 10:10–11, ESV).

"Humble yourselves, therefore, under the mighty hand of God so that at the proper time he may exalt you, [7]casting all your anxieties on him, because he cares for you. [8]Be sober-minded; be watchful. Your adversary the devil prowls around like a roaring lion, seeking someone to devour. [9]Resist Him, firm in your faith, knowing that the same kinds of suffering are being experienced by your brotherhood throughout the world. [10]And after you have suffered a little while, the God of all grace, who has called you to His eternal glory in Christ, will Himself restore, confirm, strengthen, and establish you. [11]To Him be the dominion forever and ever. Amen" (1 Peter 5:6–11, ESV).

"You are of your father the devil, and your will is to do your father's desires. He was a murderer from the beginning, and does not stand in the truth, because there is no truth in him. When he lies, he speaks out of his own character, for he is a liar and the father of lies" (John 8:44, ESV).

Do we realize that we are in a war? Satan does not go easy on us because we are women. He is out to destroy. God is here to rescue! Will you go to God today and ask for His help?

What are some insights about Satan that you need to be more aware of?

_____

_____

_____

_____

READ THE BIBLE

Read Romans 8. Write down all of the promises you come across.

_____

_____

_____

_____

Satan is trying to devour us, but God is for us and He is stronger. He helps us in our weaknesses. He will not condemn us while we are struggling, and He doesn't allow anything to separate us from His love. Remember, all of this is true because of the cross. Christ stepped in on our behalf and paved a way for us to God. Rely on Christ's righteousness to come to your Father.

WEEK 1 ....WEEK 2........WEEK 3........WEEK 4........WEEK 5........WEEK 6........WEEK 7........WEEK 8........WEEK 9........WEEK 10........WEEK 11........WEEK 12

DAY 5

PRAY

Spend at least five minutes talking to God right now.

- Ask the Lord to cause you to see and hate the ugliness of pornography, lust, sexual fantasies, and masturbation.

- Tell Jesus the things you're afraid of.

- Confess your selfishness (wanting to be first), self-sufficiency (wanting to be in control), self-gratification (wanting to be served), greed (wanting more), and pride (wanting it on your terms).

- Ask the Lord to be the Master and to make you a willing servant. (Include all of these things in your prayers every day this week.)

- Be sure to pray for other Proven Women that they, too, will hate sin. Write down their names as you pray. Be specific in your requests to God.

Write out your prayers below.

_____

_____

_____

_____

_____

_____

_____

_____

_____

PW

WEEK TWO

TESTIMONY

"I find the Proven Women curriculum so important. It allows us, as women, to know that we are not the only ones feeling this way. I am not the only woman who has struggled with sexual integrity, you are not the first, and neither of us will be the last. This curriculum lets women know that it is okay to struggle, but it is not okay to stay in your struggle. It lets you know that there is hope to change your life and the decisions you are making. We are all sinners and will continue to make mistakes, but thanks to God's mercy and grace we are forgiven. And as Christ followers we are given the choice to pick up our cross and follow him. If you are tired of the life you are living, choose today to give it all over to the Lord and choose to follow him."

Passionate for God,
Repentant in spirit,
Open and honest,
Victorious in living,
Eternal in perspective, and
Networking with other ***PROVEN Women.***

MEMORY VERSE

2 Timothy 2:22 (ESV): "So flee youthful passions and pursue righteousness, faith, love, and peace, along with those who call on the Lord from a pure heart."

WEEK 2 DAY 1 (MONDAY)

KEY THOUGHT: Sin hurts your relationship with God.

DAILY READING

Breaking the Grip of Lust—There is One Way Out!
Women are finally finding the courage to step up and seek deliverance from sexual bondage. This has been a hidden issue for so long and remains hidden for so many. Whether a woman has come forward or not, she often has a longing for freedom from sexual bondage. She shares this longing with Christ because he desires freedom for her as well.

It's important to state upfront that there are no magical formulas or quick fixes. However, there is a way out. The only road to freedom from sexual obsession is an intimate and daily relationship with Jesus Christ. Without that relationship, some form of sin will always tear you down. The good news is that Jesus loves you and wants to stand alongside you to free you. He wants to be an active part of your life. He created you in such a way that you would share your life with Him daily. Today's reading briefly explains the path for overcoming habits of sexual sin while striving toward a growing personal relationship with Christ.

Sexual Immorality Hinders Your Relationship with God.
God doesn't sit in heaven making up rules, waiting to punish you for breaking them. Instead, He purposefully created you in His image (Genesis 1:27) with the intention that you would not only love and worship Him (Matthew 4:10), but also be His child (John 1:12; 1 John 3:1) and His friend (James 2:23). The Lord is a personal God and is truly interested in a close and meaningful relationship with you.

WEEK 1 ..... WEEK 2 ..... WEEK 3 ..... WEEK 4 ..... WEEK 5 ..... WEEK 6 ..... WEEK 7 ..... WEEK 8 ..... WEEK 9 ..... WEEK 10 ..... WEEK 11 ..... WEEK 12

DAY 1

God's commandments are not designed to be a burden but to foster your relationship with Him so that you may prosper. Jesus tells you not to commit adultery in your heart (Matthew 5:27–28) or engage in other forms of sexual immorality such as lust, pornography, or masturbation, so you won't damage your relationships with Him and with others. He knows that in the end, these things lead you down the wrong path and produce shame, guilt, bitterness, hurtful feelings, emptiness, and loneliness. God wants you to avoid this pain. He calls you to be pure and holy because He is pure and holy (1 Peter 1:16). Jesus wants you to be like Him. That's what discipleship is all about.

When your thoughts or actions become self-centered, you move further away from your loving God. Sexual sins magnify this effect. Your body is a temple of the Holy Spirit who lives inside you if you have trusted in Jesus as your Savior. Therefore, sexual sins are sins against God's temple (1 Corinthians 6:18–20).

Listen carefully to what God is saying: "In view of God's mercy... offer your bodies as living sacrifices, holy and pleasing to God—this is your spiritual act of worship" (Romans 12:1, NIV). When you selfishly give yourself over to sexual desires, sex becomes your master—the focal point of your life. Jesus wants to be the center of your life. Each time you lust by masturbating, looking at pornography, or hooking up with someone in sexual immorality, you place God on a shelf and forget about the One who loves you and gave Himself for you. You turn away from Jesus and disregard the good things He alone can give. You also invite emptiness into your soul and effectively sabotage your own life.

The Root Problem

There is a deeper problem that must be addressed before bondage to sexual immorality will end. Masturbation, pornography, and sexual immorality aren't the sole sources of sin in your life. They are symptoms being fed by something else. There is a root that feeds all sin and keeps it alive. This holds true for all who face sexual struggles. The root cause is selfishness and the pride that accompanies it. *Selfishness* is choosing to appease your desires rather than choosing to obey Christ. *Pride* is thinking that you know what is best for your life better than God does. Both of these, when they work together breed entitlement, leading you to think that you deserve to be served and to have every desire fulfilled. Until you come to grips with the seriousness of selfishness and pride in your life and battle these root sins, you'll never really have lasting freedom from bondage to sexual immorality.

DAY 1

A good way to explain this is to look at your palm. In the center of your palm, imagine selfishness and pride. Each of your fingers, stemming from your palm, represents a sin, such as masturbation, lust, greed, pornography, and jealousy, flowing from selfishness and pride. Notice that selfishness and pride are fueling these sins. You may be able to fight against these sins individually, but it will be an ongoing, vicious battle because they are continually being fueled. It's not enough for you to merely remove a particular sin. It may be possible out of sheer determination to bend a finger and stop masturbating for months or years. Maybe you can even bend a few fingers at the same time. However, if you allow selfishness and pride to remain in your life, you'll still have barriers that block an intimate relationship with God, and the roots of sexual sins will still be present. Also, another selfish action, such as anger or jealousy, will likely take its place.

When you make it your goal to overcome a particular sexual sin, such as masturbation, you set your sights too low and aim at the wrong target. Failure is assured. You'll never be free from sexual bondage until you address selfishness and pride.

How do you stop being selfish and prideful? On your own, you cannot. That's why you must trust Jesus and turn complete control of your entire life over to Him. This is not merely a slogan or something for your ears to hear, and it's not about being more "religious." It's becoming a new person in Christ. The more you draw near to Jesus Christ and take on His character as your own, the less you'll be consumed with self-interest. When you live by following the Spirit of God, you won't gratify the desires of the sinful nature because the sinful nature is contrary to God's character (Galatians 5:16). It goes like this: The more you seek to love and follow Jesus, the less selfish and prideful you become. The more you withdraw from Jesus, the more self-centered you become—which leads to pursuing selfish pleasures such as lust. That's why there is no freedom from sexual immorality apart from having a real, personal, daily relationship with Jesus, one in which you seek Him with all of your heart.

When you commit sin, it often leads to feelings of guilt or shame. This, in turn, causes you to hide areas of your life. You walk away from God. Once separated, you continue to sin, heaping on more guilt and shame, leading to more hiding. Pretty soon, you're caught in a spiral leading even further downward. You also start to become numb to the sin as time goes on. The only road that leads to a restored relationship with God and freedom from the downward slope of sexual bondage is to walk the path that leads to experiencing Jesus Christ on a personal level, and becoming totally dependent upon Him each and every day.

WEEK 1...... WEEK 2 ...... WEEK 3........ WEEK 4........ WEEK 5........ WEEK 6........ WEEK 7........ WEEK 8........ WEEK 9........ WEEK 10 .... WEEK 11........ WEEK 12

DAY 1

HEARTWORK

Remember, Jesus is standing there with open arms ready to receive you, no matter what the condition of your heart is right now. He already stood in the gap for you, taking on your guilt and shame while absorbing God's judgment for you. There is a temptation to run to Jesus while clinging to our selfishness and pride, expecting Him to accept us while still expecting to be able to cling to our sin. He wants us to give Him the worst of ourselves. He will empower us and give us the strength to overcome. He loves us and is ready to rescue us in EVERY moment of temptation. 1 Corinthians 10:13 (NIV) says that, "No temptation has overtaken you that is not common to man. God is faithful, and he will not let you be tempted beyond your ability, but with the temptation he will also provide the way of escape, that you may be able to endure it."

You can trust Jesus with your life because Jesus has already given up His life to save yours. In the past, what has kept you from trusting Jesus?

_____

_____

Are you willingly turning to Jesus, ready to open your heart to Him? Why or why not?

_____

_____

Why is it important to remember the cross when you approach God with your sin?

_____

_____

WEEK 1 ..... WEEK 2 ..... WEEK 3 .... WEEK 4 .... WEEK 5 .... WEEK 6 .... WEEK 7 .... WEEK 8 .... WEEK 9 .... WEEK 10 .... WEEK 11 .... WEEK 12

DAY 1

READ THE BIBLE

Read Galatians 5.

List the works of the flesh: Circle any of the ones that seem to be a struggle in your life.

_____

_____

_____

List the Fruits of the Spirit.

_____

_____

_____

Take some time to picture the relationships in your life. How are the works of the flesh and the Fruits of the Spirit evident in your relationships? How are they affecting your relationships?

_____

_____

Do you want to have the Fruits of the Spirit? Why or why not?

_____

_____

_____

WEEK 1 .... WEEK 2 ...... WEEK 3 .... WEEK 4 .... WEEK 5 .... WEEK 6 .... WEEK 7 .... WEEK 8 .... WEEK 9 .... WEEK 10 .... WEEK 11 .... WEEK 12

DAY 1

Pick three Fruits of the Spirit and write out how you want them in your own life.

_____

_____

_____

 ## PRAY

* Ask the Lord to cause you to see and hate the ugliness of pornography, lust, fantasy, and masturbation.

* Ask Jesus how He wants you to trust Him.

* Ask Jesus to take away specific works of the flesh and to give you specific Fruits of the Spirit.

* Ask God to show you how to be His daughter.

* Be sure to pray for other Proven Women that they, too, will hate sin. Write down their names as you pray. Be specific in your requests to God.

Write out your prayers below.

_____

_____

_____

_____

_____

_____

_____

WEEK 1 ..... WEEK 2 ..... WEEK 3 ..... WEEK 4 ..... WEEK 5 ..... WEEK 6 ..... WEEK 7 ..... WEEK 8 ..... WEEK 9 ..... WEEK 10 ..... WEEK 11 ..... WEEK 12

DAY 1

MEMORY VERSE

2 Timothy 2:22 (ESV): "So flee youthful passions and pursue righteousness, faith, love, and peace, along with those who call on the Lord from a pure heart."

WEEK 2 DAY 2 (TUESDAY)

KEY THOUGHT: By being in a relationship with Jesus, He redeems every part of our lives, even our imaginations.

Yesterday, we read about our sinful nature and used the illustration of a hand: the palm representing the roots of selfishness and pride and the fingers representing different sins which stem off of these roots. This picture shows how sin is fueled by selfishness and pride. No matter how much you fight against sin in your life, if you do not deal with what is fueling it, it will always be a losing battle.

Today I want us to see a different picture, one that is used throughout Scripture.

READ THE BIBLE

John 15:1–17

What picture does Jesus give to His disciples?

_____

_____

In this picture, what does the vine represent?

_____

_____

WEEK 1...... WEEK 2 ...... WEEK 3........ WEEK 4........ WEEK 5........ WEEK 6........ WEEK 7........ WEEK 8........ WEEK 9........ WEEK 10........ WEEK 11........ WEEK 12

DAY 2

What do the branches represent?

_____

_____

How does this picture compare to the picture with the hand?

_____

_____

_____

_____

_____

DAILY READING

In this passage, Jesus is sitting with the disciples during His last week on earth before He was crucified. He had just had the Last Supper with them and washed their feet. This was a demonstration of His love for them and an example of how they were to love and serve one another. John 14–16 are the final thoughts He leaves with them before His crucifixion. It is within this context that we read about the vine and the branches. Jesus had the opportunity to live life and walk with these men for the previous three years. He knew these men and loved them, but He also knew His time with them was coming to a close. He would soon be accomplishing His chief assignment on earth, to conquer sin on the cross, after which He would conquer death through His resurrection. Then He would return to His home in heaven, but His work with His disciples was nowhere near complete.

He knew the plans He had for them, but He also knew that they would need Him as much after His departure as they had in the previous three years, if not more. He was showing them that even though He was not going to be physically with them anymore, He would still be available.

WEEK 1..... WEEK 2..... WEEK 3..... WEEK 4..... WEEK 5..... WEEK 6..... WEEK 7..... WEEK 8..... WEEK 9..... WEEK 10..... WEEK 11..... WEEK 12

DAY 2

He is the Vine and they are the branches. Apart from Him, they could do nothing. Acts 1:8 says that the disciples received power when the Holy Spirit came upon them.

It is the same for us. When we put our faith in Jesus, we receive the Holy Spirit and His power. When we abide in Christ—spending time with Him, meditating on His Word, talking with Him and trusting Him, we see His power in our lives. However, when we act on our own, apart from Christ, we will not see fruit. In fact, we will see the opposite. Yesterday, we read Galatians 5 and saw the two different lists—the works of the flesh vs the fruit of the spirit. The works of the flesh, including sexual sin, stem off of the root of selfishness and pride. It is so tempting to want to try to cut off the works of the flesh and empower ourselves to cultivate love, joy, and other fruit on our own. Do we see that apart from Christ we are powerless? If we saw a branch with rotting fruit laying on the ground by itself, we would know that the branch can do absolutely nothing to cut off the rotting fruit and start growing good fruit. It cannot fix itself. In the same way, we cannot fix ourselves. On our own, we cannot cut out evil and begin producing fruit on our own. John 15 explains that Christ is the vine and God Himself is the Vine Dresser. If we go to God and confess our sins, He is faithful and just to forgive and cleanse.

God is the one who can prune us. At times, the pruning may hurt, but He does this out of love for us. Maybe you're going through that right now. He looks at each of us and sees not only who we are right now, but who He created us to be. He is for us and will do whatever it takes to cultivate His fruit in our life. Read verse 16 (NIV) again, "You did not choose me, but I chose you and appointed you that you should go and bear fruit and that your fruit should abide, so that whatever you ask the Father in my name, he may give it to you." Do you realize that you were chosen for a purpose? God chose you so that you would bear fruit, and He is committed to His investment. Philippians 1:6 (NIV) says, "He who began a good work in you will carry it on to completion until the day of Christ Jesus."

In our picture with the hand and the fingers, sin results from the source of selfishness and pride. Jesus gives a much better picture. When we abide in Him, we are like a tree bearing fruit. He is both the root and tree and we are just branches. Yet when we allow ourselves to be fully connected to Him, we will see vibrant fruit in our lives. He will breathe life back into us.

WEEK 1 ...... WEEK 2 ...... WEEK 3 ...... WEEK 4 ...... WEEK 5 ...... WEEK 6 ...... WEEK 7 ...... WEEK 8 ...... WEEK 9 ...... WEEK 10 ...... WEEK 11 ...... WEEK 12

DAY 2

Psalm 1:1–4 (ESV)

> Blessed is the man who walks not in the counsel of the wicked,
> nor stands in the way of sinners,
> nor sits in the seat of scoffers;
> ²but his delight is in the law of the Lord,
> and on his law he meditates day and night.
>
> ³He is like a tree
> planted by streams of water
> that yields its fruit in its season,
> and its leaf does not wither.
> In all that he does, he prospers.
> ⁴The wicked are not so,
> but are like chaff that the wind drives away.

Here is another picture of a tree. God compares a man who delights in His Word and continually dwells on it to a tree that is bearing fruit. This sounds appealing! The question is, are we willing to put in the hard work and dedication to fill our mind with Scripture? Meditation on Scripture does not just happen on its own. It takes intentionality and discipline to fill our mind with Scripture. There are times that your mind is going to want to wander and dwell on sexual fantasies or ideas. Are you willing in those moments to take those thoughts captive and bring them back to Jesus' cross?

Several years ago I caved in and filled my mind with written porn. Without any effort at all, the sexual scene filled my mind. Without any prompting, these thoughts just kept coming and coming, and I really wanted to let my mind go there and stay there. By God's grace, His conviction was very strong, and I knew I couldn't remain in that state of mind. I began memorizing Proverbs 31. Over the next three days, anytime the scene popped into my head, I immediately turned it into an opportunity to go through the verses I had already memorized. I actually had to picture the words spelled out in my mind in order to push out the scene. But as I focused more and more on Scripture, the scene stopped popping into my mind, and it no longer had power over me.

To be honest, I don't think I would have recovered without fighting so hard with Scripture. The lure was strong, and I did not have the will power to say "no" on my own. Praise God for His conviction and for the promise of His Word. The cross is where Jesus meets us in our pain and weakness. And it is through meditating on the cross that Jesus redeems our imaginations.

Last year, I met with a student who was struggling with porn. She overcame moments of temptation by physically getting on her knees and praying out loud for His power and strength. When we turn to God in these moments, He comes through. He is the Vine Dresser who will cut away our sin and prune us. He cleanses and heals and grows His fruit on us.

Yesterday you read Galatians 5:16–26. Today, I want you to read it again, focusing on Galatians 5:22–23. These are the Fruit of the Spirit. God designed us for relationships, and He wants us to enjoy these relationships by allowing His fruit to encompass them. Do we desire to engage with others in the midst of love, joy, peace, patience, kindness, goodness, faithfulness, gentleness and self-control? Or do we still want to look out for ourselves and encounter sexual immorality, drunkenness, strife, division, jealousy, envy and other enticing states of the heart?

Whether we like it or not, there is a powerful source at work within us. Left unattended, that powerful source is our flesh, pulled and enticed by sinful desire and the tactics of Satan. We can attempt to fight against the works of the flesh on our own; however, if we are not intentionally abiding in Christ, we will see the works of the flesh ruling our lives.

Do you see how each of these works of the flesh leads to destruction? Destruction of relationships? Destruction of your own heart? They also bring division between God and us. This does not mean that if you see these things in your life then you are not a Christian. It is saying that you cannot be walking in an intimate relationship with the Lord while walking in these works. It is important to confess these things before the Lord and ask Him to help us crucify—put to death—these desires and passions.

HEARTWORK

Make a Commitment Now

God is calling you right now to put aside selfishness and pride and to follow Jesus Christ. If you've been sexually impure, go to Jesus right now. No matter what your sexual sin, He is faithful and willing to forgive and purify you (1 John 1:9). God wants to forgive you, but you must ask to be forgiven, and you must trust completely in Jesus Christ for healing. This happens when you: (1) acknowledge and confess that your selfishness and pride are sins

WEEK 1 ..... WEEK 2 ..... WEEK 3 .... WEEK 4 .... WEEK 5 .... WEEK 6 .... WEEK 7 .... WEEK 8 .... WEEK 9 .... WEEK 10 .... WEEK 11 .... WEEK 12

DAY 2

against God and that Christ endured the shame of these sins on the cross, and (2) give total control of all areas of your life to Jesus. True repentance must occur before God changes you. Right now, admit to the Lord that you have made satisfying your desires the focus of your life and acknowledge how your pride has blinded you to God's truth. Confess your sins and spend time asking Jesus to take total, permanent control of all areas of your life.

Record your commitment below.

_____

_____

_____

 ## PRAY

Spend some time thanking Jesus for being the True Vine. Ask Him to help you abide in Him and depend on Him. Talk to Him about the different ways you have tried to do this on your own in the past. Commit to Him that you are going to start relying on Him for fruit in your life. Open up to God about anything else that you learned in the reading today. God desires to develop a relationship with you, and open and honest prayer is a crucial part of that relationship.

Record your prayers below.

_____

_____

_____

_____

_____

WEEK 1 ...... WEEK 2 ...... WEEK 3 ...... WEEK 4 ...... WEEK 5 ...... WEEK 6 ...... WEEK 7 ...... WEEK 8 ...... WEEK 9 ...... WEEK 10 ...... WEEK 11 ...... WEEK 12

DAY 2

WEEK 1 ... WEEK 2 ... WEEK 3 ... WEEK 4 ... WEEK 5 ... WEEK 6 ... WEEK 7 ... WEEK 8 ... WEEK 9 ... WEEK 10 ... WEEK 11 ... WEEK 12

DAY 3

READ THE BIBLE

Revelation 2:18–29

18"And to the angel of the church in Thyatira write: 'The words of the Son of God, who has eyes like a flame of fire, and whose feet are like burnished bronze.' 19I know your works, your love and faith and service and patient endurance, and that your latter works exceed the first. 20But I have this against you, that you tolerate that woman Jezebel, who calls herself a prophetess and is teaching and seducing my servants to practice sexual immorality and to eat food sacrificed to idols. I gave her time to repent, but she refuses to repent of her sexual immorality. Behold, I will throw her onto a sickbed, and those who commit adultery with her I will throw into great tribulation, unless they repent of her works, and I will strike her children dead. And all the churches will know that I am he who searches mind and heart, and I will give to each of you according to your works. But to the rest of you in Thyatira, who do not hold this teaching, who have not learned what some call the deep things of Satan, to you I say, I do not lay on you any other burden. Only hold fast what you have until I come. The one who conquers and who keeps my works until the end, to him I will give authority over the nations, and he will rule them with a rod of iron, as when earthen pots are broken in pieces, even as I myself have received authority from my Father. And I will give him the morning star. He who has an ear, let him hear what the Spirit says to the churches."

This passage accurately depicts so many Christians within this generation. They love God and are living out their faith, while also not only tolerating but participating in sexual sin. God calls us to repentance. We cannot only pursue Christ and simply expect lustful desires to fall away. There needs to be a pursuit of Christ while simultaneously starving the flesh and repenting of the current sin in our life.

Loving God with all your strength.
Jesus said that the laws of God can be summed up in two commandments (Mark 12:30–31, ESV): "Love the Lord your God with all your heart and with all your soul and with all your mind and with all your strength. Love your neighbor as yourself."

Loving God with all of your heart, soul, mind, and strength means that you must pursue Jesus Christ with at least the same level of passion that you had pursued lust. The love of

WEEK 1 ..... WEEK 2 ..... WEEK 3 .... WEEK 4 .... WEEK 5 .... WEEK 6 .... WEEK 7 .... WEEK 8 .... WEEK 9 .... WEEK 10 .... WEEK 11 .... WEEK 12

DAY 3

Jesus should be on your mind all day. In practical terms, loving God includes setting aside time daily to meet privately with Jesus in open communication. Begin by simply talking to Jesus Christ as you would a friend. Tell Him about your struggles and fears. Ask Him to rescue you and to give you His strength. Pour out your heart to Him. The more you get to know and trust Jesus, the more you'll want to praise and worship Him from your heart and desire to follow His ways. Jesus wants to know all of us, not just part of us. (See Psalm 119:1–40.)

Loving the Lord also involves participating in a Bible-believing church. We see this within 2 Timothy 2:22 as well. Pursue God's Kingdom *along with those who call upon the Lord with a pure heart.* Although some are reluctant to attend church, it's important for several reasons. Jesus Himself established the church, and He loves and cares for it today (Ephesians 5:25–32). Church is where you can find support and strength, join women's fellowship and Bible studies, establish an accountability partner, develop relationships in which you share your life with other women, and encourage other believers (Hebrews 10:25). The people we are around influence us for better or for worse.

Attending church is not about being religious, doing a good deed, or performing penance. Instead, participate because you want to meet with God, to worship Him, and to join with other men and women who are seeking Him. Please, even if you've had bad church experiences in the past, find a church that really follows the Lord, where you can link your heart with others who love and serve God with pure hearts. It's time to stop walking alone.

Eliminate selfish practices from your life.
As I mentioned earlier, we cannot pursue Christ without also fleeing youthful passions. Living a Proven life involves dying to selfish desires. It's time to get rid of all sexual immorality, including fantasizing, pornography, and sexual immorality with others. This also means eliminating things which may be feeding these lustful desires. How do you eliminate immoral practices in your life without merely following a list of things to avoid? First, understand that by indulging in selfish practices, you've weakened your sensitivity to sin (Ephesians 4:19). You need to correct your thinking to bring an end to your fantasy life. The key is to recognize the sin in it and to bring Jesus into those moments with us.

Second, do as God says, which is to hate sin (Psalm 97:10; Proverbs 8:13; Romans; 12:9). If you're justifying your fantasy life or are chasing after pornography, then you're only playing a game at trying to stop. It must be viewed as an unhealthy, undesirable, unwanted evil in

WEEK 1 ..... WEEK 2 ..... WEEK 3 .... WEEK 4 .... WEEK 5 .... WEEK 6 .... WEEK 7 .... WEEK 8 .... WEEK 9 .... WEEK 10 .... WEEK 11 .... WEEK 12

DAY 3

your life that is no longer welcome. Talk to God about this; ask Him to cause you to see it as sin. Then, make a stand. Choose to hate it and hate it hard! How? By falling in love with Jesus and acknowledging Him in those moments instead of loving sin.

Having accepted the importance of loving God and hating sin, it's still wise to establish certain boundaries to help in the battle against temptation. The point to remember, however, is not to rely solely upon boundaries as a way to obtain freedom from sexual bondage. It's an open heart toward God that leads to a changed life. Again, this only occurs by daily walking with the Lord and being dependent upon Him.

Some practical things to do as part of an overall strategy of reducing temptations:

- Cut out all books, magazines, music, Instagram accounts, TV shows, websites, and anything else that fuels lust.

- Delete any apps on your phone that tempt you.

- Use an internet block on all computers or phones.

- Delete the phone numbers of guys who have been a temptation in the past.

- Look for ways to serve people rather than sexually exploit.

Take inventory on how you fuel lust, and then set boundaries that you won't cross.

If you have spent years developing habits of fantasizing, masturbating, or viewing pornography, keep in mind that you'll likely experience withdrawal symptoms, which can be nearly overwhelming. You may also feel a great temptation to continue in your prior routines or even feel like giving up. Stay the course! Although setting boundaries helps to reduce the struggle, it's only one part of the battle plan. That's why it's vitally important that you simultaneously engage in loving God and others.

Another point to remember is that when you experience a setback, you can't give up. Confess it to Jesus and talk to Him about it. He will forgive you. Then find out what caused you to stumble, and work all the harder at loving Jesus, at loving others, and at hating sin. You may also want to reexamine your boundaries and tighten them. Make all necessary changes to help prevent a reoccurrence. Finding a female accountability partner—someone you can call day or night when you begin to struggle with temptation—is so important. If you do stumble, she is someone you can confess to, and she will help you get back on your feet.

WEEK 1...... WEEK 2 ...... WEEK 3........ WEEK 4........ WEEK 5........ WEEK 6........ WEEK 7........ WEEK 8........ WEEK 9........ WEEK 10 .... WEEK 11........ WEEK 12

DAY 3

HEARTWORK

One last time, read 2 Timothy 2:22 (ESV), "Flee youthful passions and pursue righteousness, faith, love, and peace along with those who call upon the Lord from a pure heart."

Remember, this is a both/and—flee and pursue. You are not called to do this alone. Lean on others around you who will also point you to Christ!

Who can you ask to be your accountability partner?

_____

How are you committed to being in church?

_____

How are you being strategic about being in the Word?

_____

What are the boundaries you need to set in order to starve the flesh?

_____

_____

_____

_____

_____

_____

WEEK 1 ...... WEEK 2 ...... WEEK 3 .... WEEK 4 .... WEEK 5 .... WEEK 6 .... WEEK 7 .... WEEK 8 .... WEEK 9 .... WEEK 10 .... WEEK 11 .... WEEK 12

DAY 3

PRAY

Bow before the Father now and ask Him what boundaries you need to set. Ask Him to sift your heart and bring to light some of the selfish desires that you have been trying to justify.

- Flee—ask God to show you the things in your life that you need to flee from. Repent of those things and ask God to give you the strength to resist.

- Pursue—spend some time honoring God. Praise Him by talking about some of the attributes that you appreciate about Him.

- Spend some time praying for other requests and other people. It is very helpful to get the attention off of ourselves and pray for others. Write out their names.

- Thank God for willingly walking the journey with you. He won't give up!

Record your prayers below.

_____

_____

_____

_____

_____

_____

_____

_____

_____

MEMORY VERSE

2 Timothy 2:22 (ESV): "So flee youthful passions and pursue righteousness, faith, love, and peace, along with those who call on the Lord from a pure heart."

WEEK 2 — DAY 4 (THURSDAY)

KEY THOUGHT: God draws near to those who draw close to Him (James 4:8). Go draw near to God and He will draw near to you.

READ THE BIBLE

Love the Lord with All Your Heart

We are going to take the next several days to work through the PROVEN acronym. Today we are going to start with P: **[P]assionate for God.**

Psalm 101 is one of my favorite passages but it is also one of the hardest to read because it is very convicting. Take a few minutes to read and reread this passage.

Write some observations.

_____

_____

DAILY READING

Though I have always found verses 3 and 4 especially convicting (we will dive into these verses eventually), I used to skim over the first verse and ignore it. I thought the first verse was just a typical introduction into a Psalm. "I will sing of steadfast love and justice, to you oh Lord, I will make music." Yada yada yada... let's get into the good stuff. The rest of the

DAY 4

passage is powerful and a sucker punch to the gut. But one day while I was teaching this passage to a group of college students, God really got a grip on my heart with verse one. It states the goal and the purpose of not only becoming free from sexual sin, but even more so, outlines our purpose for life. We need to strive to be in a place with our mind and our heart that singing to the Lord is possible. "I will sing of steadfast love and justice. To you O Lord, I will make music." The goal is not music but to be in a mind-set of worship, to have our mind centered on the Lord with gratitude and joy.

Need another verse to show you that this is important to the Lord? 1 Thessalonians 5:16–18 (ESV) states, "Rejoice always, pray without ceasing, give thanks in all circumstances, for this is the will of God in Christ Jesus in you." Have you ever wondered what God's will is for you? This simplifies it! Rejoice, be in constant communication with the Father, and have a grateful heart. Easy enough?? Though it may be simple, it is not easy. I don't know about you, but my mind gets bombarded and distracted with so many other neutral or evil things.

One of the problems with lust is that if we leave it unattended, it will consume our mind. We cannot lust and worship God at the same time. Every time our mind entertains a thought that goes against God's will, we turn our back on God and walk away from Him and toward the object of our affection. Praise God that because of the cross, God never turns His back on us. He is standing there with arms open wide every time we repent and turn our heart away from sin and look to Jesus. God will also give us the strength in the moment to walk away from the temptation if we ask Him. It doesn't mean it will be easy, but it will be possible.

Write out 1 Corinthians 10:13.

_____

_____

As we go through this week, we are going to work through some very practical things to take our hearts back for Christ, but today I want us to spend a little more time remembering why we are going through the study. The first step in becoming a PROVEN Woman is to become passionate for God.

Ladies, I cannot put into words the beauty and wonder of Jesus. His creation, the untainted beautiful version of His creation, is a reflection of who He is. One summer, I got to travel

WEEK 1 ..... WEEK 2 ..... WEEK 3 ..... WEEK 4 ..... WEEK 5 ..... WEEK 6 ..... WEEK 7 ..... WEEK 8 ..... WEEK 9 ..... WEEK 10 .... WEEK 11 .... WEEK 12

DAY 4

to Montana and to Kazakhstan and was amazed at the beauty of the mountains. I stood in awe of my Creator those days. God is worthy, holy, loving, all-powerful, all-knowing, brilliant, wise, creative… these words can go on forever! He loves us and pursues us. He longs for our hearts and minds to be free from demeaning and destructive thoughts so that we are capable of loving Him in return, to be united with Him in perfect harmony. He paved the way for us through the cross. Jesus completed the hard work for us. Now He asks us to partner with Him in allowing the power of the cross to cleanse our mind and heart. But the goal is not just to turn into a better person. The goal is to fall completely and wholly in love with Him.

What are some things about God that you are grateful for? Do you have any favorite verses that you cherish? Spend a few minutes meditating on those verses and thanking God for His truth.

Write out at least one of the verses. If you cannot remember its reference, look it up. It is important to know where you can find these verses so that they can be a constant resource for you.

_____

_____

_____

HEARTWORK

WRITE A PSALM TO GOD
One of the best-loved books of the Bible is Psalms. It's a marvelous compilation of praise and prayers to God. Many Christians have discovered the tremendous benefit of writing their own psalms or prayer letters to God. What about you? This section will help you begin to experience the intimacy you can have with the Lord through pouring out your heart to Him in your own psalms.

WHY WRITE PSALMS?
The Lord is pleased not only when you praise Him but also when you openly talk to Him. Sometimes, however, you're not sure how to have an open and honest relationship with

WEEK 1 ... WEEK 2 ... WEEK 3 ... WEEK 4 ... WEEK 5 ... WEEK 6 ... WEEK 7 ... WEEK 8 ... WEEK 9 ... WEEK 10 ... WEEK 11 ... WEEK 12

DAY 4

God. Writing a psalm is a lot like writing a letter to a close friend and sharing yourself with her. Your friend is interested in hearing about how you are doing, not just what you are doing. She cares about the behind the scenes stuff—your hopes, dreams, fears and struggles. She also desires to hear what you appreciate about her as a friend. When you write psalms to God (or when you pray, for that matter), your goal is to build a two-way friendship. You're developing a relationship where you can be open and honest with your thoughts and feelings.

WHOM ARE YOU WRITING TO?

In any letter, what you say and how you say it depends on to whom you are writing. A scribbled note to a friend would be different from a letter to the CEO of a company you respect. The way you write a psalm will greatly depend on who you know God to be. He is your Father figure, the Sovereign King of the universe and your best friend.

You need to be careful not to think narrowly about who God is, because that will limit what you think you can or should say to Him. If you focus on only one or two of His characteristics, like His love or mercy, you miss out on so much of God. In fact, God is also good, holy, just, beautiful, perfect, life-giving, supreme, all-knowing, all-powerful, unchanging, wise, jealous, faithful, true, kind, patient, and so much more. The more you get to know God, the more you can richly communicate and have a fulfilling relationship with Him.

HOW TO WRITE YOUR PSALM TO GOD

Writing the first few words can be the hardest. Before you begin, take a quiet moment to reflect and pray. Ask God to still your heart and mind. Ask the Holy Spirit to lead you in what to write. Is your heart filled with praise, or are you struggling with something and in need of wisdom or grace? The topic you write about in your psalm should be in line with the present condition of your heart. Of the 150 psalms of the Bible, only about half are primarily praise or thanksgiving oriented. Many others are pleas for mercy, cries for help, depictions of repentance, requests for strength, or requests for wisdom. It's clear that each of the psalms in the Bible is an expression of the person's heart at the time the psalm was written. Similarly, when you write a psalm, start with how you are feeling right now. Don't think that you must write a praise psalm every time. If you're angry, it might be phony to try to write a love song to God. Instead, cry out to Him. Tell God that you're angry or hurt. Seek His mercy, grace, or love. Ask questions. Make statements. Be real! No matter how many psalms you write, wait upon God for guidance each time. Close your eyes and pray. Search your heart and ask God to speak to you. Then pick up your pen and write down a few words. Ask yourself: How do I feel? What am I thinking? What are my attitudes? What

WEEK 1 ..... WEEK 2 ..... WEEK 3 .... WEEK 4 .... WEEK 5 .... WEEK 6 .... WEEK 7 .... WEEK 8 .... WEEK 9 .... WEEK 10 .... WEEK 11 .... WEEK 12

DAY 4

circumstances am I facing? For instance, if God has answered a prayer or blessed a loved one greatly, be ready to praise Him. Listen for God. Ask Him to guide your words. A psalm may begin like this: "God, You are so good" or "Your name is beautiful." Then stop and listen to God. Ask Him to fill your heart. Seek to share your innermost thoughts and feelings. Don't become concerned about whether the next set of words rhymes or sounds eloquent.

Don't try to force things or attempt to write like someone else. Be yourself and speak from your heart. The style of writing isn't important. God isn't holding a literary contest to see who can string together the fanciest-sounding words. Rather, He wants your heart. He wants you to be eager to meet with Him in prayer and to open your life to Him as a daughter. A psalm can be a great way to tell God you love Him, as well as a way of crying out to Him for help.

_____

_____

_____

_____

_____

_____

_____

After writing a few lines, read and reread what you have written. You'll rarely need to rewrite or edit. Reviewing what you've written helps you stay focused and keeps your heart on track. A psalm of about thirty or forty lines can take fifteen or twenty minutes to write, but you don't have to spend that much time. You may need only a few minutes to write a psalm that glorifies God. Get started and stay with it!

WEEK 1 ...... WEEK 2 ...... WEEK 3 ...... WEEK 4 ...... WEEK 5 ...... WEEK 6 ...... WEEK 7 ...... WEEK 8 ...... WEEK 9 ...... WEEK 10 ...... WEEK 11 ...... WEEK 12

DAY 4

PRAY

You've been vulnerable before Him today. As we wrap up today, reflect on that in prayer.

- Pray for any concerns or distractions that may have pulled you away from the last exercise.

- Thank Him for the ability He gave you to create.

- Thank Him for His heart that hears you and delights in your relationship.

- Ask for His presence to transform you.

Record your prayers below.

_____

_____

_____

_____

_____

_____

_____

_____

_____

_____

_____

MEMORY VERSE

2 Timothy 2:22 (ESV): "So flee youthful passions and pursue righteousness, faith, love, and peace, along with those who call on the Lord from a pure heart."

WEEK 2 DAY 5 (FRIDAY)

KEY THOUGHT: God wants to experience life with us.

READ THE BIBLE

Repentant in Spirit

Yesterday we focused on the letter (P) Passionate for God. I wish I could say that my heart is always focused on the Lord with love and gratitude, but sadly that is not the reality for me or for any of us. There will be times in all of our lives when God is not our first love. It is in those times when selfishness and pride can quickly grip us and steer us away toward lustful temptation. Today I want us to focus on how to make God our first love again. At the beginning of Revelation, there are seven letters that are written to seven different churches. Each of these letters is written directly by Jesus. I want you to read the letter to the Church of Ephesus.

Revelation 2:1–5 (ESV)

> *To the angel of the church in Ephesus write: "The words of him who holds the seven stars in his right hand, who walks among the seven golden lampstands."* *²I know your works, your toil and your patient endurance, and how you cannot bear with those who are evil, but have tested those who call themselves apostles and are not, and found them to be false. ³I know you are enduring patiently and bearing up for my name's sake, and you have not grown weary.*

WEEK 1...... WEEK 2 ....WEEK 3........WEEK 4........WEEK 5........WEEK 6........WEEK 7........WEEK 8........WEEK 9........WEEK 10 ....WEEK 11........WEEK 12

DAY 5

Let's stop right there for a moment. If I had received this letter from Jesus and stopped at this point in the letter, I would be patting myself on the back. Look at all of these wonderful things that I am doing and look how Jesus noticed! Verse 4, though, starts with a dreadful word: "BUT."

> Verse 4—*But I have this against you, that you have abandoned the love you had at first.*

Ouch! Even if we are doing great things, if God isn't our number one passion, then it is all in vain. Jesus did not write this letter to condemn the Church of Ephesus. He wrote it to help them return to their first love. The very next verse shows them what they need to do.

> [5]*Remember therefore from where you have fallen; repent, and do the works you did at first. If not, I will come to you and remove your lampstand from its place, unless you repent.*

DAILY READING

Jesus gives them three simple steps to return to their first love:

Remember → Repent → Return

Remember: Remember the height from which you have fallen. Was there a time in your life when you were closer to God than you are now? What were you doing then to cultivate that relationship that you may not be doing now? Perhaps there was a time when you were daily in the Word. Perhaps you remember being a pure little girl. Perhaps you used to be a lot more faithful in church attendance and have lately been isolating yourself. Perhaps you used to prayer journal and write to God or be a part of a community group that encouraged you in your walk. And maybe there's something else I haven't even thought of. Take some time to remember who God is and what you can do to strengthen that relationship.

Additionally, there may be things you are doing now that have pulled you away from God that you were not doing then. This could be the company you keep, the things you are watching or listening to, substance abuse or something else.

WEEK 1...... WEEK 2 ...... WEEK 3........ WEEK 4........ WEEK 5........ WEEK 6........ WEEK 7........ WEEK 8........ WEEK 9........ WEEK 10 .... WEEK 11........ WEEK 12

DAY 5

Whether you have neglected something good or begun doing something destructive, we need to be mindful that these things have pulled us from our first love. The next step is vital and brings us to the next letter within our PROVEN Ministry.

Repent: We cannot skip this step. Sometimes, when I know I have done something wrong, I try to fix it and hope God and others haven't noticed. I try to change my ways on my own to regain God's approval. This is both impossible and completely contradictory to the gospel. God wants us to bow before Him as we are and repent, to see the sin as He sees the sin. We need to admit that sin is wrong and offensive to God as well as destructive to us. We must ask God to remove the sin and empower us to stand steadfast with Him.

To be honest, many of us are afraid to repent because we do not really want the sin taken away. Or we want God to snap His fingers and change our heart so that we no longer desire the sins, and it is completely effortless to turn to God. This is not how God transforms us, however. God wants to transform our heart, not just give us a quick fix every time we ask for it. He also longs to be a part of our journey, not heal us by taking away the journey.

I know we already read this passage this week, but let's look at Revelation 2:18–29 again.

Once again, in the beginning of the passage, Jesus states some good things that He has observed about this church before using the dreadful word, "but." He is writing to a church who claims to love God while also tolerating sexual sin. We can see within this letter that this behavior is repulsive to Jesus. He is not saying these things to condemn us or shame us. He is calling us to repent. Notice verse 22, "Behold, I will throw her onto a sickbed, and those who commit adultery with her I will throw into great tribulation, unless they repent of her work." This verse can sound a little scary. Jesus says He will bring on great tribulation. But upon whom is He bringing this? For those who are struggling? NO! For anyone who has sinned? NO! Only for those who refuse to repent. Ladies, repentance is the doorway into God's grace and forgiveness.

Repentance is seeing sin the way God sees sin. It is evil and offensive to Him. We cannot downplay sin. If we do, then we will not fully turn away from it, and it will continue to have a stronghold in our life.

WEEK 1 ..... WEEK 2 ..... WEEK 3 ..... WEEK 4 ..... WEEK 5 ..... WEEK 6 ..... WEEK 7 ..... WEEK 8 ..... WEEK 9 ..... WEEK 10 ..... WEEK 11 ..... WEEK 12

DAY 5

HEARTWORK

Take some time to think of a period in your life when you were pure in heart. What were some things that were different about your life then?

_____

_____

_____

_____

How have things changed, bringing you to the state you are in now? Maybe you experienced something traumatic or realized something painful from your past. Maybe it was gradual, maybe it wasn't. Write out your thoughts.

_____

_____

_____

_____

If you are a new believer, what are some things that you are doing to grow your relationship with the Lord?

_____

_____

WEEK 1...... WEEK 2 ...... WEEK 3........ WEEK 4........ WEEK 5........ WEEK 6........ WEEK 7........ WEEK 8........ WEEK 9........ WEEK 10 .... WEEK 11........ WEEK 12

DAY 5

Return: This is the final step, and it's easier said than done. After repenting, it is important to move ourselves to action. Begin doing the things you have neglected. Don't wait for the "right time." Begin investing in your relationship with God now.

Take some time and kneel before God. Ask Him to show you the areas in your life that are keeping you from loving Him first.

PRAY

My prayer is that you are feeling deep conviction as you read this and able to respond to God with repentance. Write out your prayer of repentance right here.

_____

_____

_____

_____

_____

_____

_____

_____

If you do not experience conviction over your sin, then take some time to be honest with God and ask Him to help you see sin the way He does. Pray that God will break your heart for the things that break His. Ask Him to give you a love and respect for Him so that you desire to see things the way He sees things. The ugliness of the cross is a reflection of our sin before God. Ask Jesus to help you see His cross, His deep love for you as He hung there, and the great cost.

PW

WEEK THREE

TESTIMONY

"Unfortunately, I had to learn the hard way. So much pain and brokenness comes with having sex outside of marriage, and each time you have sex with someone you give a part of yourself to them, and they will always have a space in your mind. That temporary moment of pleasure is not worth the baggage it comes with. Whether it's someone you have slept with multiple times or a one-night stand, there will be baggage, whether it be physical or mental. The Lord intended us to have one partner to have sex with as to spare us from these pains."

Passionate for God,
Repentant in spirit, Open and honest,
Victorious in living,
Eternal in perspective, and
Networking with other *PROVEN Women.*

MEMORY VERSE

Psalm 101:1–2 (ESV): "I will sing of steadfast love and justice; to you, O Lord, I will make music. I will ponder the way that is blameless. Oh when will you come to me? I will walk with integrity of heart within my house."

WEEK 3 DAY 1 (MONDAY)

KEY THOUGHT: God wants our whole hearts and we can trust Him to take care of it.

The next letter is (O), open and honest. As you sense the Lord's conviction in your heart, it is important for you to be open and honest to both God as well as other women in your Proven group. Do not allow these things to remain hidden. Even if you do not feel conviction, be open and honest about that. God knows your heart, and He cares about what is actually there. He doesn't want the masked version but the honest version of your heart. I am praying for boldness and authenticity. As you all are honest, you will also notice a deeper connection happening with the ladies in your group. This is cultivating an intimacy that God desires for His daughters. Please do not allow fear to keep things hidden. Satan wants nothing more than to use shame to shut you off from others. He knows that isolation is one of the best tactics to keep you in bondage. Ask God for help, He will empower you to be honest.

READ THE BIBLE

Read Psalm 32. Write initial thoughts:

_____

_____

_____

_____

WEEK 1........ WEEK 2........ WEEK 3 .... WEEK 4........ WEEK 5........ WEEK 6........ WEEK 7........ WEEK 8........ WEEK 9........10 WEEK.......11 WEEK.......12 WEEK

DAY 1

Reread verses 1–5 (ESV).

> Blessed is the one whose transgression is forgiven, whose sin is covered.
> ²Blessed is the man against whom the LORD counts no iniquity,
> and in whose spirit there is no deceit.
>
> ³For when I kept silent, my bones wasted away
> through my groaning all day long.
> ⁴For day and night your hand was heavy upon me;
> my strength was dried up as by the heat of summer. Selah
>
> ⁵I acknowledged my sin to you,
> and I did not cover my iniquity;
> I said, "I will confess my transgressions to the LORD,"
> and you forgave the iniquity of my sin. Selah.

DAILY READING

Last week, we talked about repentance, which is turning toward God and away from sin. I think some people try to repent without opening up and being honest about their sin. They are broken over their sin and try to turn away, but they never open up and communicate the sin before the Lord or others. Out of shame, we keep things covered, unaware that exposing the sin is the very thing that will bring God's blessing in our life. Without confession, there isn't true repentance: just sorrow over our guilt. Remember, God is always after relationship.

Notice that this passage does not say blessed is the one who has not sinned. Nor does it say blessed is the one who has remained pure. Obviously, doing so is good and God blesses those who have remained pure, but He also blesses those whom He has forgiven. This passage was written by King David, and I can only imagine that he wrote it after his encounter with Bathsheba. If you do not know the story, allow me to enlighten you. This David is the same David that we know from the story of David and Goliath. At this point in his life, he had already defeated the giant; he was God's chosen and anointed king, and he was already known as a man after God's own heart. David had quite the stellar resume. But even after all of this, he allowed himself to be in the wrong place at the wrong time and saw a beautiful woman bathing on her rooftop. He decided he wanted her. He slept with her and she became pregnant. Knowing she was married and that this would be a big problem, he brought her husband, Uriah, home from war so that she would sleep with

WEEK 1 ...... WEEK 2 ...... **WEEK 3** ...... WEEK 4 ...... WEEK 5 ...... WEEK 6 ...... WEEK 7 ...... WEEK 8 ...... WEEK 9 ...... WEEK 10 ...... WEEK 11 ...... WEEK 12

DAY 1

him, and people would assume he was the child's father. Although Uriah came home, he did not sleep with her because he wanted to honor his troops. He didn't want to have the pleasure of his wife when his men could not have the pleasure of theirs. Out of fear of getting caught, David strategized a plan to have him killed in action.

At this point, David is an adulterer as well as a murderer. Pretty big sins! David tried to keep his sin secret for a while, but he was eventually confronted about it. At this point, he was broken; he repented of his sin and confessed it to the Lord, asking for forgiveness. As it says in Psalm 32, God forgave David the iniquity of his sin. David writes this passage from experience saying, "Blessed is the one who has been forgiven." But he also writes about the miserable time he experienced between committing the sin and confessing it. He describes it saying,

> For when I kept silent, my bones wasted away
> through my groaning all day long.
> [4]For day and night your hand was heavy upon me;
> my strength was dried up as by the heat of summer.

Can you hear the misery? Sin destroys our soul, but God gives us conviction as a way to move toward Him who is able to cleanse our soul. If we did not have conviction, we would continue on in sin, which would eventually destroy us. We also would move further and further away from God. God loves us so much that He puts His heavy hand of conviction on us, not to make us cower in shame, but to draw us to Himself in repentance. We can repent because we know that "if we confess our sins he is faithful and just to forgive us and cleanse us from all unrighteousness" (1 John 1:9, ESV). Hidden sin is a very dangerous thing in our hearts. If you are feeling conviction from God, He is not pushing you away but urging you to sprint toward Him in brokenness and repentance. But as you turn to Him, do not remain silent. It is so important to acknowledge our sin before the Lord.

HEARTWORK

Open and honest Just like David, we will experience conviction over sin until we bring it to light. I want to give you three different types of confession and ask you to see which one is needed in your life.

- **Confess to God**—This one should always be included. No matter how many other people you confess to, it is very important to be open and honest with God. Do we

WEEK 1......... WEEK 2......... WEEK 3 .... WEEK 4......... WEEK 5......... WEEK 6......... WEEK 7......... WEEK 8......... WEEK 9......... WEEK 10 .... WEEK 11........ WEEK 12

DAY 1

realize that when we sin it is an offense against God? There may be something in your life that you have been trying to justify or hide from God. All He is asking of you is that you acknowledge your sin and confess it to Him, nailing it to the cross. This may be a sin just between you and the Lord and confessing to Him is enough. I believe you will know if this is the case because once you confess to the Lord, you feel the weight of conviction lifted and know you are free. Or Jesus will tell you to go to another person.

- **Confess to God and man**—More times than not, I think it is helpful to not only confess to God but also to confess to a fellow Christian. Sometimes it does not matter who you confess to, as long as you tell someone. This adds extra accountability when we confess to someone else besides God. You will know you need to confess your sin to someone if after confessing it to God, you still feel like you are hiding it and the conviction is still there. Be wise in who you confess to. When the woman caught in adultery was brought before Jesus, He said to her, "Neither do I condemn you; go and from now on sin no more" (John 8:11, ESV). This is the type of response that we hope for. Someone who will not condemn you, but who will encourage and expect you to strive toward holiness. We do not want to confess to someone we know to be judgmental, bringing on extra shame. But we also don't want to confide in someone who is flippant about sin and does not care for holiness; this person will affirm your sin rather than pointing you towards holiness. My prayer is that God will bring the right person into your life through the Proven Ministry.

- **Confess to God and a specific person**—Then there are times that you know you have to confess to a specific person. This may be your spouse, a parent, your accountability partner, or someone else. If you are in ministry, this may be your supervisor. If God is putting a specific person on your mind, you could confess to God and 100 different people, but you know you haven't dealt with the sin until you have told that specific person that God has put on your heart. How do you know if this is the case for you? If you are bartering with God about ways to not have to tell this person, yet the conviction remains heavy on you, you probably need to confess to that person. (Trust me, you will know.) This is the one time I will encourage you to confess to this person even if you do not think they will respond well. Remember, no matter how they respond, God's grace covers you. He does not condemn you. He's already given you all of His love, and He'll be with you as you speak to that person.

Notice that confessing to God is in all three of these types. When we confess to God, we know He will always listen, forgive, and cleanse. When we confess to someone else, we do not have a guarantee of how they will respond, but we can still trust God that He will lift the conviction and set us free as we have been obedient to our part. Conviction can be

WEEK 1........ WEEK 2........ WEEK 3 .... WEEK 4........ WEEK 5........ WEEK 6........ WEEK 7........ WEEK 8........ WEEK 9........ WEEK 10 ....WEEK 11........WEEK 12

DAY 1

miserable; however, it is up to you how long it lasts. Conviction is meant to draw us toward repentance. The quicker we confess our sin, the sooner the conviction will be lifted. There may still be consequences to our sin; however, we will be guaranteed that we will be in right standing with God.

Are there any sins if your life that you have been trying to justify or cover up before God? Ask God to help you sift your heart and be willing to confess the sin that He exposes. Then ask God if there is a particular person that you need to talk to about this. This may be one of your networking sisters, but it also may be someone specific in your life. Be willing to obey whatever God puts on your heart. I am praying for God to give you discernment and courage.

PRAY

Here is some very helpful direction. As you confess to God, I encourage you to not just do it in your mind. Many times when we pray in our mind, words just circle around in our head. It's similar to skimming a page rather than reading a page. Ideas get jumbled together rather than completely communicated. In the same way, when we pray in our mind, things may not get articulated that need to be expressed. I want to encourage you to either say your prayer out loud, write it out, or even mouth it silently, but make sure you are actually putting your confession to words. There is power in true confession. Be specific and be honest. Then take some time to praise God for His forgiveness. He will not hold back any good thing from those who walk with Him (Psalm 84:11). Spend ten minutes talking with Him.

_____

_____

_____

_____

_____

_____

MEMORY VERSE

Psalm 101:1–2 (ESV): "I will sing of steadfast love and justice; to you, O Lord, I will make music. I will ponder the way that is blameless. Oh when will you come to me? I will walk with integrity of heart within my house."

WEEK 3 DAY 2 (TUESDAY)

KEY THOUGHT: God transforms our hearts because He loves us.

Victorious in Living

The past several days, we have talked through *Passion for God, Repentant in spirit,* and being *Open and honest* with ourselves, God, and each other. Each of these deal with the heart and the direction it is going. Passion for God is the destination for which we are striving. Repentance is the process of acknowledging that our heart is in the wrong direction and then turning it back to the Lord. Openness and honesty are the expression of this transformation. These are so important and vital in the process of overcoming sin in our lives, but we also need practical steps which will help us get to and remain in a place of (V)ictorious living. This week, we are going to work through a few passages that will add practical steps to what we are already doing.

At some point, we need to get past words and thoughts and start declaring war on our actions as well. We have already declared war on our heart, striving to point it back to God.

READ THE BIBLE

Read **Hebrews 12** in one sitting, then come back so we can look at specific parts of it together.

Write out some of your initial thoughts.

_____

_____

WEEK 1........ WEEK 2........ **WEEK 3**........ WEEK 4........ WEEK 5........ WEEK 6........ WEEK 7........ WEEK 8........ WEEK 9........ WEEK 10........ WEEK 11........ WEEK 12

DAY 2

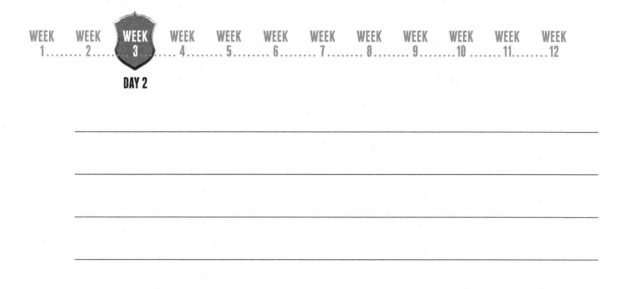

_____

_____

_____

_____

_____

DAILY READING

Hebrews 12:1–2 (ESV) *"Therefore, since we are surrounded by so great a cloud of witnesses, let us also lay aside every weight and sin which clings so closely, and let us run with endurance the race that is set before us, looking to Jesus, the founder and perfecter of our faith, who for the joy that was set before him endured the cross, despising the shame, and is seated at the right hand of the throne of God."*

Let me set the stage for you. Picture yourself in an arena full of people in the stands. You are on an important relay team, and you have already been handed the baton. You have other team members that are in the race with you, running alongside you. You are not just competing for a prize, you are on a mission together. There is purpose to this race. The people in the stands are a part of this team as well. This race has been going on for centuries, and the people in the stands are those who have already run their leg. *"Therefore, since we are surrounded by so great a cloud of witnesses..."* To whom is this referring? Read Hebrews 11, which is known as the Hall of Faith. These men and women have done their part, and they passed the baton on to us. Now we are in this race together. There is nothing more they can do. It's our turn!

"Let us also lay aside every weight and sin which clings so closely" (v1).

We have a mission, yet the pull of pornography and masturbation and other sexual sin entangles us. We get tripped up and continue to fall when we allow these things to remain in our life. Notice that this verse says both "weight" and "sin." At times, we may get rid of the big things that we consider sin, but we leave things which may weigh us down and

WEEK 1........ WEEK 2........ WEEK 3 .... WEEK 4........ WEEK 5........ WEEK 6........ WEEK 7........ WEEK 8........ WEEK 9........ WEEK 10........ WEEK 11........ WEEK 12

DAY 2

feed our craving for lust. Perhaps you got rid of hardcore porn, but you are spending all of your time watching shows and movies that celebrate sexual sin. Perhaps you have stopped having intercourse with your boyfriend, but you are still being very physical with him and allowing boundaries to be crossed. Are we willing to take this life seriously enough to lay aside not only the sin, but also the weights that will entangle?

"Let us run with endurance, the race set before us" (v1).

In a race, an athlete does not get to pick her course, the race has been set out for her. In the same way, God has a plan for your life. Ephesians 2:10 (ESV) states, *"For you are His workmanship, created in Christ Jesus for good works which God prepared beforehand that you would walk in them."* You have been created, chosen, and bought for a purpose. Let us come together for this purpose, being willing to set aside anything that will weigh us down.

"Looking to Jesus, the founder and perfecter of our faith, who for the joy that was set before him endured the cross, despising the shame, and is seated at the right hand of the throne of God. Consider him who endured from sinners such hostility against himself, so that you may not grow weary or fainthearted. In your struggle against sin you have not yet resisted to the point of shedding your blood" (v2–4).

Ladies, I do not want to downplay anything. It does no good to sugarcoat something that is hard and painful. To say this race is hard and takes a lot of endurance is an understatement. But we are not in it alone. We have each other, but even more than that we have Jesus. He is both our example and our strength. Jesus endured so much more than we will ever be asked to endure. He endured the cross on our behalf in order to empower us. But He is no longer suffering. He is alive and well and seated in heaven, interceding for us and empowering us through His Spirit.

Verses 3 and 4 show how much Christ endured so that we would not grow weary. Have we resisted to the point of shedding our blood? This is a battle. We are called to stand fast in the strength of Christ.

Many times we pray against temptation. When I pray against a temptation, I am usually praying for God to change the circumstances that I think are causing the struggle. "God, let me get married so that I am not tempted to seek intimacy elsewhere." Another common thought process is to pray that God will just make the temptation go away. But God does

WEEK 1 ..... WEEK 2 ..... WEEK 3 ..... WEEK 4 ..... WEEK 5 ..... WEEK 6 ..... WEEK 7 ..... WEEK 8 ..... WEEK 9 ..... WEEK 10 ..... WEEK 11 ..... WEEK 12

DAY 2

not just snap His fingers and make everything go away. He builds our character by **being** our strength for resistance. He is not asking us to do anything that He has not already done for us. He endured so much so that we would not grow weary when we are asked to endure *and* so that He can be our companion through it all. His goal is always to change us into His Son's image.

Saying "no" in the midst of temptation is hard. I have heard people say to just "pray harder," and that advice can easily lead to confusion and frustration. "Praying harder" makes no sense if you have the wrong concept of prayer. Prayer in these moments does not just look like asking for the temptation to fall away. If it did, "praying harder" would look like this: asking with the right words, with the right degree of intensity and the right amount of time; and if you get the ratio just right, your temptation will disappear. Praying in the moment of struggle means choosing to stand steadfast in the power of Christ and resisting the temptation with all of His might, no matter how strong the temptation or how long it lasts. It's shifting your focus off of your own strength, or lack thereof, and onto Him and His strength.

James 1:12–15 (NIV)

> [12]Blessed is the one who perseveres under trial because, having stood the test, that person will receive the crown of life that the Lord has promised to those who love him.

> [13]When tempted, no one should say, "God is tempting me." For God cannot be tempted by evil, nor does he tempt anyone; [14]but each person is tempted when they are dragged away by their own evil desire and enticed. [15]Then, after desire has conceived, it gives birth to sin; and sin, when it is full-grown, gives birth to death.

Did you hear that? God is not ashamed of you that you are struggling with the temptation of pornography, masturbation, or fantasies. He is ecstatic when, in those moments, you choose steadfastness rather than caving into the temptation. He stands with you in those moments. Jesus understands the amount of strength it takes in those moments to endure because He already endured incomparable shame during his time on the cross. So yes, pray harder, but this does not mean praying from a distance, expecting God to shut off the temptation. This prayer is partnering with Christ as you both stand steadfast together with His strength.

WEEK 1 ...... WEEK 2 ...... **WEEK 3** ...... WEEK 4 ...... WEEK 5 ...... WEEK 6 ...... WEEK 7 ...... WEEK 8 ...... WEEK 9 ...... WEEK 10 ...... WEEK 11 ...... WEEK 12

DAY 2

HEARTWORK

When you pray against a temptation, what are you expecting God to do for you?

_____

_____

_____

_____

In your own words, what do you think it means to stand steadfast with Christ?

_____

_____

_____

_____

God's discipline versus God's wrath

What is the difference between punishment and discipline?

_____

_____

If we receive grace, why do we also receive discipline?

_____

_____

WEEK 1........ WEEK 2........ WEEK 3 .... WEEK 4........ WEEK 5........ WEEK 6........ WEEK 7........ WEEK 8........ WEEK 9........ WEEK 10........ WEEK 11........ WEEK 12

DAY 2

Punishment is about justice. It gives the person what they deserve. Discipline is for the good of the person, training them in the way they should go. God extends mercy by not giving us what we deserve. Jesus got the punishment we deserve on the cross. Then He extends grace by giving us discipline. Discipline is conviction as well as His companionship as we navigate the consequences of our sin. He lovingly and gently walks us through the things that He knows will draw us to Him, to repentance, and to His way.

Imagine a five-year-old, just tall enough to reach his hand up and touch a hot burner on the stove. A loving mother would tell him to not touch the stove because she knows it's painful. When he comes crying into her arms after touching the burner out of rebellion, she comforts the child and says something like, "Please, listen to me and don't touch the stove again. I know it hurts and I'm sorry." She shows mercy by not punishing him for his rebellion. She shows grace by holding him as he cries and helping him understand that her "way" is not only right, but it comes from a place of love.

Disclaimer: Discipline is very different from something evil happening to us. God doesn't abuse us for the sake of discipline. Jesus knows what it is like to be abused by evil. It is not something He uses against us. He does not find pleasure in watching us get hurt.

PRAY

Spend some time remembering what Jesus endured for you on the cross. Respond to Him with thanksgiving. Are there some areas in which you are having a hard time persevering? Open up to God about where you may be struggling and why this is hard. Ask Him to give you the same strength that He gave Jesus in order to endure the cross. That divine power is available to you as well. You just have to ask. This doesn't mean the endurance will be easy or pleasant. The cross was not easy or pleasant, but Jesus had the power to endure it. He will give the same power to you if you ask Him to.

_____

_____

_____

WEEK 1........ WEEK 2........ WEEK 3 .... WEEK 4........ WEEK 5........ WEEK 6........ WEEK 7........ WEEK 8........ WEEK 9........ WEEK 10 .... WEEK 11........ WEEK 12

DAY 2

MEMORY VERSE

Psalm 101:1–2: "I will sing of steadfast love and justice; to you, O Lord, I will make music. I will ponder the way that is blameless. Oh when will you come to me? I will walk with integrity of heart within my house."

WEEK 3 DAY 3 (WEDNESDAY)

KEY THOUGHT: God empowers us to replace lies with truths.

DAILY READING

Are you willing to fight your thoughts? Most of the time, temptation starts with a thought. Without asking for it, a thought pops into our head. It may be the image of a sexual scene you have seen. It may be something that you did in the past with your boyfriend. Perhaps it is a sudden urge to go somewhere in your mind or start the process toward masturbation or text a guy you know you could hook up with tonight. There are times we go searching for something, but so many times, it starts with a fleeting thought. The thought just pops into our mind uninvited.

I believe this is a tactic of Satan. When the thought pops, our desires begin luring us toward it while he stands there and accuses us. "You're already guilty of this, why not give in?" "You know you're going to cave anyways. You don't have the power to withstand this." "God is disgusted with you because of this thought, you can't go to Him now for help. He will reject you because of your filth." These are all lies.

Many times, when a lustful thought or urge arises, we are already ashamed because of its content. Perhaps we feel the need to turn away from God in shame during that moment in order to rid ourselves of the thought. We think we need to overcome it and clean ourselves up in order for God to welcome us back. But as soon as we turn away from God, game over. We will not have the strength to turn away on our own.

WEEK 1........ WEEK 2........ WEEK 3 .... WEEK 4........ WEEK 5........ WEEK 6........ WEEK 7........ WEEK 8........ WEEK 9........WEEK 10 ....WEEK 11........WEEK 12

DAY 3

Because of God's grace and because of the cross, we have the ability to sprint to God with our thoughts, no matter how despicable they are. We do not need to hide anything from Him. When a thought pops into your mind, it becomes a moment of decision for you. You can either allow it to lure and entice your desires, taking you down the path toward sexual sin, or that exact same thought can become an opportunity to know Him. It is either an invitation to sin or to stand with Christ, becoming the person in James 1:12 (ESV): *"Blessed is the man who remains steadfast in the midst of a trial, for when he has stood the test he receives the crown of life which God has promised to those who love him."*

Satan does not want you to realize that you are free to run to God in your weak moments. Every temptation is an opportunity for intimacy. We can know Jesus in our weakness and find life, or we can know sin, which will leave us feeling dead inside.

2 Corinthians 10:3–5 (ESV) *"For though we walk in the flesh, we are not waging war according to the flesh. For the weapons of our warfare are not of the flesh but have divine power to destroy strongholds. We destroy arguments and every lofty opinion raised against the knowledge of God, and take every thought captive to obey Christ."*

When we turn to God, we have divine power to destroy the strongholds in our mind and imagination, but we have to be willing to declare war on any thought that goes against who God is and who He says you are.

Hebrews 4:14–16 (ESV) *"Since then we have a great high priest who has passed through the heavens, Jesus, the Son of God, let us hold fast our confession. [15]For we do not have a high priest who is unable to sympathize with our weaknesses, but one who in every respect has been tempted as we are, yet without sin. [16]Let us then with confidence draw near to the throne of grace, that we may receive mercy and find grace to help in time of need."*

This passage calls us to run to God with confidence. It does not say you can boldly run to God when you are worthy and doing well. It says you can run to His throne of grace in your time of need. We always need God's grace, but when do we especially need it? When we are in the midst of temptation or sin. God doesn't just want to know you at your best, He wants to know you at your worst.

Let's say that an impure thought pops into your mind. Like we said earlier, you have a choice to either dwell on it and allow it to lead you toward pornography or masturbation, or you have the choice to run to God. Let's say you start dwelling on it. A couple minutes

WEEK 1........ WEEK 2........ **WEEK 3** WEEK 4........ WEEK 5........ WEEK 6........ WEEK 7........ WEEK 8........ WEEK 9........ WEEK 10........ WEEK 11........ WEEK 12

DAY 3

in, you think… "what am I doing?" At this moment, you once again have the choice to continue or to sprint to God. He is still waiting there, ready to empower you to say "no" as soon as you ask. Let's say you decide to continue to dwell and you get out your phone and start to click on certain sites, or you feel yourself start to get stimulated and begin the act of masturbation. Even at this moment, you have the freedom to turn toward God, and He will welcome you and rescue you. You have not disqualified yourself from turning to God. But make sure you are going to confess and repent and turn away from the sin rather than turning to Him, expecting affirmation for the sin and permission to continue. You have to be ready to say "no" to it and turn away from it. There is not a point of no return. Yes, it gets incredibly difficult to say "no" once you start down the path. But it is still possible! Don't let the fact that you already started make you feel that you no longer have a choice. At the same time, don't let the fact that you can turn away at any point be an excuse to start down the path with the intention of turning away before it gets too bad. Don't play with fire. Let's take captive EVERY THOUGHT that goes against Christ.

HEARTWORK

Satan is so good at filling our minds with lies in our moments of temptation. Have there been any particular thoughts that have come up when you are being tempted? Thoughts that made you think you had to give in and couldn't turn to God?

_____

_____

_____

_____

What can you do with these thoughts when they arise?

_____

_____

WEEK 1 .... WEEK 2 .... WEEK 3 .... WEEK 4 .... WEEK 5 .... WEEK 6 .... WEEK 7 .... WEEK 8 .... WEEK 9 .... WEEK 10 .... WEEK 11 .... WEEK 12

DAY 3

It is good to recognize these lies so that when you hear them in your mind in the future, you will see them as lies and be willing to take them captive. It is hard to know that we can take them captive if we think they are accusations coming from God. I guarantee you this is not coming from God. He draws you to Himself with conviction. As you get nearer to God, you will be broken over your sin and desire rescue and freedom. Satan pushes you away with shame.

Or you may be distancing yourself. If you do not want to be broken over your sin, you will be the one to isolate yourself from God so that you can continue to be comfortable with your sin. If this is the case for you, are you willing to ask God to begin the work on your heart to convict you of your sin and set you free from this prison?

READ THE BIBLE

Read James 1 and write down any insights.

_____

_____

_____

_____

PRAY

Spend time talking to Jesus about the lies you believe—about feeling like you need sexual intimacy. Ask Him to show you why you think that is true. Also, ask Him to teach you to take your thoughts and memories captive.

_____

_____

_____

WEEK 1 .... WEEK 2 .... WEEK 3 .... WEEK 4 .... WEEK 5 .... WEEK 6 .... WEEK 7 .... WEEK 8 .... WEEK 9 .... WEEK 10 .... WEEK 11 .... WEEK 12

DAY 3

MEMORY VERSE

Psalm 101:1–2 (ESV): "I will sing of steadfast love and justice; to you, O Lord, I will make music. I will ponder the way that is blameless. Oh when will you come to me? I will walk with integrity of heart within my house."

WEEK **3** DAY 4 (THURSDAY)

KEY THOUGHT: What we pursue influences why we believe. What are you pursuing?

DAILY READING

Yesterday we talked about declaring war on our thoughts. We often have thoughts that pop into our mind uninvited. Even though these thoughts come uninvited, there are ways that we can lessen their frequency. Today we are going to work through a passage that will address this. You read Psalm 101 a few days ago. I want you to read it again, and we will dissect the rest of the passage. Today is going to look a little different. We are going to meditate through Psalm 101 and use it as an inventory for our heart and mind. This passage is one of the most convicting passages I have ever read. Every time I read it, I realize that there are things of which I should be repenting. It always comes down to this question: Do I love God enough to hate the things that pull me from Him? Please read this with an open mind. Also, please know I am not condemning or judging you. I am simply trying to shed light on what God says about our entertainment and how it affects us. My prayer is that you will invite God into this with you, and wherever He convicts you, you will repent and obey Him. Turn toward Him and know freedom.

Psalm 101 Challenge

Read through Psalm 101 completely, then come and read through it as it is broken down below and answer the questions.

WEEK 1........ WEEK 2........ WEEK 3 .... WEEK 4........ WEEK 5........ WEEK 6........ WEEK 7........ WEEK 8........ WEEK 9........ WEEK 10 .... WEEK 11........ WEEK 12

DAY 4

Write down some initial thoughts.

_____

_____

_____

I will sing of steadfast love and justice;
to you, O LORD, I will make music.

1. What is your view of God? For the psalmist, steadfast love and justice color his picture of God. What words come to mind when you think about God?

_____

_____

_____

²I will ponder the way that is blameless.
Oh when will you come to me?

2. How is your thought life? The psalmist uses his imagination to envision a life with God instead of a life with lust. Do you care about being blameless? Notice that this verse says "ponder." Pondering is more than just fleeting thoughts. It is the place where you allow your mind to dwell and imagine. Are the dwelling places of your mind blameless?

_____

_____

_____

I will walk with integrity of heart
within my house;

3. It is easy to be a different person depending on who we are around. Perhaps you put on a pretty face when you are with others. How are you doing when you are in your own

WEEK 1........ WEEK 2........ WEEK 3 .... WEEK 4........ WEEK 5........ WEEK 6........ WEEK 7........ WEEK 8........ WEEK 9........ WEEK 10........ WEEK 11........ WEEK 12

DAY 4

space and no one is watching? Can you say you walk with integrity of heart when it is just you and your screen, or you and your thoughts, or you and your boyfriend? Who are you when no one is around?

_____

_____

_____

> [3] *I will not set before my eyes*
> *anything that is worthless.*

4. Let me share how this verse has impacted my life. Lust definitely starts as a battle of the mind. When I am very careful to guard my mind by being strict with what I watch or listen to, I don't have to put as much effort toward fighting against sexual temptations. Sexual thoughts, on which I would have to declare war, do not often pop into my mind when I am carefully guarding it. When I put my guard down, however, and allow myself to be entertained by shows or movies that feed these desires, the fight for sexual purity in the mind becomes a lot harder. Thoughts pop into my mind with much more frequency, causing a mental battle that consumes my mind and time.

This does not mean that I do not watch TV at all, although that may be something that God could be asking of some of you for a while. My rule is that I can watch a show, but if I am watching a show and begin to hope for sexual sin within the show, I have to turn it off. Also, if I am going through a series and begin to notice that thoughts start to pop into my mind throughout the day that are luring me toward sexual fantasies, then I have to quit that series, no matter what. I don't wait to get through the next cliffhanger. I don't wait until the season is over. If I see that a show is beginning to stimulate thoughts that lure me toward sexual sin, I shouldn't watch it. Fighting those thoughts takes so much mental effort. I don't know about you, but I have way too much life to live to spend that much effort on constantly taking thoughts captive. The same can be true with music as well.

This is not about being legalistic but about realizing that we are in a battle for the mind. We want to strip Satan of any ammunition that He has to lure us toward sexual sin. We need to remember that sexual sin does not only take place when we act on it. Allowing

WEEK WEEK **WEEK** WEEK WEEK WEEK WEEK WEEK WEEK WEEK WEEK WEEK
1........2........**3**........4........5........6........7........8........9........10.......11.......12

DAY 4

our mind to dwell on sexual fantasies is already sin. Our mind was created to love God and know Him. We pollute the core of our imagination when we entertain it with sin.

I hate the work of those who fall away;
it shall not cling to me.

5. Do we see sexual sin as destructive? The world wants us to be amused by sin. God wants us to be repulsed by it. Can we say that we not only avoid, but actually hate the work of those who fall away? Notice that it says, "it shall not cling to me."

_____

_____

[4]A perverse heart shall be far from me;
I will know nothing of evil.

6. Are you able to see the way the world influences you?

_____

_____

[5]Whoever slanders his neighbor secretly
I will destroy. Whoever has a haughty look
and an arrogant heart I will not endure.

7. How is our attitude? What are your words toward or about others? Sometimes I am able to control my words; however, if someone were to take an inventory of my mind, they would see a lot of slander. Evil thoughts toward others also stem from selfishness and pride and should be dealt with by confessing them to the Lord and taking them captive.

_____

_____

_____

_____

DAY 4

> *⁶I will look with favor on the faithful in*
> *the land, that they may dwell with me;*
> *he who walks in the way that is blameless*
> *shall minister to me.*
>
> *⁷No one who practices deceit*
> *shall dwell in my house;*
> *no one who utters lies*
> *shall continue before my eyes.*
>
> *⁸Morning by morning I will destroy*
> *all the wicked in the land,*
> *cutting off all the evildoers*
> *from the city of the LORD.*

8. Are you living in true authenticity? Do you value honesty and integrity?

_____

_____

_____

_____

_____

HEARTWORK

How would I describe my thought life?

_____

_____

WEEK 1........ WEEK 2........ WEEK 3........ WEEK 4........ WEEK 5........ WEEK 6........ WEEK 7........ WEEK 8........ WEEK 9........ WEEK 10....... WEEK 11....... WEEK 12

DAY 4

Are there any forms of media or entertainment that you need to be willing to give up after going through today's reading?

_____

_____

_____

Take an inventory on the type of things you click on while scrolling through social media. Are the things that you are feeding yourself edifying? Mindless? Evil?

_____

_____

PRAY

Spend some time talking to God about this and praying through the Psalm. God is not an overbearing parent who just says "no" without explanation. Talk to Him about the ways that you are spending your time. Tell Him your concerns, but also explain why you may not want to give up your schedule or priorities. Allow His conviction or peace to be your guide.

Spend some time also praising God and thanking Him for other people in your life. Pray for the other Proven Women in your group who will also do this inventory. Pray that they will have the humility needed to allow God to guide their hearts through today's reading. Pray that Satan will not have any footholds in anyone's lives. Pray that this will be a powerful day for each lady in your group.

Record your prayers below.

_____

_____

_____

WEEK 1 ...... WEEK 2 ...... WEEK 3 ...... WEEK 4 ...... WEEK 5 ...... WEEK 6 ...... WEEK 7 ...... WEEK 8 ...... WEEK 9 ...... WEEK 10 ...... WEEK 11 ...... WEEK 12

DAY 4

MEMORY VERSE

Psalm 101:1–2: "I will sing of steadfast love and justice; to you, O Lord, I will make music. I will ponder the way that is blameless. Oh when will you come to me? I will walk with integrity of heart within my house."

WEEK 3 DAY 5 (FRIDAY)

KEY THOUGHT: By knowing Jesus, we can have eternal joy.

DAILY READING

[E]ternal Perspective

I know the last couple of days may have been a little intense. We are so saturated in a sexually-stimulated culture, and it is hard to guard our thoughts and eyes. Today, I want to remind us again of why we are working so hard to guard our minds and take captive every thought. It isn't just to clear our heads so that we are free to live life however we want. We have been chosen, redeemed, and appointed to live life with Christ for His purpose. Do we realize the big picture? And that we are a part of it? Today we are going to talk about having an eternal perspective.

I have a friend who compares life to a book. He says life on this earth is just the prologue and the actual story takes place in heaven. I have also heard life compared to a 1,000-mile journey. Life on this earth is just the first inch, which makes sure you are going in the right direction. The wording that resonates with me is that this life is not the main event. No matter what I face on this earth, it will be okay because this is not the main event. No matter what I do not get to experience on this earth, I will not be missing out because this is not the main event. One day, all of us who have put our faith in Christ will be united with Christ in perfect harmony and intimacy with Him and one another for all of eternity. God tells us to have this eternal perspective.

Several years ago, I was really going through a "woe is me" time. Once again, a guy I liked was pursuing another girl, and that completely drained all joy and energy from me. During

WEEK 1........ WEEK 2........ WEEK 3 .... WEEK 4........ WEEK 5........ WEEK 6........ WEEK 7........ WEEK 8........ WEEK 9........ WEEK 10........ WEEK 11........ WEEK 12

DAY 5

this time, I was teaching a Bible study to girls and telling them that we need to rely on God's truth for our well-being rather than relying on our circumstances, perspective, or mood.

2 Peter 1:3–4 (ESV) says, "His divine power has granted to us all things that pertain to life and godliness, through our knowledge of Him who has called us to His glory and excellence, in which he has granted to us His perfect and very great promises so that through them we can participate in His divine nature having escaped from the corruption in this world because of sinful desire."

This verse says that He has given us promises so that we can participate in His divine nature. We can experience His joy, His peace, His love, His power, and more. Well, that morning I was in a slump, and I knew that I could not summon up a good mood on my own no matter how much I tried. I was not going to be able to fake joy that morning. I decided that if I teach ladies to rely on God's promises, I should probably practice what I teach. I got on my Bible app and said a little prayer like, "Well Lord, let's see what You got. If You have any promises about joy, You are going to need to show me, because I am not doing it today." Honestly, I had no expectation that He would come through. I typed the word joy into the search engine and scrolled through the list.

One of the verses that popped up was Psalm 16:11 (ESV) *"You make known to me the path of life; in your presence there is fullness of joy; at your right hand there are pleasures forevermore."* I decided to read the entire chapter like a good little Bible scholar because it's good to read a verse in its context. So I began reading all of Psalm 16. When I got to verse 6, I got really mad. *"The lines have fallen for me in pleasant places; indeed, I have a beautiful inheritance."* My prayer turned into something a little more like… "God, of course King David had joy. Look at his circumstances. He was king. He was married. His lines had fallen into pleasant places and he had a great inheritance. If he is talking about joy while in the midst of being grateful for his circumstances, then that disqualifies this as a verse that will promise joy." I know, I know—I was in a really bad mood that morning. But then I had this next thought that I knew was from the Lord, "Emily, do you have an inheritance?"

Immediately, I stopped. I do have an inheritance. One that is greater than I can imagine. One that can never be taken away from me. I knew of another passage that had the word inheritance, so I flipped over to 1 Peter 1:3–5 (ESV): *"Blessed be the God and Father of our Lord Jesus Christ! According to his great mercy, he has caused us to be born again to a living*

WEEK 1 ... WEEK 2 ... WEEK 3 ... WEEK 4 ... WEEK 5 ... WEEK 6 ... WEEK 7 ... WEEK 8 ... WEEK 9 ... WEEK 10 ... WEEK 11 ... WEEK 12

DAY 5

hope through the resurrection of Jesus Christ from the dead, to an inheritance that is imperishable, undefiled, and unfading, kept in heaven for you, who by God's power are being guarded through faith for a salvation to be revealed in the last time."

We have so much promised to us. This inheritance is beyond what we can imagine. And God calls us to put all of our hope in that day. If I put all of my hope in something on this earth, then I will be disappointed and can easily lose my joy. And by the way, it really would be "my" joy—my response to good circumstances. But if I put my hope in the things that God has called me to hope in, I get to participate in His joy, which is sustaining. By rising from the dead, Jesus has promised us a resurrected joy from all of our pain, toil, and even heartbreak. I read through that passage again and decided to be grateful for the eternity that has been promised to me. When I keep that perspective, I do not need to have FOMO—fear of missing out. This is not the main event!

After choosing to be grateful, I turned back to 1 Peter and kept reading, picking up in verse 6 (ESV): *"In this you rejoice, though now for a little while if necessary, you have been grieved by various trials so that the tested genuineness of your faith—more precious than gold that perishes though it is tested by fire—may be found to result in praise and glory and honor at the revelation of Jesus Christ."*

"In this you rejoice"—God had brought me back to a verse that shows me where true joy comes from. He knows that not all of our circumstances are pleasant. Joy is not identical to happiness. Joy is a deep contentedness, even when life is hard. Sometimes, when I only look at the things on this earth, it does not feel like my lines have fallen into pleasant places like David said. But I do have a great inheritance. And so do you! In this we rejoice! That morning, I was able to get up and walk into the day with a joy that I had not forced on myself. I was still sad about the guy, but I had purpose for that day. I had a man who conquered death to love me that morning, more than any man on earth ever could.

Ladies, this is why it is so important to have an eternal perspective! When we get tunnel vision on our desires and what we do not have, it is so easy to feel like we deserve a little pleasure and succumb to sexual sin. But when we keep our eyes fixed on Jesus and on all that He has promised us, joy comes. He went through death on the cross so that He could know us in our pain. And He rose from the dead so that He could give us life in our brokenness.

WEEK 1........ WEEK 2........ WEEK 3 .... WEEK 4........ WEEK 5........ WEEK 6........ WEEK 7........ WEEK 8........ WEEK 9........ WEEK 10 .... WEEK 11........ WEEK 12

DAY 5

HEARTWORK

What are some circumstances that are stealing your joy right now? Please understand that I am not trying to downplay anyone's circumstances. Some of our circumstances are very hard and very painful and God grieves with us in those. Yet when we have an eternal perspective, there is joy in the midst of the pain. What are you facing today that is stealing your joy?

_____

_____

_____

_____

Now picture yourself 100 years down the road. You are in God's Kingdom with Jesus and other believers. No more tears, no more regrets. Take a few minutes to meditate on what it will be like and write out your thoughts.

_____

_____

_____

_____

Now come back to your present circumstances and view them through the lens of eternity and the inheritance that Jesus promises. Is there anything about your perspective that has changed? Is there anything for which you can be grateful?

_____

_____

WEEK 1 .... WEEK 2 .... WEEK 3 .... WEEK 4 .... WEEK 5 .... WEEK 6 .... WEEK 7 .... WEEK 8 .... WEEK 9 .... WEEK 10 .... WEEK 11 .... WEEK 12

DAY 5

_____

_____

God has a plan for your life. You have purpose. In order to be as equipped as possible for His purpose, we need to have His perspective, an eternal perspective.

READ THE BIBLE

Read 1 Peter 1.

PRAY

Spend some time thanking God for the inheritance that He is keeping for you. Ask God to help you to put your hope in it. If you are placing your hope in other things right now, talk to God about those things and about why you are doing so. Ask Him to help you place a greater hope in His promises. This does not mean we cannot desire things on this earth. God gives us many good desires. But we cannot rely on these things for joy.

Keeping an eternal perspective reminds us that we are also called to share this good news with others. Are there unsaved people in your life? Spend some time praying for them, that God will draw them to Himself and give you an opportunity to share the gospel with them. It is important to pray for God's Kingdom to be expanded on this earth. That's where a lasting joy is found.

_____

_____

_____

_____

WEEK 1 .... WEEK 2 .... WEEK 3 .... WEEK 4 .... WEEK 5 .... WEEK 6 .... WEEK 7 .... WEEK 8 .... WEEK 9 .... WEEK 10 .... WEEK 11 .... WEEK 12

DAY 5

PW

WEEK FOUR

TESTIMONY

"Since my first serious relationship in high school I have struggled with sexual integrity. As fallen beings we want to fit in and feel as though we belong, even when it doesn't always line up with what the Lord has laid out in his word. We don't want to feel as though we are missing out on anything, and sometimes it can feel as though God's rules are restricting and unnecessary, but this is so far from the truth. The guidelines the Lord has set in place for sexual integrity are to protect us physically, mentally, and emotionally."

Passionate for God,
Repentant in spirit,
Open and honest,
Victorious in living,
Eternal in perspective, and
Networking with other ***PROVEN Women.***

MEMORY VERSE

James 1:14 (ESV): "But each person is tempted when he is lured and enticed by his own desire."

WEEK 4 DAY 1 (MONDAY)

KEY THOUGHT: Our desires need to be redeemed.

Ladies, this week we are going to change gears a little bit. The past two weeks have really been about waging war against this struggle with lust. I wanted to start out by equipping you as much as possible for the fight. By now, I hope you realize that God is in this with you. He will empower you. You can always turn to Him. He will forgive and cleanse. We also need to realize that we also have our part in guarding our mind, which encompasses both what we feed our mind and what we allow our mind to dwell on. These are all great and important, but now we are going to dive into the heart, which is a very powerful yet delicate place.

DAILY READING

Our heart is powerful because it is the center of our desires, emotions, and imagination. If we are not careful, we will be controlled by our desires and emotions rather than having control over them. Desire is what really drives us, which is why our heart is powerful. Our heart is also delicate, because our heart can easily be violated. As we journey together in the weeks ahead, we will work through both desires and emotions and the impact that they can have on this struggle with lust. I'm not going to lie, this will not be easy, and for some of you, it will be downright rough. My prayer is that it will be very insightful as we learn both God's truth about our hearts and also discover the deep things within our own hearts.

This also brings us to the last letter of our acronym—(N)etworking. Ladies, I hope you have already been doing this with a group of women, but if not, I am going to ask you to

WEEK 1........ WEEK 2........ WEEK 3........ **WEEK 4**........ WEEK 5........ WEEK 6........ WEEK 7........ WEEK 8........ WEEK 9........ WEEK 10........ WEEK 11........ WEEK 12

DAY 1

at least find one woman to share these things with as we move forward. God has called us to be in communion with one another. He never expects us to carry our burdens on our own. Romans 12:15 (NIV) says, "Rejoice with those who rejoice and mourn with those who mourn." As we work through the issues of the heart, there are going to be great things to rejoice over, but there will also be some hurts that will be uncovered. We are a sisterhood, we are called to experience these things together. Please do not attempt to work through all of these things on your own. There is such power in sharing our heart with others and also having the opportunity to be there for others. Jesus has called us to live in the light.

Understanding Desires

Now let's jump into what the Bible says about the heart. We have already looked at this verse several times, but it contains another aspect we need to focus on. James 1:13–15 (ESV) says, "Let no one say when he is tempted, 'I am being tempted by God,' for God cannot be tempted with evil, and he himself tempts no one. ¹⁴But each person is tempted when he is lured and enticed by his own desire. ¹⁵Then desire when it has conceived gives birth to sin, and sin when it is fully grown brings forth death."

We live in a culture that believes they are entitled to pleasure. Do what you want if it makes you happy. If it doesn't blatantly harm someone, if it is consensual, do it. It's a "do what you feel is right" ideology. Feel free to try anything that will get you closer to some shallow standard of success: money, sex, power, attention, possessions. It might not be grandiose. It might be called financial security, intimacy and romance, leadership, friends, and items that hold memories or express your personal style. See? Sin can be appealing. The point is that these are selfish standards that ignore God's wisdom. Remember, God wants what's best for us.

Psalm 37:4 (ESV) says, "Delight yourself in the Lord and He will give you the desires of your heart."

When we delight in the Lord, He changes our hearts to want what He wants for us. Then He gives us what we want. When we are delighting in Him, we want to be even closer. We want purity. We want healing. He is faithful to give us those things.

WEEK 1 ..... WEEK 2 ..... WEEK 3 ..... **WEEK 4** ..... WEEK 5 ..... WEEK 6 ..... WEEK 7 ..... WEEK 8 ..... WEEK 9 ..... WEEK 10 ..... WEEK 11 ..... WEEK 12

DAY 1

READ THE BIBLE

Galatians 5:18–24 (ESV)

¹⁸But if you are led by the Spirit, you are not under the law. ¹⁹Now the *works of the flesh are evident: sexual immorality, impurity, sensuality,* ²⁰*idolatry, sorcery, enmity, strife, jealousy, fits of anger, rivalries, dissensions, divisions, envy, drunkenness, orgies, and things like these.* I warn you, as I warned you before, that those who do such things will not inherit the kingdom of God. But the fruit of the Spirit is love, joy, peace, patience, kindness, goodness, faithfulness, gentleness, self-control; against such things there is no law. And those who belong to Christ Jesus *have crucified the flesh with its passions and desires.*

Do we see that the list consisting of the works of the flesh stems from the flesh with its passions and desires?

Jeremiah 17:9 (KJV)

The *heart* is deceitful and desperately wicked, who can know it?

2 Peter 1:4 (ESV)

By which he has granted to us his precious and very great promises, so that through them you may become partakers of the divine nature, having escaped from *the corruption that is in the world because of sinful desire.*

Ephesians 2:1–3 (ESV)

And you were dead in the trespasses and sins ²in which you once walked, following the course of this world, following the prince of the power of the air, the spirit that is now at work in the sons of disobedience—³among whom we all once *lived in the passions of our flesh, carrying out the desires of the body and the mind,* and were by nature children of wrath, like the rest of mankind.

Romans 7:5 (ESV)

While we were living in the flesh, our *sinful passions,* aroused by the law, were at work in our members to bear *fruit for death.*

WEEK 1........ WEEK 2........ WEEK 3........ WEEK 4 .... WEEK 5........ WEEK 6........ WEEK 7........ WEEK 8........ WEEK 9........ WEEK 10 .... WEEK 11........ WEEK 12

DAY 1

Romans 8:5–10 (ESV)

For those who live according to the flesh set their minds on the things of the flesh, but those who live according to the Spirit set their minds on the things of the Spirit. [6]For to set the mind on the flesh is death, but to set the mind on the Spirit is life and peace. [7]For the mind that is set on the flesh is hostile to God, for it does not submit to God's law; indeed, it cannot. [8]Those who are in the flesh cannot please God. [9]You, however, are not in the flesh but in the Spirit, if in fact the Spirit of God dwells in you. Anyone who does not have the Spirit of Christ does not belong to him. [10]But if Christ is in you, although the body is dead because of sin, the Spirit is life because of righteousness.

1 Peter 4:1–6 (ESV)

Since therefore Christ suffered in the flesh, arm yourselves with the same way of thinking, for whoever has suffered in the flesh has ceased from sin, [2]so as to live for the rest of the time in the flesh no longer for *human passions* but for the will of God. [3]For the time that is past suffices for doing what the Gentiles *want* to do, living in sensuality, passions, drunkenness, orgies, drinking parties, and lawless idolatry. [4]With respect to this they are surprised when you do not join them in the same flood of debauchery, and they malign you; [5]but they will give account to him who is ready to judge the living and the dead. [6]For this is why the gospel was preached even to those who are dead, that though judged in the flesh the way people are, they might live in the spirit the way God does.

1 John 2:15–17 (ESV)

Do not *love the world* or the things in the world. If anyone loves the world, the love of the Father is not in him. [16]For all that is in the world—*the desires of the flesh* and *the desires of the eyes* and *pride of life*—is not from the Father but is from the world. [17]And the world is passing away along with its *desires*, but whoever does the will of God abides forever.

The common theme in all of these passages is that, left unattended, the desires of our heart will lead us away from God and toward sin. God warns us; He asks us to crucify the flesh with its desires and to allow Him to transform our hearts. We already looked at Galatians 5:24 (ESV) which calls us to "crucify the flesh with its passions and desires." Now look at Galatians 2:20 (ESV): "I have been crucified with Christ. It is no longer I who live, but Christ who lives in me. And the life I now live in the flesh I live by faith in the Son of God, who loved me and gave himself for me."

WEEK 1........ WEEK 2........ WEEK 3..... WEEK 4 .....5........ WEEK 5........ WEEK 6........ WEEK 7........ WEEK 8........ WEEK 9........ WEEK 10 ....11........12

DAY 1

HEARTWORK

You have just been presented with many passages of Scripture, which clearly inform us that the desires of our heart can lead us astray. This becomes a constant crossroads that each of us must face. Here lies the big question that only you can decide for yourself. Who has the most authority in your life? Are you willing to fight against these desires based on God's declaration that they are evil? Do you still believe that you have the right to follow your own path and run after each of the desires of your heart? Or is the fact that the Bible calls these things wrong enough for you to agree and then declare them unfit for your life?

After reading all of these passages, what are your thoughts on desire's role in temptation?

_____

_____

_____

_____

How do these passages challenge what society is teaching us about following your heart no matter where it leads?

_____

_____

_____

_____

Why do you think God calls us to declare war on our desires and thoughts rather than let them be?

_____

_____

WEEK 1........ WEEK 2........ WEEK 3........ WEEK 4 .... WEEK 5........ WEEK 6........ WEEK 7........ WEEK 8........ WEEK 9........ WEEK 10 .... WEEK 11........ WEEK 12

DAY 1

Are there any desires that you are allowing to rule over you?

_____

_____

How have you seen your own desires lead you in the wrong direction?

_____

_____

_____

PRAY

Spend time with God. Ask Him to give you eyes to see His Majesty and His worthiness, to be Lord of your life. Humble yourself before God and call Him Lord. Confess where you have allowed your heart to be lord over your life. If you are having a hard time bowing down to God as Lord, talk to Him about it. Tell Him what is holding you back. If you don't know, ask Him to show you. God wants to help you dig into your heart. He is not afraid to find out what is deep down inside. If it is painful, He will comfort. If it is evil, He will cleanse and forgive. There is no reason to fear opening up to God unless you don't want anything to change.

Don't forget to spend time praying for others. It is very healing to get our mind off of ourselves and onto others. Thank God for others in your life. Pray for needs of others that you are aware of. Pray with expectation that God is both listening and responding in power.

_____

_____

_____

WEEK 1 .... WEEK 2 .... WEEK 3 .... WEEK 4 .... WEEK 5 .... WEEK 6 .... WEEK 7 .... WEEK 8 .... WEEK 9 .... WEEK 10 .... WEEK 11 .... WEEK 12

DAY 1

MEMORY VERSE

James 1:14 (ESV): "But each person is tempted when he is lured and enticed by his own desire."

WEEK 4 DAY 2 (TUESDAY)

KEY THOUGHT: God cares about our hearts.

DAILY READING

Now that I have painted a very ugly picture of our desires and hearts, I want to show you the other side of this. Not all desires are evil. God intends to transform our heart so that we can live out our desires in a way that compels us to know and honor Him. God wants to conform our heart to reflect His. He delights in fulfilling the desires that He has placed in the heart of a woman. I believe that there are good, God-given desires deep within the heart of each one of us. It is good and natural for a woman to desire to be found beautiful, to be chosen, needed, protected, adored, and valued. God delights in seeing these desires fulfilled, but God also knows the best way and timing for meeting these longings within us.

Matt Heard's book, *Life with a Capital L*,[1] has a lot to say about longing. He differentiates between longings and pursuits. We all have a longing to be loved, pursued, and chosen. One pursuit of these longings is marriage, or at least a romantic dating relationship with a man. However, we may become so focused on the pursuit that we are missing how God is meeting that longing.

Why do you think God doesn't always fulfill our longings as soon as they arise?

_____

_____

WEEK 1........ WEEK 2........ WEEK 3........ WEEK 4 .... WEEK 5........ WEEK 6........ WEEK 7........ WEEK 8........ WEEK 9........ WEEK 10 .... WEEK 11 .... WEEK 12

DAY 2

_____

_____

Why do you think God doesn't always fulfill our longings the exact way we want Him to?

_____

_____

_____

We are designed to long for God and love Him with all of our heart. If God chose to fulfill each of these desires in a tangible way on this earth every time we desired or asked Him for something, then we would see Him as a great genie who always gives us what we want, rather than seeing Him as a holy, righteous God who deserves our allegiance, love, and affection. Also, God is so much wiser than us. He knows what we long for even more than we do. He fashioned our heart while we were still in the womb. Before we ever took our first breath, he already saw every one of our days; He knows exactly how things will turn out. He knows what will draw us toward Him and what will distract us from Him.

The same desire that leads us to God can get twisted along the way and lead us toward destruction. God understands our heart and our circumstances so much better than we do. He knows when granting our desires will be a blessing or when it will become a curse. He also knows when saying "no" will cultivate our character and a deeper longing for Him and His kingdom. God desires to transform each of us into the woman He designed us to be. The questions we have to ask ourselves are whether or not we trust Him and whether we are willing to see these desires fulfilled in His way.

For the next several weeks, we are going to look through each of these desires and discover what they look like in their truest form; we are also going to see how selfishness and pride can twist these desires along the way. We touched on this in the introduction, but I believe God planned for these desires to begin forming as moms and dads dote on their daughters. A young girl delights as she twirls in her little dress, knowing that her dad finds her beautiful. She blossoms as she is nurtured by the loving care of her mom. She feels cherished

WEEK 1 ...... WEEK 2 ...... WEEK 3 ...... WEEK 4 ...... WEEK 5 ...... WEEK 6 ...... WEEK 7 ...... WEEK 8 ...... WEEK 9 ...... WEEK 10 ...... WEEK 11 ...... WEEK 12

DAY 2

and protected. Because she is given dignity, she feels confident in exploring her life. But there are times when dad is distracted or negligent. Perhaps he has even been downright dismissive or abusive. Every little girl has experienced disappointment because her desires are never completely fulfilled.

Not only have we experienced disappointment, but Satan strategically works with our flesh and the culture around us to twist and distort these simple yet deep desires. The desire for beauty distorts into the need to be perceived as sexy and superior. The desire to be accepted turns to rivalry as each girl wants to become the favorite. These beautiful, God-honoring desires become starving vacuums that we feel desperate to fill. At some point, we realize our brokenness and our need for Christ. He loved us so much that He gave Himself completely on the cross. He conquered death for us by raising from the dead. He did this so that nothing could stand in the way of a loving, personal, intimate relationship with Him. He desires for us to be able to go to Him with our dreams, our fears, our disappointments, and our struggles. Hopefully we have all put our trust in Christ forever by now. But are we trusting God to be our everything now? Do we trust Him to be enough?

I have literally talked with hundreds of women over the years. I have rattled off this list of desires (to be beautiful, chosen, adored, protected, valued) to many of them and then asked if any of the desires resonated with them. At this point, I almost always come across a sea of faces all nodding adamantly. When I ask which ones, I often get the answer, "All of them." There have been times when a girl will sit there and get defensive, saying that one of these desires doesn't hit home for her. As I asked questions and dug a little into her heart, it became evident that the desire was there at one point, but after years of disappointment and pain, she stopped believing that it would be fulfilled. Therefore, she calloused her heart in that area, convincing herself that she would be fine without it. Deep, deep down inside, a part of her that wants to hope again still remains, but out of fear of disappointment or of wounded pride over being wronged, she has quenched the desire.

Ladies, I don't know if you are chasing after every whim to try to fulfill these desires or if you have hardened your heart against any of them, but I want to help you dream again. I want you to dream the dreams that God has given. God wants to do immeasurably more than we can ask or imagine (Ephesians 3:20).

WEEK 1 ...... WEEK 2 ...... WEEK 3 ...... **WEEK 4** ...... WEEK 5 ...... WEEK 6 ...... WEEK 7 ...... WEEK 8 ...... WEEK 9 ...... WEEK 10 ...... WEEK 11 ...... WEEK 12

DAY 2

READ THE BIBLE

Read Psalm 37.

What strikes you in this Psalm?

_____

_____

_____

_____

_____

_____

_____

_____

_____

Now reread Psalm 37:3–7.

HEARTWORK

God wants to fulfill the desires of our heart, but in order to do that, we need to delight in Him. I can take each of these desires and show you within Scripture how each of these desires are ultimately and truly fulfilled in Christ. This is what we are going to do over the next few weeks.

WEEK 1 . . . . WEEK 2 . . . . WEEK 3 . . . . WEEK 4 . . . . WEEK 5 . . . . WEEK 6 . . . . WEEK 7 . . . . WEEK 8 . . . . WEEK 9 . . . . WEEK 10 . . . . . . WEEK 11 . . . . . . WEEK 12

DAY 2

Why is it important for us to delight in God?

_____

_____

What are you doing to stir your affection for the Lord?

_____

_____

Psalm 37:4 is not a formula for receiving a loving marriage. We often believe that if we will just love God more, He will bless us with a loving man. Or we think, "If I love God more, He will grant me one of my pursuits that I am on a quest for." That is not the promise within this verse. If we love God more, then we will cherish His love for us and move into deeper intimacy with Him. He is calling us deeper. He has so much to shower on us, but we have to be willing to pursue Him with thanksgiving.

PRAY

Pray through Psalm 37:3–7.

Spend some time proclaiming to God why He is trustworthy. What are some ways that you have learned about God lately that you appreciate? Ask Him to help you to both delight in Him and wait on Him. Remember, as you wait, God may be doing something different than what you are anticipating. Ask God to help you trust that His way and His timing are best. Spend some time meditating on verse 5 (ESV): "Commit your way to the Lord; trust in him, and he will act." Part of committing your way to the Lord is committing that you will do things God's way. Where are you still following your own path?? Confess these things to the Lord and thank Him for His ever-present love and forgiveness.

Spend some time praying for others in your community. Pray for churches in the area. Pray for neighbors that may not know the Lord. Pray that God will give you opportunities to get to know others. As we grow to love God more, we will love others more as well. This helps fight against the selfishness and pride in our lives. I am praying that you are seeing God's transformation taking place in your own heart and life.

MEMORY VERSE

James 1:14 (ESV): "But each person is tempted when he is lured and enticed by his own desire."

WEEK 4 DAY 3 (WEDNESDAY)

KEY THOUGHT: Pride isolates us, but God calls us to trust Him.

Remember to highlight and take notes as you read through the study today; let truth speak to you.

DAILY READING

So far this week, we have taken time to look at the heart. God gave us desires that would lead us toward Him. These same desires, when mixed with selfishness and pride, can drive us in the opposite direction. Before we move forward, we need to take some time to remember that we cannot fix our sin nature on our own. Never forget that healing comes only from God. In fact, the Lord says that apart from Him you can do nothing of eternal significance (John 15:5). It's prideful to think that you can bring about any achievement through your own merits or ability. In fact, you actually oppose God when you strive to free yourself from bondage to sexual immorality in your own strength. (See James 4:6, ESV: "God opposes the proud but gives grace to the humble.")

Not one of us deserves heaven; we must trust in Christ to see our sins forgiven and our eternity secured. Still, people often seek to set aside their faith when it comes to living a holy life, somehow deceiving themselves into thinking that the ability to refrain from evil is found in their own strength. Let's read Galatians 3:2–3 (ESV): "Let me ask you only this: Did you receive the Spirit by works of the law or by hearing with faith? ³Are you so foolish? Having begun by the Spirit, are you now being perfected by the flesh?"

WEEK 1......... WEEK 2......... WEEK 3......... **WEEK 4**......... WEEK 5......... WEEK 6......... WEEK 7......... WEEK 8......... WEEK 9......... WEEK 10....... WEEK 11......... WEEK 12

DAY 3

This passage reminds us that we are saved by faith. We also are transformed through faith in the Spirit rather than by our own willpower. When you face a crisis or problem, is your first reaction to take matters into your own hands? If so, why?

_____

_____

_____

_____

For some people, self-sufficiency was forced upon them because they never had someone else to rely on. Perhaps there has been so much disappointment that you have decided to take matters into your own hands. Maybe it became easier to control things because there seems to be a smaller chance of being hurt. For others, this may simply be pride. Or perhaps it feels like you are an inconvenience if you have to depend on someone else, so you want to be able to achieve everything on your own. In any of these circumstances, these attitudes demonstrate a lack of faith in God. If you are not willing to rely on God for your transformation, perhaps you have projected your fear of being let down onto Him. You don't believe He will come through for you. Or maybe it's a matter of pride again. You want to achieve the transformation on your own in order to boast in yourself, rather than trusting God.

But we simply cannot do this without Jesus. Whatever success we have will be short-lived without Him. It is quite ironic that we cling to our own sense of control rather than allowing ourselves to fall into God's trusting arms, especially when there is no more reliable rock to stand firm on than God.

A lifestyle of self-effort and self-striving produces a self-centered and prideful heart, which is a barren field yielding mainly weeds of selfish practices, including pornography, fantasy, lust, and masturbation.

Where should you turn? The problem with all self-help techniques and efforts is that they are of human origin and will eventually crumble. You'll remain puffed up or deceived. Just as pornography or fantasy brings only momentary pleasure, self-effort only grants temporary relief. The weeds are never fully uprooted, and total freedom remains out of reach. There is no real freedom if we only change our actions but leave our hearts broken and fearful.

WEEK 1 ..... WEEK 2 ..... WEEK 3 ..... **WEEK 4** ..... WEEK 5 ..... WEEK 6 ..... WEEK 7 ..... WEEK 8 ..... WEEK 9 ..... WEEK 10 ..... WEEK 11 ..... WEEK 12

DAY 3

Regardless of the number of times you've failed before, don't remain in despair or self-pity. Although God alone heals, you are not exempt from responsibility. Your duty is to position yourself to receive God's gift of healing and then cooperate, purposefully walking in step with Him.

The Lord will not force you to participate or receive His help. You must earnestly want God's healing, ask for it, and carry it out. How? By making the pursuit of God—knowing and loving Him—your top priority! (Read those lines again.) As you embrace this truth, you'll finally understand and accept that you really are needy and utterly dependent on Him after all. This mentality allows a godly form of humility to develop that breaks down any pride. In fact, it's pride that keeps each person from God and also rejects His power to overcome evil.

Rejoice in this knowledge! God promises to raise up the humble. Seek the Lord diligently and dependently. Seek to be the opposite of proud. Seek Him in failure and seek Him in success. Begin your new life of seeking the Lord with this prayer:

> Rescue me, Lord; I am lost without you. I have been striving in my own strength, living to please myself. I have turned away from You and I rejected Your love and grace. I am in great need. I call upon You. I turn to You and yield my entire life to You. This time, I submit myself in every area of my life. Lord, I now understand how I have allowed my desires to drive me away from your presence. I want these desires to draw me to You, but I need You to transform my heart. I cannot do this on my own, so I bow before You, asking that You will do this work in me.

This humble state of heart isn't something we move on from when we get stronger in our faith. On the contrary, this state of heart actually makes us strong in our faith. The gospel is something we need every day because we need to be in relationship with Him every day. A true prayer for God to change you is one that is always heard. Place your faith in Christ and ask Him to strengthen you. God always gives you a choice to either rely on His power or to attempt to use your own.

Get into a practice of reviewing the Daily Readings, jotting down key points as well as new insights or commitments. Make your notes here. (It's never enough simply to hear truth; it must be adopted as your own.)

WEEK 1........ WEEK 2........ WEEK 3........ WEEK 4 ....5........ WEEK 6........ WEEK 7........ WEEK 8........ WEEK 9........ WEEK 10 ....WEEK 11........WEEK 12

DAY 3

READ THE BIBLE

Read John 15 right now. (We have already read this once, but we are going to meditate on it again and ask new questions.)

Consider the following questions and carefully think through your answers:

How does the healing of sexual impurity impact in my life?

_____

_____

Verse 5 (NIV) says, "apart from me you can do nothing." Do you fully believe that you cannot do any of this apart from God?

_____

_____

Why is it tempting to attempt this on our own?

_____

_____

What is holding you back from relying completely on God and relinquishing your self-effort?

_____

_____

WEEK 1........ WEEK 2........ WEEK 3........ WEEK 4 .... WEEK 5........ WEEK 6........ WEEK 7........ WEEK 8........ WEEK 9........ WEEK 10........ WEEK 11........ WEEK 12

DAY 3

Why does it matter whether I think I do the work with God's help or that God does the healing and I am the obedient servant?

_____

_____

What does it mean to reject self-effort, and how do I do this?

_____

_____

How do you see the Father pruning you at this point in your life?

_____

_____

PRAY

Now that you've written out your answers, talk through them with Jesus. Share with Him how you are growing and learning to trust Him more. Ask Him to help you trust Him completely with the areas that you are still nervous about opening up. Spend some time praying for other people in your life as well.

Record your prayers below.

_____

_____

_____

WEEK 1........ WEEK 2........ WEEK 3........ WEEK 4........ WEEK 5........ WEEK 6........ WEEK 7........ WEEK 8........ WEEK 9........ WEEK 10 .... WEEK 11........ WEEK 12

DAY 3

MEMORY VERSE

James 1:14 (ESV): "But each person is tempted when he is lured and enticed by his own desire."

WEEK 4 DAY 4 (THURSDAY)

KEY THOUGHT: Beauty matters and it runs deeper than our skin.

DAILY READING

Beauty

The first desire we are going to look at is beauty. According to Merriam-Webster, beauty is defined as (a) "the quality or aggregate of qualities in a person or thing that gives pleasure to the senses or pleasurably exalts the mind or spirit" and (b) "a particularly graceful, ornamental, or excellent quality."[2] Some synonyms and related words include loveliness, appeal, attraction, radiance, charm, delightfulness. Reading these words may resonate with a longing within us. These are good things. I believe beauty is the imagery of God's goodness. It should be wonderful and delightful. It should naturally bring about a smile and gratitude when we encounter it. Beauty is the radiance of truth and goodness.

God is the Creator of beauty. If you have ever had the opportunity to see a breathtaking sunset over a beach or a waterfall cascading down a mountainside, you understand the allure of beauty. It catches our eye and draws us toward it with awe. However, our awe should not end with the scene, but instead call us toward the one who created the scene. Beauty is meant to bring us delight, but it also turns our hearts upward in gratitude. There is something so pure and good about beauty. It is something that we as women especially long for. We long to see it but we also long to possess it. We find delight in looking around and seeing beauty around us, but we especially desire to see beauty in the mirror. We are embodied souls, and we can see the way we are valuing our soul by how we measure our external beauty. Let's spend time looking into that.

WEEK 1 .... WEEK 2 .... WEEK 3 .... **WEEK 4** .... WEEK 5 .... WEEK 6 .... WEEK 7 .... WEEK 8 .... WEEK 9 .... WEEK 10 .... WEEK 11 .... WEEK 12

DAY 4

READ THE BIBLE

God longs for us to see it in the mirror as well. Read Psalm 139. Write your initial thoughts.

_____

_____

We are going to look again at verses 13–16 (ESV).

For you formed my inward parts;
you knitted me together in my mother's womb.
[14]I praise you, for I am fearfully and wonderfully made.
Wonderful are your works;
my soul knows it very well.
[15]My frame was not hidden from you,
when I was being made in secret,
intricately woven in the depths of the earth.
[16]Your eyes saw my unformed substance;
in your book were written, every one of them,
the days that were formed for me,
when as yet there was none of them.

God knit you together in your mother's womb. You are fearfully and wonderfully made. He put thought into your eye color, your bone structure, your height, and so many other countless details. He fashioned you in a way that brings Him delight. God designed your outward appearance, but it was never meant to be your identity. 1 Samuel 16:7 reminds us that man looks on the outward appearance, but God looks at the heart. Although God uses beauty to draw people to Himself and to one another, we have an enemy that has twisted and distorted the purity of beauty.

The root of all sin is selfishness and pride. Keep this in mind as we read two passages that most scholars believe describe the fall of Satan.

WEEK 1........ WEEK 2........ WEEK 3........ WEEK 4 .... WEEK 5........ WEEK 6........ WEEK 7........ WEEK 8........ WEEK 9........ WEEK 10........ WEEK 11........ WEEK 12

DAY 4

Read Ezekiel 28:11–19 and Isaiah 14:12–17 now.

List some of the descriptions of Satan before his fall.

_____

_____

_____

_____

List ways that you see selfishness and pride at work within these passages.

_____

_____

_____

_____

List some of the descriptions of Satan after his fall.

_____

_____

_____

_____

The story of Satan is a devastatingly sad one. He was one of God's beautiful angels. He was perfect in beauty, but he wanted more. Selfishness and pride sparked an ambition in him to ascend even higher. This obsession with "more" brought about violence and destruction within Satan that eventually led to his being cast away from heaven. This is the one who now seeks to destroy us; he does so with the same type of temptation.

WEEK 1........ WEEK 2........ WEEK 3........ WEEK 4 .... WEEK 5........ WEEK 6........ WEEK 7........ WEEK 8........ WEEK 9........ WEEK 10....... WEEK 11........ WEEK 12

DAY 4

Beauty is an area of huge insecurity for many if not most girls. There are many in the world who do not feel "beautiful enough," even though God says that we are "fearfully and wonderfully made."

What is "beautiful enough"? What would it take for you to consider yourself "beautiful enough"?

_____

_____

_____

If you already do find yourself "beautiful enough," what gives you that confidence?

_____

_____

_____

When I did some soul-searching, asking myself this same question, I was very disturbed by my answer. "Beautiful enough" for me was becoming the most beautiful. This is even worse than desiring perfection. If we could reach perfection, which we cannot, this would still not be enough. We would not be willing to share the pedestal with someone else who had also achieved perfection. The same was true for Satan. He was perfect in beauty, but he wanted more. Unfortunately, he is the same one who continually breathes lies to us such as:

• You are not enough

• You deserve more

• You have been forgotten

• You are unworthy

• You have no value

• Nobody loves you

WEEK 1........ WEEK 2........ WEEK 3........ WEEK 4 .... WEEK 5........ WEEK 6........ WEEK 7........ WEEK 8........ WEEK 9........ WEEK 10........ WEEK 11........ WEEK 12

DAY 4

I have definitely seen this happening in my own life. There are times when I am not insecure about my beauty, but those are the times I look around the room and judge myself as best. All it takes is one person whom I deem better than myself to walk into the room, and all of a sudden, the insecurities erupt within. Let's be honest, insecurity is a sugarcoated word to describe what is going on. This is pride and selfishness rearing its ugly head, and we are not willing to hand over the title of "the fairest of them all" to someone else.

When our flesh gets in the way, something that God intended to draw us to Him and to one another has been distorted into a debilitating and divisive desire. It can be debilitating because some women who feel that they have never been the prettiest shut down the desire for beauty completely. This shuts down part of their heart. God has placed His fingerprint of beauty on each of us. It is something we are to enjoy, not to compare and calculate.

Beauty mixed with selfishness and pride can be divisive, because others who see themselves as a contender for "the fairest of them all" spend their days primping, priming, and perfecting, constantly measuring themselves against others. Sisters in Christ enter into competition rather than the God-given community that we need. As disciples of Jesus, we are to love our neighbors as we love ourselves. If we can't rightly value ourselves, then we will never properly value others.

This fuels the desire for attention from men. We want to outshine all other women by bringing attention to ourselves and away from others. Bodies get more in shape. Skirts get shorter. Clothes become tighter. Are we starting to see how selfishness and pride can distort our desire for beauty into unquenchable lust? Please hear me. There is absolutely nothing wrong with taking time to get ready in the morning. I enjoy looking nice and put make-up on just about every day. We just need to check our motives as we get ready in the morning. Are we trying to outdo others? Have our looks become an obsession? Or are we simply accentuating the gift that God has given us? When we get ready in the morning, we should ask ourselves two questions: Do I like the way I look? Also, am I dressing in a way that flaunts myself or that reflects a woman of dignity who walks closely with God?

We often say that we should be modest in order to guard the hearts of our brothers. It is true that guys are driven visually, and we should be mindful and respectful of them. However, we should be modest primarily to guard our own hearts instead of seeking to guard theirs. In the same way their minds are driven to see, we are driven to be seen. Satan's demise did not come because he chased after things he saw. His demise came because he worked to promote himself.

WEEK 1 .... WEEK 2 .... WEEK 3 .... **WEEK 4** .... WEEK 5 .... WEEK 6 .... WEEK 7 .... WEEK 8 .... WEEK 9 .... WEEK 10 .... WEEK 11 .... WEEK 12

DAY 4

HEARTWORK

After reading today's passages, is there anything that God has brought to light about your desire for beauty?

_____

_____

_____

Ladies, there is good news! God is here to forgive, cleanse, and transform our hearts. Beauty is something to celebrate, not compare. We are called to celebrate one another's beauty as well as our own beauty without comparing the two.

In the past, my pride made me strive for all or nothing. Often, if I couldn't be the best, I gave up. So many times I shut down rather than becoming the best that God created me to be. When we stop comparing and simply strive to be our own best potential, then we won't fear being overshadowed by someone else. Are you willing to fully blossom in someone else's shadow? Are you willing to celebrate your beauty and the beauty of others without comparing the two? We value beauty because our Father in Heaven is beautiful. When we live in His shadow, there is infinite room to grow. All other shadows are suffocating.

PRAY

Spend some time opening up to God about anything that today's reading stirred up within you. Be willing to confess the ways you have struggled with identity in beauty. Ask God to show you whether you have been viewing any other women as rivals.

Spend time praying for the other women in your life. It is hard to view them as rivals while praying for them. Ask God to help you love your sisters in Christ and see them as a sisterhood rather than competition.

If competition is not something that you struggle with, spend time praising God for freedom in this area. Pray for the same to be true for the other women in your Proven Group.

MEMORY VERSE

James 1:14 (ESV): "But each person is tempted when he is lured and enticed by his own desire."

WEEK 4 DAY 5 (FRIDAY)

KEY THOUGHT: Our beauty is a vice when it is viewed as a competition with others. We can find joy in our beauty when we are humble.

READ THE BIBLE

Yesterday, we spent some time looking into Satan's passion for greatness, which eventually led to his fall. Now read Philippians 2:1–11. Write down your initial thoughts.

_____

_____

_____

_____

Verses 1–2: "So if there is any encouragement in Christ, any comfort from love, any participation in the Spirit, any affection and sympathy, ²complete my joy by being of the same mind, having the same love, being in full accord and of one mind."

Within these two verses, we see encouragement, comfort, love, affection, sympathy, joy, and unity. These are some of the good things that God designed for us to walk in. This is unseen beauty, and it is good.

WEEK 1 ...... WEEK 2 ...... WEEK 3 ...... WEEK 4 ...... WEEK 5 ...... WEEK 6 ...... WEEK 7 ...... WEEK 8 ...... WEEK 9 ...... WEEK 10 ...... WEEK 11 ...... WEEK 12

DAY 5

Verses 3–4: "Do nothing from selfish ambition or conceit, but in humility count others more significant than yourselves. ⁴Let each of you look not only to his own interests, but also to the interests of others."

God knows that selfishness and pride are the biggest threats to our unity with other believers, so He warns us to put others' interests above our own. How do these verses apply to our desire to be beautiful?

_____

_____

_____

Verses 5–8: "Have this mind among yourselves, which is yours in Christ Jesus, ⁶who, though he was in the form of God, did not count equality with God a thing to be grasped, ⁷but emptied himself, by taking the form of a servant, being born in the likeness of men. ⁸And being found in human form, he humbled himself by becoming obedient to the point of death, even death on a cross."

How does this description of Jesus contrast with yesterday's description of Satan?

_____

_____

_____

_____

 ## DAILY READING

Jesus is the only One who deserves the top pedestal. He is the name above all names. He is the King of Kings and the Lord of Lords. He is God. He was with God in creation, designing the beauty of this world and the intricate parts of each of us. He is worthy beyond what we

WEEK 1........ WEEK 2........ WEEK 3...... WEEK 4 ...... WEEK 5........ WEEK 6........ WEEK 7........ WEEK 8........ WEEK 9........ WEEK 10 .... WEEK 11........ WEEK 12

DAY 5

could possibly imagine. Isaiah 9:6 (ESV) says, "For to us a child is born, to us a son is given; and the government shall be upon his shoulder, and his name shall be called Wonderful Counselor, Mighty God, Everlasting Father, Prince of Peace."

I wish I could put His beauty and worth into words, but He is immeasurably more than any of us could express. He is all-deserving, yet He does not act out in pride and selfishness. He is clothed in both splendor and humility.

What does it mean that Jesus emptied Himself?

_____

_____

Why did Jesus empty Himself, then humble Himself to the point of death?

_____

_____

Verses 9–11: "Therefore God has highly exalted him and bestowed on him the name that is above every name, ¹⁰so that at the name of Jesus every knee should bow, in heaven and on earth and under the earth, ¹¹and every tongue confess that Jesus Christ is Lord, to the glory of God the Father."

What was God's response to Jesus' humility and obedience?

_____

_____

What was God's response to Satan's selfishness and pride?

_____

_____

WEEK 1........ WEEK 2........ WEEK 3..... WEEK 4 .... WEEK 5........ WEEK 6........ WEEK 7........ WEEK 8........ WEEK 9........ WEEK 10 .... WEEK 11........ WEEK 12

DAY 5

Both Satan and Jesus are at work in our lives. Satan is breathing lies. Jesus is breathing life. One tells us we are not enough. The other says we are "fearfully and wonderfully made." One wants us to follow in his footsteps of self-promotion, which ultimately leads to destruction. The other calls us to follow Him into humility, which leads to abundant life.

Yesterday I gave a definition of beauty with some synonyms. Let me add a few more synonyms that I found listed in the same resource (Merriam-Webster online). Beauty—seductiveness, sex appeal, flamboyance, flashiness, showiness and shapeliness.[3]

Satan has woven selfishness and pride into something good, which has led culture to distort beauty into sexiness. Society says that beauty = value = sexiness. Therefore, many women feel the need to find their sex appeal to feel like they have any worth at all. Couple this with the desire to outshine all others, and we quickly speed down the road toward lust. Sexiness is great between a husband and a wife, but it is not meant to be flaunted to the world. It is definitely not meant to be our worth.

God says:

> Proverbs 31:30 (ESV) "Charm is deceitful, and beauty is vain, but a woman who fears the LORD is to be praised."

> 1 Peter 3:3–4 (ESV) "Do not let your adorning be external—the braiding of hair and the putting on of gold jewelry, or the clothing you wear—[4]but let your adorning be the hidden person of the heart with the imperishable beauty of a gentle and quiet spirit, which in God's sight is very precious."

Society says that beauty is the most praiseworthy thing about a person. What does God call praiseworthy?

_____

_____

WEEK 1........ WEEK 2........ WEEK 3........ WEEK 4 .... WEEK 5........ WEEK 6........ WEEK 7........ WEEK 8........ WEEK 9........ WEEK 10........ WEEK 11........ WEEK 12

DAY 5

How does God define imperishable beauty?

_____

_____

Sometimes, Satan uses selfishness and pride. Sometimes, however, Satan is just outright mean. For some of you, the problem isn't that you desire to be the favorite. Some of you have lost hope in beauty altogether. To be honest, this used to be me. To give you the very short version, when I was in junior high, I had two different guys at different times make it very clear to me that they didn't think I was beautiful. After the second guy said it, I believed it. I simply accepted the fact that beauty wasn't a trait I would be known for. I thought I was fine with that. But every time a guy passed over me for another girl, the wound of not being "beautiful enough" kept getting deeper and deeper without me even realizing it. A few years ago, I was at a women's conference and we were talking about our deepest hurts. Being in my mid-thirties and still single, rejection easily came up for me. But out of nowhere, I began sharing this story from junior high. I hadn't thought of that story in years, and I had no idea how powerful those moments had been in shaping me. One lady listened to me, then she told me that those boys had been agents of the enemy. Satan had used them to feed lies into my mind. Then she said I had shaken hands with the enemy and accepted these lies as truth rather than what my Heavenly Father says about me. She asked me to confess these lies to the Lord and ask God to help me see myself the way He sees me.

I finally realized how painful it had been to believe that I wasn't beautiful enough. I thought it was prideful to want to be beautiful, so I took pride in not caring about beauty. Oh the irony. But in order to do so, I had to shut down a part of my heart that God had designed. I had to be honest with God about this desire. I was honest about the pain and also about how I had tried to protect my heart by not caring. It was painful, but God has brought about such healing. I am not saying I don't still struggle; however, I am able to celebrate others' beauty while also celebrating my own. And when I see jealousy or lust starting to take root, I simply confess it to the Lord and allow Him to continue to transform and cleanse my heart.

WEEK 1........ WEEK 2........ WEEK 3........ **WEEK 4** .... WEEK 5........ WEEK 6........ WEEK 7........ WEEK 8........ WEEK 9........ WEEK 10 .... WEEK 11........ WEEK 12

DAY 5

There is nothing wrong with the desire to feel beautiful. The problem comes when our worth is wrapped up in our physical appearance or when we desire to outdo everyone else in beauty. Beauty is an attractiveness that God designed to draw us to one another in unity, not to create division or lust.

HEARTWORK

Have there been any situations in your life which have threatened your freedom to desire beauty?

_____

_____

_____

_____

_____

How can you celebrate others' beauty while also celebrating your own?

_____

_____

_____

_____

_____

WEEK 1 .... WEEK 2 .... WEEK 3 .... **WEEK 4** .... WEEK 5 .... WEEK 6 .... WEEK 7 .... WEEK 8 .... WEEK 9 .... WEEK 10 .... WEEK 11 .... WEEK 12

DAY 5

PRAY

Who has the louder voice in your life? To whom are you listening? Satan and society? Or your Creator? The one who takes life from you or the one who gave His life for you?

Spend some time being honest with God. If there is any selfishness and pride in your heart (or life?), be willing to repent of it. You do not need to change your heart on your own. Allow God to convict you where conviction is needed. As He brings things to mind, talk to Him about them. Allow Him to speak His truth about your beautiful identity! If you've given up on beauty, ask Jesus to breathe life back into that part of your soul. During your time in prayer, ask Jesus how He thinks that you are beautiful.

Record your prayers below.

_____

_____

_____

_____

_____

_____

_____

_____

WEEK 1 .... WEEK 2 .... WEEK 3 .... WEEK 4 .... WEEK 5 .... WEEK 6 .... WEEK 7 .... WEEK 8 .... WEEK 9 .... WEEK 10 .... WEEK 11 .... WEEK 12

DAY 5

PW

WEEK FIVE

TESTIMONY

"Maintaining sexual integrity in today's culture is extremely difficult as a Christian. It's like having the little angel and devil on your shoulders: Your faith is telling you what is right, and when you act outside of those guidelines you feel convicted. Then society and culture are telling you that sex is a natural thing, and it is perfectly fine to explore that."

Passionate for God,
Repentant in spirit,
Open and honest,
Victorious in living,
Eternal in perspective, and
Networking with other *PROVEN Women.*

MEMORY VERSE

Hebrews 4:15–16 (ESV): "For we do not have a high priest who is unable to sympathize with our weaknesses, but one who in every respect has been tempted as we are, yet without sin. Let us then with confidence draw near to the throne of grace, that we may receive mercy and find grace to help in time of need."

WEEK 5 DAY 1 (MONDAY)

KEY THOUGHT: What do you desire most?

To begin this week, read Psalm 63.

What does this passage reveal about God?

_____

_____

_____

What does this passage reveal about us?

_____

_____

_____

DAILY READING

Have you ever felt longing in the way it is described in Psalm 63:1 (ESV)? I seek you "as in a dry and weary land where there is no water." Have you ever felt that way in your heart about anything? I am not necessarily talking about a spiritual desire at this point. We can

WEEK 1........ WEEK 2........ WEEK 3........ WEEK 4....... WEEK 5 .... WEEK 6........ WEEK 7........ WEEK 8........ WEEK 9........ WEEK 10 .... WEEK 11........ WEEK 12

DAY 1

want something so much that we literally feel the longing physically. There is a pain in our gut or our chest. You can almost feel that void, and the void is miserable. We will do almost anything to fill that void. Perhaps we settle for unhealthy relationships because we desire the attention. Perhaps there is a huge longing for physical pleasure, so we give in to pornography and masturbation.

When Psalm 63 talks about desire, however, it is describing it in its truest form. King David accurately identifies his desires. He realizes that the deep longing within his soul is for His God. One of the most miserable feelings is a desire unfulfilled. Fortunately, this is not David's experience, at least not at this point in his life. Verse 5 (ESV) says, "My soul will be satisfied as with fat and rich food, and my mouth will praise you with joyful lips." Satisfaction, joyful lips—these are things we want to experience. Each of us can experience satisfaction and joy if when we choose to steer our heart toward the Lord and recognize that we long for Him, and that He brings satisfaction.

When our heart is satisfied with the Lord, we can also enjoy the other things in our life. With a full heart, we can also enjoy relationships and pursuits and adventures. However, when we turn to these things first to fill the hole which God is meant to fill, these same relationships and pursuits are "not enough." We keep needing more and more. We easily become dissatisfied. I am sure those who are turning to relationships, pornography and masturbation have discovered that the longing only grows deeper. Eventually harder porn and more frequent masturbation are needed. This becomes a vicious cycle.

READ THE BIBLE

Let's read another passage about someone who had a longing and got herself into this vicious cycle. Read John 4:1–45.

Write down any initial thoughts.

_____

_____

_____

WEEK 1 ...... WEEK 2 ...... WEEK 3 ...... WEEK 4 ...... **WEEK 5** ...... WEEK 6 ...... WEEK 7 ...... WEEK 8 ...... WEEK 9 ...... WEEK 10 ...... WEEK 11 ...... WEEK 12

DAY 1

Jesus sat and waited by the well. The disciples ran off to get food, but He stayed behind because He had an appointment. It was a weird time to meet someone at the well, for the women did not normally come during the heat of the day. However, Jesus knew this was her time. He knew who was coming, and He was going to make sure He was there to greet her. It was time. Time to cleanse and heal her heart. He also had a mission for her, one that she had no idea she was about to embark on.

He already knew everything about her. He knew how thirsty her heart was for love and affection. He also knew where those desires had driven her. She was spiraling downward in a cycle of marriage, rejection, another man, marriage, rejection, another man. We do not know if she was being rejected or if she was the one rejecting. Either way, she was emotionally and spiritually starving, and she was chasing after the wrong things. Her soul was thirsting for more than water and far more than other relationships could provide.

Was Jesus angry at her? No. Did He reject her because of the things that she had done? No. Did He avoid her in case she rejected what He had to offer her? No.

Knowing both the condition of her heart and her past and present actions, Jesus created an appointment to spend time with her. He gently confronted her in her sin but also revealed Himself to her as the Christ. He saw her and accepted her. Then she turned and told her entire town about Him, and many believed. Here are a few lessons we can glean from this story:

- Jesus understood the longing of her heart better than she did.

- The things that she had done and that she was currently doing did not keep Jesus away.

- God had a mission and purpose for her life. The things she had done did not disqualify her.

- Jesus pursued her even though she was at her worst.

HEARTWORK

Do you believe God knows your heart better than you do? Do you think what He has to offer is better than the things you are chasing?

_____

_____

WEEK 1 ...... WEEK 2 ...... WEEK 3 ...... WEEK 4 ...... **WEEK 5** ...... WEEK 6 ...... WEEK 7 ...... WEEK 8 ...... WEEK 9 ...... WEEK 10 ...... WEEK 11 ...... WEEK 12

DAY 1

If you and Jesus met in person today, what are some things He might point out in your life?

_____

_____

_____

_____

When this woman heard the truth and found Jesus, she immediately told others about Him. Who are others with whom you need to share how God is transforming your life so that they can have hope that God can do it for them as well?

_____

_____

_____

_____

PRAY

"ACTS" is a commonly used tool to help your mind not get scattered as you pray. You may find it useful.

Adoration—spend some time quieting your heart and remembering who God is. Praise Him for some of His attributes for which you are thankful.

Confession—be honest with God about how your thoughts and actions have been the past couple days. Confess where you have fallen short and thank Him for His forgiveness and grace.

Thanksgiving—celebrate ways you are seeing God working in your life today.

WEEK 1........ WEEK 2........ WEEK 3........ WEEK 4........ WEEK 5 .... WEEK 6........ WEEK 7........ WEEK 8........ WEEK 9........ WEEK 10 .... WEEK 11........ WEEK 12

DAY 1

Supplication—pray for others in your life. Pray especially for those that God has put on your heart that you need to share His good news with. Pray for opportunities to share with them.

Pray for anything else that God puts on your heart. Have faith and expectation that He hears you and that He is responding in power.

Record your prayers below.

_____

_____

_____

_____

_____

_____

_____

_____

_____

_____

_____

_____

_____

_____

MEMORY VERSE

Hebrews 4:15–16 (ESV): "For we do not have a high priest who is unable to sympathize with our weaknesses, but one who in every respect has been tempted as we are, yet without sin. Let us then with confidence draw near to the throne of grace, that we may receive mercy and find grace to help in time of need."

WEEK 5 DAY 2 (TUESDAY)

KEY THOUGHT: God has made us to have relationships.

DAILY READING

The desire to be chosen hits home for most girls. Once again, this desire begins with our earthly fathers. We want our dad to choose to spend time with us. We want him to choose to come to our track meet, debate, or dance recital rather than staying late at work. We want him to join us on the trampoline rather than shushing us so he can watch TV. We want him to tell us that he loves us and delights in us. Why does this matter so much to us? Because our little hearts long to know that we are seen and loved by him. We want to know that we are worth the time, effort, and words of affirmation. We need to know that we have value.

Whether you have an amazing dad, a poor father figure, or no father at all, eventually a dad's affection is not enough. In some way, he falls short and we long for a deeper intimacy. This is good, because we are designed to leave home and cling to our husband. But before this happens, we are meant to find our completeness in Christ.

But, our heart doesn't always identify this longing as being for Christ. As young women, we often ask ourselves, am I worth the attention of any of the young men around me? Do I have what it takes to catch someone's eye? It is amazing how much stock we put into this question, as if all of our value is wrapped up in whether or not we get chosen. We want to know that there is someone who values us enough to choose us above all others. If we are already married and are not careful, we can place our worth in whether or not our husband loves and appreciates us today. Don't get me wrong, we blossom more when we know we

WEEK 1........ WEEK 2........ WEEK 3........ WEEK 4........ **WEEK 5** .... WEEK 6........ WEEK 7........ WEEK 8........ WEEK 9........ WEEK 10........ WEEK 11........ WEEK 12

DAY 2

are loved. We are meant to be loved. Our worth, however, is not determined by how much we are loved by a man. Our worth is determined by how much we are loved by God.

We can do some crazy things to get chosen. We manipulate our looks, our personalities, our schedules, and our interests. For some of us, we will do anything and everything to be chosen. For some, this includes chasing after men and feeling valued when men find pleasure in their body. For others, they feel like they will never become chosen and lose heart. Some choose to live vicariously through porn or fantasies. Pornography hits the heart from two angles at this point. It brings false intimacy, allowing her to feel like she is chosen in that moment. On the other hand, pornography can provide an escape, momentarily numbing the pain of rejection.

The same can be true of a woman who is in a relationship but has become discontent in it. An unappreciated or insecure wife or girlfriend can also become desperate to fill this void. When we place our value and worth on whether or not a man is choosing us above everyone and everything else, our heart and foundation begin to unravel.

Once again, something that God intended for good, our flesh and Satan have distorted into something destructive. There is nothing wrong with desiring to be chosen. In fact, God instilled this desire within our hearts. It is part of God's design. It is a beautiful thing when a father loves his daughter. God finds delight in watching a man pursue and marry his wife. He is pleased when a husband daily loves and seeks after his wife. These are things that God designed because they are symbolic of His love and pursuit of us.

Did you just hear those very important words? Human relationships are *symbolic of His love and pursuit of us.* Our identity is not decided by whether or not a man chooses or accepts us today, but rather that our God and Savior created us, knit us together in our mother's womb, rescued us, laid down His life for us, chose us, and daily chooses to pursue an even deeper and more intimate relationship with us.

HEARTWORK

When we go through a painful circumstance, Satan is usually right around the corner to kick us while we are down. He wants to infuse lies into these memories, which makes the wound even deeper. For instance, if a dad did not love his daughter well, the daughter often blames herself, believing the lie that she was not lovable enough to keep him around.

WEEK 1........ WEEK 2........ WEEK 3........ WEEK 4........ **WEEK 5** WEEK 6........ WEEK 7........ WEEK 8........ WEEK 9........ WEEK 10 .... WEEK 11........12

DAY 2

When someone gets rejected, Satan wants them to believe they are a disappointment. When someone is in a hard marriage, Satan wants that person to feel like a failure. He pins shameful labels on us that go along with these painful circumstances. Only God has the authority to define us. However, it is the responsibility of each person to decide whom they will believe. Will they agree with the shameful label that feels true, or will they believe their Heavenly Father who redeems and restores?

Several years ago, I was walking down the hallway at work, having a pity party for myself. I had just found out that another woman in her late twenties to early thirties got engaged. I wanted the ground to swallow me up because I felt like I walked around with singleness stamped across my forehead, like people were wondering what was wrong with me. God doesn't speak to me audibly, but somehow, He gets thoughts across to me. God stopped me in my tracks and just said, "Stop. Stop calling yourself a single woman. I haven't given you that label. You are just woman. Fully woman and a beloved woman. You are who I want you to be and where I want you to be. You are walking in a shame I didn't give you." That day brought a lot of freedom for me.

Is there any label that you are carrying that God never intended for you to carry? Singleness was mine, but that doesn't belong to everyone reading this. Perhaps yours is divorced? Rejected? Unloved? Unseen?

_____

_____

_____

_____

Is there any fear that you have when it comes to relationships? How have you personalized that fear? For instance, do you fear that they will leave you someday because you are not lovable enough to make them stay? Do you fear that you will never be chosen because you have become the one who is always looked over? Are you afraid you are not pretty enough? Smart enough? Feminine enough?

_____

_____

WEEK 1 ...... WEEK 2 ...... WEEK 3 ...... WEEK 4 ...... **WEEK 5** ...... WEEK 6 ...... WEEK 7 ...... WEEK 8 ...... WEEK 9 ...... WEEK 10 ...... WEEK 11 ...... WEEK 12

DAY 2

_____

_____

READ THE BIBLE

Read Isaiah 54 and write out your initial thoughts.

_____

_____

_____

_____

_____

I used to get frustrated with this passage because I was afraid that if I allowed this passage to speak to me, then I was allowing God to tell me that I would never have a husband, that He would be the only husband I would ever get. But that is not the message of this passage.

Verses 4–6: "Fear not, for you will not be ashamed; be not confounded, for you will not be disgraced; for you will forget the shame of your youth, and the reproach of your widowhood you will remember no more. For your Maker is your husband, the Lord of hosts is his name; and the Holy One of Israel is your Redeemer, the God of the whole earth he is called. For the Lord has called you like a wife deserted and grieved in spirit, like a wife of youth when she is cast off, says your God."

Whether your pain of rejection comes from a parent, your husband, or constantly being overlooked, know that God sees your pain and gathers you to Himself in compassion. He takes away any lies we have been carrying. God sees us completely. God loves us and pursues us. His love is consistent. No matter what lie or label Satan has smeared across your reputation, know that God can cleanse and wash it away. He brings ultimate healing.

WEEK 1 .... WEEK 2 .... WEEK 3 .... WEEK 4 .... **WEEK 5** .... WEEK 6 .... WEEK 7 .... WEEK 8 .... WEEK 9 .... WEEK 10 .... WEEK 11 .... WEEK 12

DAY 2

PRAY

If you have any of these fears, confide in the Lord about them. He wants to hear everything that is going on in your mind. He brings peace, joy, and love where you have fear and pain. Are you willing to trust God with your heart? Spend some time talking to the Lord about how you trust Him. If you are having a hard time trusting Him, be honest about why. Ask God to help you to love Him with all your heart and to trust Him completely. Thank Him for loving you enough that He gave everything to rescue you.

Record your prayers below.

_____

_____

_____

_____

_____

_____

_____

_____

_____

_____

MEMORY VERSE

Hebrews 4:15–16 (ESV): "For we do not have a high priest who is unable to sympathize with our weaknesses, but one who in every respect has been tempted as we are, yet without sin. Let us then with confidence draw near to the throne of grace, that we may receive mercy and find grace to help in time of need."

WEEK 5 DAY 3 (WEDNESDAY)

KEY THOUGHT: God gives us so much safety in our relationship with Him that we have nothing to fear in relationships with others.

DAILY READING

God has designed us to be in perfect relationship with Him and with one another. We want to belong and know that we are accepted. An emotionally healthy person who is walking in close intimacy with the Lord is free to enter into healthy relationships with others.

One of the deepest emotional pains a person can experience is the pain of rejection. We were designed to be in perfect relationship with God and one another. Rejection was not part of God's original plan; however, there is no way to avoid experiencing it now. Some people will experience it at higher degrees than others, but every one of us will experience rejection at one point or another. Our hearts will naturally try to avoid the pain of rejection. The problem is, many try to avoid this pain through unhealthy means. We have a tendency to build a fortress around our heart in order to keep it from experiencing pain. Some use walls, keeping everyone at arm's length, never being vulnerable. Other's use various ways to escape. It is easier to escape into lust, substance abuse and busyness than to feel our own pain.

What walls do we put up in order to protect our hearts?

- Some people have shut down all desires and expectations. They do not expect anything from anyone. You cannot be let down by someone if you don't expect anything from them. Pornography, fantasy, and masturbation become very attractive to this person because it is within their control. They serve themselves and don't have to rely on anyone

WEEK 1......... WEEK 2......... WEEK 3......... WEEK 4......... WEEK 5 .... WEEK 6......... WEEK 7......... WEEK 8......... WEEK 9......... WEEK 10 .... WEEK 11........ WEEK 12

DAY 3

else in the process. For this person, the main problem is not the pornography but the condition of their heart. Even if they were to say "no" to the lustful behavior, they would eventually find something else to self-soothe until they actually deal with their heart.

- Some people avoid being hurt by going from relationship to relationship to relationship. If they are rejected by one person, they quickly fill the void by instantly jumping into the next relationship. They may not know how to stand on their own two feet. They do not realize that they are whole and complete in Christ. The fear of feeling the pain of rejection propels them into the next relationship.

- Some isolate themselves. They have a hard time trusting others. They were mistreated and deeply wounded by someone. They live in fear that it will happen again, so they focus on healing themselves and try to adapt to self-reliance. They are not only shutting out the bad, they are shutting out the good. It's hard for them to hear that this is pride in the midst of pain. Their heart will need to learn to trust that God wants to heal them and wants them to have healthy, loving relationships.

HEARTWORK

What walls have you built to guard your heart?

_____

_____

Unfortunately, many well-meaning people have cultivated this avoidance of pain by misusing the verse Proverbs 4:23 (NIV): "Above all else, guard your heart, for everything you do flows from it." Many times when I stand before a group of girls and ask them how they have seen this verse used in their life, they say, "guard it from being broken. Guard it from liking a boy who may not like you back." We are taught to build a fortress around our heart that no one can penetrate.

But this perspective leads to lies like these: Don't worry, because when the right knight in shining armor rides into town, the king will give him a key to your heart. All of the walls will magically come tumbling down for him and him alone. Your fear of vulnerability will dissipate because this knight will be understanding in all of your conversations. Your fear of rejection will instantly melt away because the right man will never leave you.

WEEK 1........ WEEK 2........ WEEK 3........ WEEK 4........ **WEEK 5** .... WEEK 6........ WEEK 7........ WEEK 8........ WEEK 9........ WEEK 10 .... WEEK 11........ WEEK 12

DAY 3

But this way of thinking isn't true! There is not a perfect guy that is going to magically fix your heart. We are broken. The man that is in your life or the man who will potentially come into your life is broken. Each of us is responsible for our own heart. We are called to guard it, but we have to guard it His way.

SPECIAL NOTE:

We need to ask God for discernment. If there is someone in your life who has been abusive, then it is very important to put proper boundaries in place. God does not ask us to be a doormat to those who take advantage of us. What I am saying is that we should not put up walls out of fear of rejection or fear of the unknown.

So, if God is not calling us to put up walls to guard our heart from pain, what is He saying?

READ THE BIBLE

When God called us to guard our heart above all else, He was definitely not calling us to build a fortress around it so we would never experience pain. Remember, He says our heart is the wellspring of life. When we put up walls that shut people out, can life flow out of it?

Read Proverbs 4, then re-read Proverbs 4:20–27.

When you put Proverbs 4:23 in its context, what is God asking us to guard our hearts from? He asks us to guard it from evil, crooked speech, devious talk and impurity. We need to guard it from lust, pride, and selfishness. We should also be guarding it from the labels and stigmas that we talked about yesterday. We are going to experience pain in this life. We cannot love well without experiencing pain. But there are things that we need to guard our heart from along the way.

We need to guard our hearts from sin. As soon as you see jealousy, rivalry, lust, selfishness, pride, bitterness, or other sinful desires stirring up within your heart, it is crucial that you deal with this instantly. Don't bury it. Confess it to the Lord and let Him cleanse your heart. Make every effort to guard your heart from these things.

WEEK 1 .... WEEK 2 .... WEEK 3 .... WEEK 4 .... WEEK 5 .... WEEK 6 .... WEEK 7 .... WEEK 8 .... WEEK 9 .... WEEK 10 .... WEEK 11 .... WEEK 12

DAY 3

We also need to guard our hearts from the lies of Satan. Like we said yesterday, along with the pain of rejection comes the label "rejected." If we think getting chosen proves our worth, then getting rejected does the complete opposite. If we let it, rejection strips us of our dignity. Satan tells us we are not enough. We were trying so hard to stand up with our chest puffed up and our head held high. Rejection sucks all of the air out of us. We deflate and see lifeless versions of ourselves. Rejection seems to prove what we feared all along, that we are not worthy.

At least that's what Satan wants us to think. Don't forget, he is the father of lies and the accuser. He does not play fair. He wants nothing more than to blind you of your true worth. He knows you are so much more than your relational status, but he doesn't want you to know that. He knows that even if a man rejects you on this earth, that does not make you unworthy. Yet, he still attempts to smear that label across your heart. He knows that you are a beloved daughter. You belong to the church which is the bride of Christ. You are the holy temple of the most high God. He knows you have been sought after, paid for, rescued, clothed, crowned, and set on a mission. *He also knows that you don't believe it,* so he whispers to you over and over and over and over: "You are not enough. You are not enough. You are not enough. Fill this void with sexual pleasure. You will never get these desires fulfilled in God's way because you are not worth it."

God, on the other hand, also knows your worth. He knows you have dignity because He gave it to you. He sees you and He loves you. He knows you are enough. He also knows you will be rejected from time to time. He does not expect you to be okay with rejection. He knows it will hurt and He grieves with you. He wants you to run to Him with your aching heart and allow Him to comfort you. He wants to reassure you that although it hurts when a man rejects you, it does not define you. You have just as much worth the day before the rejection as you do the day after your rejection. Because God defines your worth, not man's view of you.

Pornography as an Escape

- Some people use physical intimacy as prevention. They stick to physical intimacy rather than engaging with people in order to protect themselves from future hurt. This is such a false sense of security. It is true that these individuals are keeping others from hurting them, but they are also starving themselves of true intimacy. Meanwhile, they are destroying their heart with physical intimacy. We should be making every effort to guard our heart from physical intimacy and other sexual sins, rather than using sexual sin to barricade our heart from experiencing intimate relationships.

WEEK 1 ...... WEEK 2 ...... WEEK 3 ...... WEEK 4 ...... **WEEK 5** ...... WEEK 6 ...... WEEK 7 ...... WEEK 8 ...... WEEK 9 ...... WEEK 10 ...... WEEK 11 ...... WEEK 12

DAY 3

- Others use physical intimacy to escape the current pain they are experiencing. Rather than going to God for comfort, they go to porn or fantasies for an escape. For a short time, the pain is numbed. This is also destructive to the heart. Numbing the pain does nothing toward bringing healing, so it prolongs the pain in the long run.

- Physical intimacy also feeds the sex drive, magnifying the very desire that is being starved of true intimacy. This makes people need more and more, creating an addictive pattern.

PRAY

Yesterday, you talked to God about some lies and labels you may have been believing about yourself. Today, I want you to talk to God about how He identifies you. Then spend time praising Him. Thank Him for attributes of His character that are evident in your life. Think back over the past couple days and remember ways that God was at work in your life. Take some time to praise Him for these things.

Pray for other Proven Women as well. God doesn't just call us to love Him. He calls us to love others as well. This helps us walk away from selfishness. Ask God to show you ways you can be serving others.

_____

_____

_____

_____

_____

_____

_____

MEMORY VERSE

Hebrews 4:15–16 (ESV): "For we do not have a high priest who is unable to sympathize with our weaknesses, but one who in every respect has been tempted as we are, yet without sin. Let us then with confidence draw near to the throne of grace, that we may receive mercy and find grace to help in time of need."

WEEK 5 DAY 4 (THURSDAY)

KEY THOUGHT: God comforts us in our pain.

This week, we have been talking about the desire to be chosen and the pain of rejection. We have talked about guarding our heart from lies and labels that can bombard us during our time of pain. We have also been warned about not escaping pain by turning toward pornography and other sexual sin. You may be saying, "that's great, Emily, but I have no idea what to do with all of the pain that I am experiencing, and it seems impossible to just sit here and feel it." Pain can be very overwhelming. Let's jump right to Scripture to see what God has to say about this through our brother Paul.

DAILY READING

Read 2 Corinthians 1:3–11 (ESV):

> Blessed be the God and Father of our Lord Jesus Christ, the Father of mercies and God of all comfort, [4]who comforts us in all our affliction, so that we may be able to comfort those who are in any affliction, with the comfort with which we ourselves are comforted by God. [5]For as we share abundantly in Christ's sufferings, so through Christ we share abundantly in comfort too. [6]If we are afflicted, it is for your comfort and salvation; and if we are comforted, it is for your comfort, which you experience when you patiently endure the same sufferings that we suffer. [7]Our hope for you is unshaken, for we know that as you share in our sufferings, you will also share in our comfort.
>
> [8]For we do not want you to be unaware, brothers, of the affliction we experienced in Asia. For we were so utterly burdened beyond our strength that we

WEEK 1........ WEEK 2........ WEEK 3........ WEEK 4........ **WEEK 5** .... WEEK 6........ WEEK 7........ WEEK 8........ WEEK 9........ WEEK 10........ WEEK 11........ WEEK 12

DAY 4

despaired of life itself. [9]Indeed, we felt that we had received the sentence of death. But that was to make us rely not on ourselves but on God who raises the dead. [10]He delivered us from such a deadly peril, and he will deliver us. On him we have set our hope that he will deliver us again. [11]You also must help us by prayer, so that many will give thanks on our behalf for the blessing granted us through the prayers of many.

What is Paul's explanation for suffering?

_____

_____

_____

How did God use Paul to bring hope to others?

_____

_____

_____

In this passage, Paul is writing to a group of people who were suffering. He writes to remind them that God is the Father of mercy and God of all comfort. Paul is speaking from experience. God's comfort is not just a concept that Paul was taught in a Sunday school room and chose to believe. It is something that He had personally experienced. I love verse 7: "Our hope for you is unshaken, for we know that as you share in our sufferings, you will also share in our comfort." Paul does not try to downplay their suffering or fix it for them. Rather he has such hope for them because he believes with all of his heart that God will meet them in their suffering and comfort them.

In the next few verses, he shares his own experience with them. He was so overwhelmed with his own suffering that he despised life itself, yet he learned to rely on God during that time. God is a powerful, loving being who delivers us from our despair.

WEEK 1........ WEEK 2........ WEEK 3........ WEEK 4........ **WEEK 5** .... WEEK 6........ WEEK 7........ WEEK 8........ WEEK 9........ WEEK 10 .... WEEK 11........ WEEK 12

DAY 4

I don't know what you are experiencing. I don't know how overwhelmed you are by your pain, your loneliness, or your darkness. But I do know that God will come and meet you where you are. He is the God of all comfort.

How does God comfort us?

- **With His presence**—Psalm 23:4 (ESV)—"Even though I walk through the valley of the shadow of death, I will fear no evil for you are with me. Your rod and staff comfort me."

- **With His strength**—Psalm 73:26 (ESV)—"My flesh and my heart may fail, but God is the strength of my heart and my portion forever."

- **With empathy**—Jesus wept with Mary and Martha before raising Lazarus (John 11). We will look into this in greater depth tomorrow.

- **By acknowledging the situation or pain**—Psalm 56:8 (ESV)—"You have *kept count of my tossings;* put *my tears* in your bottle. Are they not in your book?"

- **By listening and caring**—Hebrews 5:7 (ESV)—"In the days of his flesh, Jesus offered up prayers and supplications, with loud cries and tears, to him who was able to save him from death, and *he was heard because of his reverence.*"

Anytime we are suffering, we are entering into a place where Christ has already been. Jesus understands pain. While on the earth, He was rejected, mocked, scorned, and betrayed. He felt the shame of all of our sin. As if the emotional pain was not enough, He also endured more physical pain than I can imagine. Jesus went through all that pain and despair so that He can know you in your despair.

 ## READ THE BIBLE

Read Psalm 22.

This is a prophetic Psalm, describing Christ on the cross. Spend time meditating on the suffering that Christ endured.

Write out any thoughts that come to mind as you meditate on Christ.

_____

_____

WEEK 1 ...... WEEK 2 ...... WEEK 3 ...... WEEK 4 ...... **WEEK 5** ...... WEEK 6 ...... WEEK 7 ...... WEEK 8 ...... WEEK 9 ...... WEEK 10 ...... WEEK 11 ...... WEEK 12

DAY 4

_____

_____

Do you realize all of this suffering was for your sake? Hebrews 12:2–4 (ESV): "Looking to Jesus, the founder and perfecter of our faith, who for the joy that was set before him endured the cross, despising the shame, and is seated at the right hand of the throne of God. ³Consider him who endured from sinners such hostility against himself, so that you may not grow weary or fainthearted. ⁴In your struggle against sin you have not yet resisted to the point of shedding your blood."

According to these verses, why did Christ suffer?

_____

_____

How does this impact the way you view the cross?

_____

_____

HEARTWORK

Once again, I want to warn you of a tactic of evil. Some of you may be reading this and think that God's comfort does not apply to you because you have brought on your own pain. Perhaps you are experiencing pain over a relationship you should have never been in, so you think you do not deserve God's comfort. Do not believe this lie! Let's read 2 Corinthians 1:3 (ESV) again: "Blessed be the God and Father of our Lord Jesus Christ, the Father of mercies and God of all comfort." He is the Father of *mercy* and God of all *comfort*. Mercy is such a beautiful word. He comes to us with peace even when we deserve wrath. I believe that God was very strategic in putting these two words together. He wants you to know that you are not exempt. No matter the reason for your pain, no matter whose fault it is, God will come. Because of the cross, Jesus stands in the gap, taking on our shame, so that

WEEK 1........ WEEK 2........ WEEK 3........ WEEK 4........ WEEK 5 .... WEEK 6........ WEEK 7........ WEEK 8........ WEEK 9........ WEEK 10 .... WEEK 11........ WEEK 12

DAY 4

nothing stands in the way of your Father's love for you. First He showers you with mercy, and then He comes in to hold you.

Do you believe that God will comfort you today?

_____

_____

Of the ways God comforts (presence, strength, empathy, acknowledging pain, and listening), which one means the most to you? Why?

_____

_____

PRAY

Spend time thanking Christ for His suffering on your behalf.

Open up to God about painful circumstances you have experienced. Trust God to listen and care about every detail.

Ask God to give you the strength needed to be present in this pain, allowing Him to come and comfort you. Resist escaping into pornography or other sexual sins.

Be honest with God about anything else you may be trying to bury and hide. He already knows and He wants to free you from these things. If it is painful, he will comfort. If it is ugly, He will cleanse and forgive. He is yours.

_____

_____

_____

_____

MEMORY VERSE

Hebrews 4:15–16 (ESV): "For we do not have a high priest who is unable to sympathize with our weaknesses, but one who in every respect has been tempted as we are, yet without sin. Let us then with confidence draw near to the throne of grace, that we may receive mercy and find grace to help in time of need."

WEEK 5 DAY 5 (FRIDAY)

KEY THOUGHT: God feels our pain with us and aches to comfort us.

DAILY READING

Getting raw before the Lord

Most women have lots of layers. I don't know if you would rather be compared to an onion or a parfait, but let's be honest, we can be very complicated. Many times we don't even understand ourselves. We may be unaware of what is deep in our own innermost layers. It is usually things that are under the surface that wreak the most havoc in our lives.

Many people are afraid to open up their heart for two reasons—shame and pain. Some of us are afraid to open up our hearts and dig deep because we are afraid of how ugly and dirty it is. We don't want to reveal motives because we know that they are selfish and prideful. Perhaps we have been good at managing our outward appearance and behavior, but if we dig in too deep, we don't know if we could continue managing it. So we leave things buried under the surface, claiming that ignorance is bliss.

Another reason to leave our hearts untouched and guarded is because we may not know how deep wounds run, and it scares us to death to uncover how broken our heart truly is. We will do anything and everything to avoid pain. Sometimes we harden our heart and try to be okay all the time. Sometimes we try to escape through staying busy, always being in a relationship, Netflix, or porn and masturbation.

Do we have the courage to open our heart and be raw with God, no matter what is beneath the surface? It took me awhile to get this vulnerable with the Lord. I was afraid He would

WEEK
1........
WEEK
2........
WEEK
3........
WEEK
4........
WEEK
5
WEEK
6........
WEEK
7........
WEEK
8........
WEEK
9........
WEEK
10........
WEEK
11........
WEEK
12

DAY 5

be so disappointed with the ugliness beneath the surface. To be honest, I think I was more afraid that I would be disappointed with how ugly it was. I really wanted to be known as a good, godly Christian girl, so it just became easier to leave things buried. I also thought that if I was a strong Christian, then things shouldn't bother me. I believed that being surrendered to God would mean that I was okay with whatever I had to face, so I buried the pain. I thought God was so pleased with my strength. But I could not have been more wrong. Burying things under the surface actually kept God at arm's length when He wanted to be up close and personal. Remember, God is pursuing an intimate relationship with us, so all of these hidden secrets and walled-off parts of our hearts create distance rather than create intimacy.

Here I thought God would be so pleased with my strength. It wasn't strength. It was pride. God doesn't want us to be strong. He wants to be our strength.

Hebrews 4:12–16 (ESV) became such an important passage for me. It gave me the courage to be raw before the Lord.

"For the Word of God is living and active, sharper than any two-edged sword, piercing to the division of soul and of spirit, of joints and of marrow, and discerning the thoughts and intentions of the heart, and no creature is hidden from his sight, but all are naked and exposed to the eyes of him to whom we must give account. Since then we have a great high priest who has passed through the heavens, Jesus the Son of God, let us hold fast our confession. For we do not have a high priest who is unable to sympathize with us but one who in every respect has been temped as we are, yet without sin. Let us then with confidence draw near to the throne of grace, that we may receive mercy and find grace to help in the time of need."

This passage tells us to picture the Word of God as a two-edged sword. I used to picture a huge sword that someone would use in battle. But someone else pointed out to me that this is more like a surgeon's scalpel. As I read the verse in its context, I can picture not only the scalpel but the entire surgical room. I lie on a surgeon's table with my heart fully opened to the Lord. Everything within me wants to reach up and cover my heart with my hands. There are things that I want to shield and hide. But the loving surgeon reminds me that He is gentle and kind. He also is very discerning, knowing what to cut away and what to leave. As He takes the scalpel and cuts into my heart, He cleanses and forgives everything that is ugly. As He gets to a scar that stirs up the pain of a memory,

WEEK 1 ...... WEEK 2 ...... WEEK 3 ...... WEEK 4 ...... WEEK 5 ...... WEEK 6 ...... WEEK 7 ...... WEEK 8 ...... WEEK 9 ...... WEEK 10 ...... WEEK 11 ...... WEEK 12

DAY 5

He cries tears with me as He empathizes with me. He brings healing and comfort to my heart. I have nothing to fear.

Read Hebrews 4:12–16 again.

Jesus is my great high priest. He walked on this earth and experienced so many of the things I have experienced. He was rejected, betrayed, tempted, neglected, and mocked. He can empathize with us no matter what it is we are experiencing. We are safe to confide in Him. Not only has He experienced these things, but He always responded well. He did not cave into lust, pride, selfishness or substance abuse or other things we use to catch the pain we go through. Jesus was tempted in every way that we are, yet He remained without sin.

He is our great role model. He also is the One who empowers us. His Spirit is within us. When we need to know how to respond within a situation, He is right there to step in. He will give us the discernment to know how to respond. He will also give us the strength needed to stand steadfast with us. I love that this passsage says Jesus sympathizes with our weaknesses. He does not stand at a distance to judge us. He enters into the struggle with us to empower us.

READ THE BIBLE

Read John 11.

This is the story of Jesus raising Lazarus from the dead. For Mary and Martha, however, for the first few days, this wasn't the story of their brother being raised but of their brother dying, because Jesus did not show up. Mary and Martha sent word to Jesus that Lazarus was sick. Read verses 5–6 with me again: "Now Jesus loved Martha and her sister and Lazarus. So, when he heard that Lazarus was ill, he stayed two days longer in the place where he was."

Ummm... Excuse me? What? Because He loved them, He stayed away two days longer? How is that loving them? We need to remember that God is all-knowing and all-loving. He always sees the big picture. Jesus knew that those present at Lazarus's resurrection were about to experience the greatest miracle that He had performed up to this point. He knew they would temporarily experience pain, yet the kingdom work that would come from this would outshine the momentary hurt.

DAY 5

When Jesus arrived, Lazarus had already been in the grave four days. Martha came out to greet Jesus. I love this conversation between Jesus and Martha. Martha usually gets a bad rap for her busyness in the other story of Mary and Martha with Jesus. This is Martha's redeeming moment. Let's reread her conversation with Jesus.

John 11:21–27 (NIV)

Martha said to Jesus, "Lord, if you had been here, my brother would not have died. But even now I know that whatever you ask from God, God will give you." Jesus said to her, "Your brother will rise again." Martha said to him, "I know that he will rise again in the resurrection on the last day." Jesus said to her, "I am the resurrection and the life. Whoever believes in me, though he die, yet shall he live, and everyone who lives and believes in me shall never die. Do you believe this?" She said to him, "Yes, Lord; I believe that you are the Christ, the Son of God, who is coming into the world."

Despite the fact that Jesus did not immediately show up, Martha still trusts Jesus as the Christ. She says that she still believes that God will do whatever Jesus asks. I don't think she is saying this to get Jesus to miraculously raise Lazarus from the dead. The reason I don't think this is her agenda is that later, when Jesus says to open the tomb, she tries to stop Him because it will smell bad. She is not expecting any physical miracle from Jesus at this point. Yet she confirms that she still believes that He is the Christ. Her faith in Jesus was not dependent on His intervention on her circumstances. Her belief in Christ was on Who He is.

How often do we choose to doubt God's goodness when He allows us to walk through painful times?

Now we get to my favorite part of the story. John 11:33–35 (NIV) says, "When Jesus saw her weeping, and the Jews who had come with her also weeping, he was deeply moved in his spirit and greatly troubled. And he said, 'Where have you laid him?' They said to him, 'Lord, come and see.' Jesus wept."

I used to think that Jesus wept because He was grieving for Lazarus as well, but that makes no sense because He knew what He was about to do. Rather, Jesus saw how much these women were hurting and it greatly moved Him. Think of how easy it would have been to simply shush them by telling them that He was about to raise Lazarus. Instead, His compassion compelled Him to weep with them before turning and fixing the problem.

WEEK
1........

WEEK 1 .... WEEK 2 .... WEEK 3 .... WEEK 4 .... WEEK 5 .... WEEK 6 .... WEEK 7 .... WEEK 8 .... WEEK 9 .... WEEK 10 .... WEEK 11 .... WEEK 12

DAY 5

This passage revealed to me how much God cares. I used to picture God up in heaven with arms crossed, asking me if I was willing to surrender and obey. I often felt the need to shut down any negative emotions such as disappointment, sadness, or pain. I felt like if I trusted God, I would be okay with whatever He asked me to walk through. But this passage taught me that God cares about the pain. He sheds tears when I shed tears.

HEARTWORK

Are there any layers of your heart that you consider still unavailable to God and/or others?

_____

_____

What holds you back from opening up about these areas?

_____

_____

_____

_____

How did it hit your heart today to hear that God aches with you in the painful times?

_____

_____

_____

_____

WEEK 1 ...... WEEK 2 ...... WEEK 3 ...... WEEK 4 ...... WEEK 5 ...... WEEK 6 ...... WEEK 7 ...... WEEK 8 ...... WEEK 9 ...... WEEK 10 ...... WEEK 11 ...... WEEK 12

DAY 5

PRAY

Spend ten minutes today being as open and honest as you can with God. If there are areas of your life that you have still not articulated to the Lord, ask Him for the courage to open up. Ask God to reveal to you His compassion and empathy today.

Record your prayers below.

_____

_____

_____

_____

_____

_____

_____

_____

_____

_____

_____

_____

PW

WEEK SIX

TESTIMONY

"I think there needs to be a warning at the start of the workbook. I would suggest something like, 'This book will stir up emotions and reveal things to you that will not make you happy, and show you how you really live.' When I first started the workbook I was so convicted over seeing for the first time my selfishness (wanting to be first), self-sufficiency (wanting to be in control), self-gratification (wanting to be served), greed (wanting more), and pride (wanting it on my terms), that I closed the book and ran and hid in pornography. But the Holy Spirit drew me back to Christ, the only One who can save and heal me. I felt such a longing to return to the Lord, so I returned to the study and am using it to go to Jesus and am making it a part of my daily prayer time."

Passionate for God,
Repentant in spirit,
Open and honest,
Victorious in living,
Eternal in perspective, and
Networking with other ***PROVEN Women.***

MEMORY VERSE

Philippians 2:3–5 (ESV): "Do nothing from selfish ambition or conceit, but in humility count others more significant than yourselves. Let each of you look not only to his own interests, but also to the interests of others. Have this mind among yourselves, which is yours in Christ Jesus."

WEEK **6** DAY 1 (MONDAY)

KEY THOUGHT: We were made to worship God, but were born worshiping ourselves. We need Him to redeem our nature.

DAILY READING

The Mind of Christ

There are so many things about God that we can love and worship. He is so holy, loving, and worthy of our praise. Many people have different attributes of God for which they are most grateful. Some people are most grateful for God's love. Some most appreciate God as Father or God as protector. I am grateful for these, but the one aspect of God that gets me to stand in awe of Him over and over again is God as Creator and Designer. I cannot believe how brilliant our God is. He thought through everything. Do we realize that God designed a perfect version of every relationship? He created every relationship, such as father/daughter, brother/sister, husband/wife, and friend/friend. He designed each person's role within these relationships. He knew how each should be loved, accepted, and nurtured. Also, each of these relationships are symbolic and reflects His relationship to us. God wants us to be loved and nurtured on this earth, but He also knows that He loves us more than we can ever imagine. His relationship with us is so beautiful and perfect and will last for all eternity. His love for us is more than what we're able to comprehend.

Not only did God design relationships, He also designed our hearts and minds to be able to act and respond well within these relationships. He gave us the ability to give and receive love, to trust, to be vulnerable, and to confide in one another. These things bring intimacy

WEEK 1........ WEEK 2........ WEEK 3........ WEEK 4........ WEEK 5........ WEEK 6 .... WEEK 7........ WEEK 8........ WEEK 9........ WEEK 10 .... WEEK 11........ WEEK 12

DAY 1

and depth to our relationships both with God and with each other. When all of this is played out within God's design, we are beautiful and whole.

The problem is, things are not as they are supposed to be. The world did not stay within God's design. Through one man, sin entered the world and death through sin (Romans 5:12). Now there is brokenness, rejection, betrayal, and abuse. We live in a world that does not treat us the way God desires for us to be treated and that grieves the loving and just heart of God.

The brokenness, however, is not only in the world around us. It is also within us. We are born into this world with a twisted mind and heart. From the beginning of our life, we are developing and learning. It is so fun to watch a baby start to mature and interact with the world. You can almost see the wheels turning in their little minds as they start to mimic what they see in others. But as they develop, you also start to see their selfishness and pride come about as well. It is a hard truth that you do not have to teach a little kid to say "no" or "mine." We are born putting ourselves first.

It is sad to say we are in a lose-lose situation. We are born into a selfish, prideful world, and we ourselves are selfish and prideful. But God: God has been in the business of redemption and reconciliation for as long as the world has been in existence. He desires to rescue us, redeem us, and heal us, but we have to be willing to allow Him to do it His way, by putting faith in Jesus as our Savior. We are transformed by trusting that He is our Creator. He knows what works and what does not work. His way is always better than our way, even if it does not make sense within our framework of thinking. We need a new way of thinking.

I recently spoke with a counseling professor who has spent years studying the neurology of the mind. She explained that our brain develops over the first twenty-five years of our life. There are two parts of the brain that develop to work together well, the prefrontal cortex (PFC) and the limbic system. "The PFC is responsible for focus, impulse control, planning, empathy, insight, forethought, organization, judgment, emotional control, and learning from one's mistakes. It is where we spend most of our time."[4] The limbic system is referred to as the fight-or-flight area of the brain. The limbic system's functions are the formation and storage of memory, regulating emotion, bonding, fight or flight, modulating motivation, appetite and sleep, and sexual arousal.[5] God gave us a gut instinct that knows when we are in danger: our senses are heightened, and we are hyper-aware of our surroundings. When we are in this mode, we can become irrational. Adrenaline is pumping, and we are ready to defend ourselves or ready to flee. Once the danger subsides and we find ourselves

WEEK 1........ WEEK 2........ WEEK 3........ WEEK 4........ WEEK 5........ WEEK 6........ WEEK 7........ WEEK 8........ WEEK 9........ WEEK 10........ WEEK 11........ WEEK 12

DAY 1

again in safety, our brain transitions back to our normal, more rational way of thinking. A calmness comes back over us, and we return to a peaceful state.

The best way to describe the development of the brain is to picture roadways inside of it. Now, just like God designed life, He also designed what the "roads" in our brain are supposed to look like. These pathways allow us to transition from fight-or-flight mode back into the area of our brain that allows for love, trust, acceptance, decision-making, vulnerability, and more. These roads develop best when they have been nurtured by love and security throughout our years of development. They also function best when we have a foundation of love, selflessness, and humility. When our brains are unhealthy, then fear, selfishness, and pride become major contributors to the roads in our mind. If we begin down a road that leads us to discomfort and possible betrayal, then we put up a wall and make a detour. That detour will be something that we think will protect our hearts from experiencing that pain again. The detour could be pornography. It could be isolation. It could be using humor to mask an insecurity.

Here's the deal: Our minds tend to use the road most traveled. So, if you have gone to pornography over and over again, that has become a well-worn path in your mind. Without any effort at all, your mind will instantly go in that direction. This path has gotten comfortable for you. It feels good and makes you feel safe. You hear that this path leads to destruction, but for the moment it just feels good. But there is hope because God can help us make new roads in our mind. In fact, God calls us to transform our mind.

What would it look like to have a good, healthy mind while living in this broken world? What if I open myself up and begin to trust and become vulnerable, only to be hurt in the end? Becoming healthy does not guarantee that my world will become better. I may risk loving someone and still go through the pain of rejection. I may trust someone only to have them betray me. It sounds like a scary thing to have a healthy mind in this broken world. Would God really call us to that?

There is one person that we can look to as an example of this, Jesus! He is the one person on this earth who had a perfectly healthy mind. Just like ours, His had to develop over time. He went through all of the stages of human development, but His lacked the fear, pride, and selfishness that rule within ours. Jesus experienced betrayal, false accusations, abandonment, and great suffering throughout His earthly life. Yet Jesus loved, He grieved, He trusted, He forgave and He set up relational boundaries. He is the great example of who we should be.

WEEK 1........ WEEK 2........ WEEK 3........ WEEK 4........ WEEK 5........ **WEEK 6**....... WEEK 7........ WEEK 8........ WEEK 9........ WEEK 10........ WEEK 11........ WEEK 12

DAY 1

READ THE BIBLE

Read Romans 12:1–2 (ESV) and Philippians 2:1–11 (ESV):

"I appeal to you therefore, brothers, by the mercies of God, to present your bodies as a living sacrifice, holy and acceptable to God, which is your spiritual worship. [2]Do not be conformed to this world, but be transformed by the renewal of your mind, that by testing you may discern what is the will of God, what is good and acceptable and perfect."

"So if there is any encouragement in Christ, any comfort from love, any participation in the Spirit, any affection and sympathy, [2]complete my joy by being of the same mind, having the same love, being in full accord and of one mind. [3]Do nothing from selfish ambition or conceit, but in humility count others more significant than yourselves. [4]Let each of you look not only to his own interests, but also to the interests of others. [5]Have this mind among yourselves, which is yours in Christ Jesus, [6]who, though he was in the form of God, did not count equality with God a thing to be grasped, [7]but emptied himself, by taking the form of a servant, being born in the likeness of men. [8]And being found in human form, he humbled himself by becoming obedient to the point of death, even death on a cross. [9]Therefore God has highly exalted him and bestowed on him the name that is above every name, [10]so that at the name of Jesus every knee should bow, in heaven and on earth and under the earth, [11]and every tongue confess that Jesus Christ is Lord, to the glory of God the Father."

God wants us to have the mind of Christ. Jesus walked this earth fully alive. His heart and mind were at its full capacity. "Above all else, guard your heart, for everything you do flows from it" (Proverbs 4:23, NIV).

The roads we create which steer us away from a vulnerable life are avenues that Satan can use to keep us in those ruts.

Our mind will take the paths it knows best. Think of a trail through the woods that you often ride your bike on. After years and years of taking this path, a crevice develops that your tire fits into—a well-worn path. You may steer off a bit and the tire jumps out of this crevice for a while, but eventually it finds its way back into the crevice.

WEEK 1........ WEEK 2........ WEEK 3........ WEEK 4........ WEEK 5........ **WEEK 6** .... WEEK 7........ WEEK 8........ WEEK 9........ WEEK 10 .... WEEK 11........ WEEK 12

DAY 1

HEARTWORK

For some of you, pornography has become a well-worn path. It gives you a type of release that you feel like you need. Something has triggered you, and all of a sudden you find yourself in fight-or-flight mode. You feel backed into a corner, and the only way out is through that release.

Porn may be the primary road that your brain has right now, but this is not your destiny. God is the One who can build new roadways in your mind. He is ready with hard hat on and tool belt around his waist. But He isn't just going to build this for you. He has a hard hat and tool belt for you as well. We have to join Him in the work.

What are the most well-worn paths in your brain? When you are going through a rough time, what is your go-to method of getting through it?

_____

_____

My dad builds decks for a living, and I used to work with him. Our relationship grew during that year when I worked with him. I know my dad looks forward to the day that he can build a deck for me on my own house. Rather than building one for me, he would find even more joy if I jumped out there and worked with him.

Ladies, I have no idea how to build a deck on my own. Even if my dad sent all of the instructions and a blueprint, I would not be able to do it. My dad has never asked me to go build a deck for him, but he invites me into the work he is doing. He is the one with the tools and the lumber. My dad hands me a tool belt. He hands me the lumber that he has cut and shows me where to place it. When I cannot hammer something right, I tell him and he helps me. He guides me step-by-step-by-step. Some parts I know how to do well, because it is a skill I have already mastered over time; but we talk about life and enjoy each other's company during these times.

This is the picture I want you to have of building a new road system with God. There are ways out of that trapped corner without using the well-worn path of pornography and

WEEK 1........ WEEK 2........ WEEK 3........ WEEK 4........ WEEK 5........ **WEEK 6**........ WEEK 7........ WEEK 8........ WEEK 9........ WEEK 10........ WEEK 11........ WEEK 12

DAY 1

masturbation or destructive relationships. God is patient and loving. No matter how long it takes, He is willing to show up every single day to help you build this new road. Even on the days you don't show up, He is there, ready and waiting.

PRAY

The reason that you are encouraged to pray every day is because prayer is now becoming a well-worn path in your brain. When you are going through a tough time, prayer needs to become your most natural response. Prayer becomes more natural the more you do it. Spend time today talking to God about anything that comes to mind. Praise Him, confess to Him where your heart has gone astray, pray for others, and be honest about the things going on in your heart. I hope God is becoming one of your closest friends!

Record your prayers below.

_____

_____

_____

_____

_____

_____

_____

_____

WEEK 1 ...... WEEK 2 ...... WEEK 3 ...... WEEK 4 ...... WEEK 5 ...... **WEEK 6** ...... WEEK 7 ...... WEEK 8 ...... WEEK 9 ...... WEEK 10 ...... WEEK 11 ...... WEEK 12

DAY 1

_____

_____

_____

_____

_____

_____

_____

_____

_____

SPECIAL NOTE:

Become a Proven Women partner today. Is your heart changing? Do you want to see other women break free and live out sexual integrity? You can help by joining the sisterhood of Proven Women by praying for the ministry, making a tax-deductible donation, and volunteering to lead or be a resource for other women who need support. Visit our website to learn more about how you can partner with us to advance this important work: *www.ProvenWomen.org.*

MEMORY VERSE

Philippians 2:3–5 (ESV): "Do nothing from selfish ambition or conceit, but in humility count others more significant than yourselves. Let each of you look not only to his own interests, but also to the interests of others. Have this mind among yourselves, which is yours in Christ Jesus."

WEEK 6 DAY 2 (TUESDAY)

KEY THOUGHT: Where do you find your value?

DAILY READING

Have you ever daydreamed about being a damsel in distress and a knight in shining armor comes to save the day? Well, perhaps in your daydream you didn't picture yourself as Rapunzel with hair that flowed down to the bottom of a tower. Perhaps your daydream was more along the lines of the guy you like stepping in and rescuing you from a night of loneliness. Perhaps it involves hoping that your husband will stand up and defend you when one of the kids is being rude to you. One of our other God-given desires is the desire to be protected.

Don't get me wrong, women are strong. Proverbs calls us to clothe ourselves with strength and dignity (Proverbs 31:25). Yet, as women, we are wired to desire to be protected. That is why we so often hear about a knight in shining armor. This does not say we are weak. This does not mean that we cannot fend for ourselves. We want to be protected to demonstrate that we are valued. Having someone willing to fight for us and protect us means that they care about us. And once again, we want to know that we are worth the fight.

I remember a youth speaker at a retreat telling all of us high school students that he cared about all of us, and if there was a fire in the building, he would work hard to get all of us out. But then he made a distinction about his family. If there was a fire and his wife and kids were in the midst of all of us, you better be sure that he was going to forget about all of us and first get his wife and kids out. Then he would come back and try to rescue us. I don't even remember what the point of his illustration was, but that little story stuck with

WEEK 1 ..... WEEK 2 ..... WEEK 3 ..... WEEK 4 ..... WEEK 5 ..... **WEEK 6** ..... WEEK 7 ..... WEEK 8 ..... WEEK 9 ..... WEEK 10 ..... WEEK 11 ..... WEEK 12

DAY 2

me and not necessarily in a good way. It became ammunition that Satan has used to get me down. I will be in the midst of a crowd and all of a sudden I get this thought, "If something were to happen in here, I am not anyone's priority to save."

Does this make me feel unsafe? Nope. At least for me, it has nothing to do with safety, and everything to do with not feeling valuable. In that moment, I have this defeating thought that I will be overlooked and neglected. People will run past me to save others who are valued more than I am. It is a very self-defeating thought, and it is evil at its core.

What thoughts pop into your mind that make you question your value?

_____

_____

_____

What do you do when you have these thoughts?

_____

_____

There was another time when I was a resident director at Liberty University. One particular night, I had several major things happen on a few different dorms. I had to go from one to another to another making sure that everything was all right. This was after an already exhausting week, and I felt like I was at my wits end. When I got back to my apartment very late that night, I crawled into a closet that I had made into a prayer room. I curled into a ball and cried out to the Lord: "Lord, I am always making sure everyone else is okay. Who makes sure I am okay?"

Have there been any experiences that have made you feel like you were not important enough to be protected?

_____

_____

WEEK 1 ...... WEEK 2 ...... WEEK 3 ...... WEEK 4 ...... WEEK 5 ...... WEEK 6 ...... WEEK 7 ...... WEEK 8 ...... WEEK 9 ...... WEEK 10 ...... WEEK 11 ...... WEEK 12

DAY 2

_____

_____

When a thought like this pops into my mind, it is very easy to go into "woe is me" mode. "Woe is me" mode can become a dangerous place to be. Our thoughts turn introspective and we can become self-absorbed. If we do not fight against this mentality, but rather follow it effortlessly, then we will begin spiraling downward. It can go downward into despair, into anxiety, into lust, or anything else. No matter what it is spiraling into, this thought pattern veers away from God and toward a destination chosen by our enemy. The farther down that road we venture, the easier of a target we become for lustful temptations. We begin hearing the whispers: "You aren't worth protecting. You are weak. You will not be able to say 'no' to pornography tonight, so why don't you just go ahead and cave now?" "No one protects you. Even God doesn't protect you, so why are you trying so hard to fight this for Him? He doesn't care, so give in to what really brings you pleasure." These lies are nothing but evil.

Yesterday we talked about transforming our mind. We need to take action with our thoughts. When a thought like this pops into our mind, we have a choice to make. We can listen and follow it downward, or we can take that thought captive and replace it with truth. We can say "NO" to the downward spiral and stand steadfast with God. We must recognize this as a strategy of Satan and refuse to be pawns in his hands. Satan does not get to degrade our value. Each of us has intrinsic value that was placed in us the moment we were knit together in our mother's womb. **Nothing** can add or take away from our value. Satan threw away his value, and he hates that Jesus has given us the value that he tried to steal.

If that is hard for you to believe, then it is so important to continue spending time with God each day so that He can remind you of these truths. He wants to transform our minds. He wants to clothe us in His affection and value.

WEEK 1........ WEEK 2........ WEEK 3........ WEEK 4........ WEEK 5...... WEEK 6 ...... WEEK 7........ WEEK 8........ WEEK 9........ WEEK 10 .... WEEK 11........ WEEK 12

DAY 2

READ THE BIBLE

Read Psalm 139. We have read this before, but this is a passage worth meditating on.

Write down any insights that come to your mind.

_____

_____

_____

_____

Sometimes thoughts will randomly enter our minds. Other times we are faced with these thoughts because we are in the midst of tough circumstances. No matter the reason for the thoughts, we are faced with a choice as soon as they come: either dwell on the negative or intentionally turn to God. These thoughts put us in that fight-or-flight mode. Taking thoughts captive and turning to God will build the roads that you need to return to a logical, peaceful thought process. If we do not act intentionally, our mind will act in autopilot, and pornography and masturbation may seem like the only option.

That night as a resident director, while I lay in my closet sobbing, God gently reminded me that I am His. He sees me! He cares about my well-being. He gave me the perseverance and strength that I needed to make it through that night. He was by my side every step of the way. He comforted me and filled me back up after I had poured myself out completely for my girls. It would have been nice in the moment to have strong arms to hold me as I cried on a physical shoulder. But I also realized that although it would have been nice, it was not something that I needed. What I truly needed had already been provided.

Psalm 139 reminds me that no matter where I go, God is there. There will not be a second of my life when I am on my own. He knows my thoughts. He knows when I get up and when I sit down. Even when I forget that He exists, He is still intentionally watching me, caring for

WEEK 1........ WEEK 2........ WEEK 3........ WEEK 4........ WEEK 5........ **WEEK 6**........ WEEK 7........ WEEK 8........ WEEK 9........ WEEK 10........ WEEK 11........ WEEK 12

DAY 2

me, guiding me, and protecting me. There are so many times that I am unaware of Him, yet He is never unaware of me. "Such thoughts are too wonderful for me" (Psalm 139:6, ESV).

When we train our minds to be more aware of God, we have instant access to His peace, comfort, wisdom, and strength. But when I am left to my own thoughts, I can easily become a slave to the lies that assail me.

HEARTWORK

Think back through the last week. Have there been any downward thought spirals similar to what was presented today? Do you find yourself more susceptible to lust when you are in the midst of these thoughts?

_____

_____

How have you been proactive in taking these thoughts captive in your relationship with Jesus?

_____

_____

There is one thing I want to make clear to each of us. God loves and values us, and He wants us to accept this as true and believe that we have value. But the purpose of us knowing our own value is not so that we can walk around with head held high and look down our nose at others. He does not want us sitting around and dwelling on how great we are. He wants you to understand that you are loved and valued so that your heart is free to love Him and love others. He fills us so that we can pour into others.

WEEK 1........ WEEK 2........ WEEK 3........ WEEK 4........ WEEK 5........ **WEEK 6** .... WEEK 7........ WEEK 8........ WEEK 9........ WEEK 10 .... WEEK 11........ WEEK 12

DAY 2

PRAY

Spend some time thanking God for other people He has placed in your life. Talk to Him about how you want His protection in your life. Be honest about how you have thought He fell short in the past. Ask Him to help you trust Him completely. Ask for the eyes to see Him and the ears to hear Him.

_____

_____

_____

_____

_____

_____

_____

_____

_____

_____

_____

_____

_____

MEMORY VERSE

Philippians 2:3-5 (ESV): "Do nothing from selfish ambition or conceit, but in humility count others more significant than yourselves. Let each of you look not only to his own interests, but also to the interests of others. Have this mind among yourselves, which is yours in Christ Jesus."

WEEK 6 DAY 3 (WEDNESDAY)

KEY THOUGHT: God is always protecting us.

READ THE BIBLE

Read Psalm 20.

Do you trust God as much as you would trust a tangible protection like a security system or a person who is there to protect you? David was not being metaphorical when he talked about chariots and horses. Time and time again, God came through when His people were outnumbered. Some trust in chariots, but we trust in the name of the Lord our God (Psalm 20:7). Is God's presence a place where you find security?

_____

_____

_____

_____

WEEK 1 .... WEEK 2 .... WEEK 3 .... WEEK 4 .... WEEK 5 .... WEEK 6 .... WEEK 7 .... WEEK 8 .... WEEK 9 .... WEEK 10 .... WEEK 11 .... WEEK 12

DAY 3

DAILY READING

Read Exodus 14.

Put yourself in the shoes of the Israelites during this time. Things looked hopeless. They were trapped by the sea and an angry army was pursuing them. It's so easy for us to read this story and say, "Don't worry, just trust God," because we know the outcome. The Israelites are about to face an incredible miracle. I cannot imagine what it was like for them to actually get to see the parting of the Red Sea and gaze out upon the dry land before them.

The Israelites did not know what they were about to experience. That is the case for all of us. We are blind to the future. We have no idea what we will face. But there is One who does know. I know it is very cliché, but I love the sentence, "I do not know what the future holds, but I know the One who holds the future." This sentence is only comforting if we actually know and trust the One who holds the future. Some people know that God commands the future; however, they do not trust in His love or goodness, so this brings no peace. That is why it is so important for us to walk with God and grow to know and love Him more and more every day. Everything we experience is filtered through His love and holiness.

Trusting God does not guarantee that I will not go through tough times. Trusting God does not guarantee that I will not face pain. Trusting God does not mean that I will never face harm, never be rejected, or never face my worst nightmare. I would be giving you false hope if I told you that. In fact, God calls us to suffering. But Jesus suffered more than any of us. He is not calling us to anything that He has not done for us. Jesus sympathizes with us and extends His strength and peace to us in the midst of hardship.

Trusting God also reminds me that I will never face life alone. God is always in the midst of our circumstances offering strength, peace, and comfort. He is our loving, gentle Father who grieves with us when our situation hurts. He is our protective Father who hates all sin done against His children. Also, He can provide divine protection in the midst of what seems to be an impossible situation. Just to be clear, God absolutely has natural tools to keep us safe. Trusting God does not mean we reject conventional wisdom—like locking our front door at night.

WEEK 1........ WEEK 2........ WEEK 3........ WEEK 4........ WEEK 5........ **WEEK 6** .... WEEK 7........ WEEK 8........ WEEK 9........ WEEK 10........ WEEK 11........ WEEK 12

DAY 3

HEARTWORK

Today, we had a shorter reading section so we can spend more time in prayer. Don't rush through the following meditation, but turn your attention toward meeting with God. In order to learn to more fully trust God, it is important for us to spend time with Him and get to know Him.

1. Begin by allowing your mind to dwell on who God is. Allow yourself to be overwhelmed by God and His great love, mercy, and grace. Is there any part of you that is questioning His love and/or goodness? If so, talk to Him about it.

2. Picture yourself fixing your eyes on Jesus as He hangs on the cross, perfecting your faith (Hebrews 12:2). He willingly gave up everything and suffered on your behalf in order to stand steadfast with you. What does it mean to you to know that Jesus suffered on your behalf? To know that He is well acquainted with pain?

3. Contemplate the Lord's character in your heart right now, knowing that because of all that He endured you will not grow weary or lose heart as you remain under His wing (Hebrews 12:1–3).

4. Ask God to illuminate your face with the glory of the Lord—the glory that dims as you drift away. Pray that your countenance becomes ever-increasing in brightness as you draw nearer to the Source, experiencing more of the likeness of Christ (2 Corinthians 3:18). Purpose to be grateful, thankful, and content.

5. Right now, confess any sin you have committed this week and ask Jesus to heal your soul.

6. Confess ways that you have been withholding love from others or not being a friend.

7. Confess ways you have been avoiding or ignoring God.

8. Ask the Lord to instill in you a deep desire to worship and praise Him. Commit to spending intentional time meeting with God with zeal and passion.

9. Ask the Holy Spirit to reveal any areas where you treat God like a vending machine, demanding what you think you deserve or need.

10. Ask God to show you ways in which you do not fully turn to or trust in Him.

11. Openly discuss with the Lord whether you see Him as good. Keep going to God in prayer and petition, asking Him to open your eyes to His faithfulness, forgiveness, and unconditional love. Soak in the promise that if you seek Him with all of your heart, He will make Himself known to you. Ask God to help you stop pretending to trust in Him or simply going through the motions of trying to get to know Him.

12. Ask the Lord to cause you to truly believe that His Word is trustworthy and true and that it has daily application in your life. Keep reading the Bible to know God, meeting with Him in your heart and soul, not merely to gain knowledge about Him.

WEEK 1 .... WEEK 2 .... WEEK 3 .... WEEK 4 .... WEEK 5 .... WEEK 6 .... WEEK 7 .... WEEK 8 .... WEEK 9 .... WEEK 10 .... WEEK 11 .... WEEK 12

DAY 3

13. Ask God to change your inner desires so that you make pursuing the Lord your number one priority in life.

Record some of your prayers below.

_____

_____

_____

_____

_____

_____

_____

_____

_____

_____

_____

_____

_____

_____

MEMORY VERSE

Philippians 2:3–5 (ESV): "Do nothing from selfish ambition or conceit, but in humility count others more significant than yourselves. Let each of you look not only to his own interests, but also to the interests of others. Have this mind among yourselves, which is yours in Christ Jesus."

WEEK 6 DAY 4 (THURSDAY)

KEY THOUGHT: The walls around our heart don't protect us, they constrict us.

DAILY READING

We cannot address pain without addressing abuse. Chances are pretty high that many of you have experienced some form of abuse (emotional, physical, or sexual), that has contributed to (1) walls still being around your heart, (2) you shying away from vulnerable and intimate relationships and engaging in unhealthy styles of interaction with people, or (3) hidden anger. Additionally, it's important to realize that sexual abuse is not limited to forced intercourse. It can take many forms, including exposure to pornography, seeing naked adults, uncomfortable touching of your body by another, or being teased about your body. Emotional abuse, such as shame-based criticism, withholding love, and not permitting feelings to be expressed, can be very destructive. Perhaps you were teased a lot as a child or called names. Maybe your dad or mom was cruel or physically abusive. The effects of all forms of abuse frequently carry over into adulthood. The key to healing is a commitment to being open and honest about these issues, not locking away your feelings.

Have you been the victim of abuse, whether physical, verbal, emotional, or sexual? Many people have. Sadly, adults who had been inappropriately used by others in a sexual manner as children often find it hard to acknowledge that they were victims. Many incorrectly view the abuse through the lens of adulthood. For instance, if someone showed you pornography or touched you inappropriately when you were ten or twelve years old, you may

WEEK 1 .... WEEK 2 .... WEEK 3 .... WEEK 4 .... WEEK 5 .... WEEK 6 .... WEEK 7 .... WEEK 8 .... WEEK 9 .... WEEK 10 .... WEEK 11 .... WEEK 12

DAY 4

not appreciate that you were not in the same position to say "no" as you are today. Perhaps you thought you were responsible for the abuse because you responded to or received it rather than standing against it.

Take the time to watch the behavior of children. At moments, they seem all grown up; but as you watch longer, you'll see that they are in need of protection. They are vulnerable and impressionable. That's how you were as a little girl, but it could be that others violated you and used you for their selfish pleasure without regard to the lasting emotional harm it would bring you.

If you have been a victim of abuse, it is important to understand that it is not your fault, nor did you commit a sin. A victim is never the guilty party, and you are no exception. Even if you later developed some sinful habits as a result of this abuse, God understands and freely forgives. The unconditional love of Christ awaits us all, drawing us to Him. It permits us to live again. The beauty of the cross, ironically, is how ugly it is. The horror of Jesus' torture and death is that it reflects the condition of our souls. But because of that horror, we know with certainty that God sees the worst of our brokenness and still gives up His life as an act of love. When you open yourself to the Lord and to His healing and soothing love, His mercy and grace melt away self-condemnation, bitterness, and apathy.

Many, if not most, children exposed to some form of inappropriate sexualization (such as pornography or physical touch) develop unhealthy self-judgments. This also opens the door to all sorts of unhealthy sexual responses, ranging from chasing after sex as a form of vindication to viewing sex as dirty, even as a married woman. Abuse victims often cast blame inward. They think they brought it on or attracted the sexual advance.

Others blame God for not stopping the abuse. In each person, a battle rages inside. Victims suffer deep wounds to their souls, having self-respect torn from them. Anger—even hatred— is planted. Many build thick walls around their hearts, vowing never to be vulnerable again. Therefore, relationships remain shallow and unfulfilling. The walls once designed to protect now constrict. While you seek to keep out pain, you also block out love, and you won't let anyone in.

How about you? Do you run from real intimacy because of hurt from past relationships or the fear of being harmed again?

WEEK 1......WEEK 2......WEEK 3......WEEK 4......WEEK 5......**WEEK 6**......WEEK 7......WEEK 8......WEEK 9......WEEK 10......WEEK 11......WEEK 12

DAY 4

Can you trust again? In your own strength, you cannot. Instead, you will constantly turn to false forms of intimacy, ones you dictate and control, ones that do not require giving completely of yourself.

The healing path for victims of abuse begins by embracing God the Father in a real and vulnerable way. Will you turn to God and trust Him? Perhaps you have nagging thoughts, such as "Where were You, God?" or "Why did You let it happen?" You may never have full answers to these questions, but you can trust God that He is loving and good. He embodied your pain on the cross and He hurts with you. He absolutely hates that this happened to you. He desires to heal and redeem everything that has taken place in your life. Once you find healing, this can become an area in your life that you may be able to look back on and use to more effectively empathize with and comfort others. You will be able to relate to and minister to people in ways that others cannot. But God first wants you to come to Him for healing. He cares about you and your pain. He is a loving Father who wants to sit with you in your pain, soothing and comforting you, no matter how deep the pain is.

Last week we talked about God as comforter. He comforts with His presence, His words, His care and empathy. I cannot fathom the depth of your pain, but God sees it all the way to its inner core and desires to heal and soothe you in your pain. He does not expect you to be strong for Him. He does not expect you to be okay. God desires to free you from the pain as well as any shackles of bitterness which you may be using to ease your own pain. Bitterness is a false sense of relief from pain; but ultimately, it is not protecting your heart but destroying it. The problem is that the bitterness numbs pain, so those harboring bitterness are unaware that the heart is being destroyed. I am sure you have heard the saying before, "Bitterness is like taking poison and waiting for the other person to die."

You don't have to live with bitterness or rage. The more time you spend getting to know God personally, the softer your heart will become. You'll be able to trust again, and you'll be drawn irresistibly to the Lord. As you do, you'll experience more and more of His character, including the richness of His mercy, grace, kindness, and love. He will help you to forgive, and you'll even come to want enemies to be blessed as you keep the focus off yourself. This isn't a fairy tale that only happens to others. God chose you before the creation of the world to be His blessed and dearly loved child (Ephesians 1:4–5). Angels also rejoiced when you turned from sin (Luke 15:10). The Lord has a kingdom prepared for you, and He has many good works for you to do together with Him now (Ephesians 2:10). The solution to a lifetime of hurt is to gaze upon the beauty of the Lord and fix your attention upon the love of His cross and the hope of His resurrection. You'll be constantly and increasingly

WEEK 1 .... WEEK 2 .... WEEK 3 .... WEEK 4 .... WEEK 5 .... **WEEK 6** .... WEEK 7 .... WEEK 8 .... WEEK 9 .... WEEK 10 .... WEEK 11 .... WEEK 12

DAY 4

transformed into the likeness of your perfect heavenly Father, guaranteed. So fix your hope and trust in Him.

HEARTWORK

List points that stuck out to you or any decisions that you need to make.

_____

_____

_____

_____

_____

_____

_____

_____

_____

_____

_____

_____

_____

WEEK 1........ WEEK 2........ WEEK 3........ WEEK 4........ WEEK 5........ WEEK 6 .... WEEK 7........ WEEK 8........ WEEK 9........ WEEK 10 .... WEEK 11........ WEEK 12

DAY 4

PRAY

Right now, go to God in relational prayer.

- Ask God to show you what walls you have around your heart. What are you trying to protect? Ask Him why those walls are there.

- Give the Lord permission to take control of all areas of your heart and life. This means you'll have to give up the right to remain angry, the right to run away from conflict, and the right to flee from vulnerable love and true intimacy. God will heal you if you let Him. Go to Him.

- Tell God you want to experience feelings. Now give Him permission to open your heart.

- Spend time pouring out your heart to the Lord. Talk to Him as your Lord, One who is listening.

_____

_____

_____

_____

_____

_____

_____

_____

_____

WEEK 1 ...... WEEK 2 ...... WEEK 3 ...... WEEK 4 ...... WEEK 5 ...... WEEK 6 ...... WEEK 7 ...... WEEK 8 ...... WEEK 9 ...... WEEK 10 ...... WEEK 11 ...... WEEK 12

DAY 4

MEMORY VERSE

Philippians 2:3–5 (ESV): "Do nothing from selfish ambition or conceit, but in humility count others more significant than yourselves. Let each of you look not only to his own interests, but also to the interests of others. Have this mind among yourselves, which is yours in Christ Jesus."

WEEK 6 DAY 5 (FRIDAY)

KEY THOUGHT: God fights for us.

DAILY READING

Yesterday we mentioned the importance of forgiveness, but today we are really going to focus on it. I think we all know that forgiveness is important and something that God asks us to do. However, this is also something that is very hard to do. In fact, without the help of the Holy Spirit, I believe this is something that is impossible for us to do. Part of the reason why forgiveness is so hard is that many of us have a skewed view of it. I believe that there is human forgiveness and then there is divine forgiveness. Let me show you the difference between the two:

Human forgiveness takes place when we can say, "That's okay. It's not a big deal." Many times this happens when we can put ourselves in the other person's shoes and understand why they did what they did. Or maybe it really wasn't that big of a deal, so it is small enough that we can just overlook it and sweep it under the rug. For instance, a friend wrongs you in some way and you are upset so you confront them. Then they respond by saying, "Oh, I am sorry, I didn't mean it to come across that way. I just meant this. I didn't mean to hurt you." Then you say, "Oh I understand, okay, I forgive you.'

This is not true forgiveness. This is merely excusing or justifying the wrong behavior.

There are times when people say, "Well, what they did to me is just not forgivable." What they mean by this is that there is no way to make the wrong done against them small enough that they can sweep it under the rug and pretend that it didn't happen. No matter what

WEEK 1 .... WEEK 2 .... WEEK 3 .... WEEK 4 .... WEEK 5 .... WEEK 6 .... WEEK 7 .... WEEK 8 .... WEEK 9 .... WEEK 10 .... WEEK 11 .... WEEK 12

DAY 5

angle they look at the wrong, it is still wrong. The wrong that was done is not unforgivable. It is inexcusable. But by definition, in order to forgive someone, there has to be something done wrong. This will require divine forgiveness.

Many people don't want to forgive because they fear that by saying they forgive someone, they are saying that what happened to them is okay. If we do not have a real definition of forgiveness, then we can also adopt a skewed view of God. If we think that He is asking us to say that a wrong done against us is okay and to sweep it under the rug, then it looks like He also is looking the other way and sweeping it under the rug. It looks like God doesn't care.

This could not be further from the truth. God cares about how you have been wronged and hurt more than you can imagine.

Anytime someone has sinned against you, God has seen it and has been incredibly angry. In His Word, He tells us how we should live because He wants us to love one another. He wants to see His children treated well. When someone goes against this and sins against you, they are sinning against Him by violating you. He absolutely hates it when his beloved daughter has been abused, hurt, wronged, abandoned, or deceived. He sees every single incident. He has never once turned a blind eye to a single way you have been hurt. He aches when you ache and He desires vengeance on the one who wronged you. He is a just God! Nothing has been swept under the rug. No one has been let off the hook. Yet, God asks us to forgive. Isn't forgiveness saying it's okay that something happened? Absolutely not!

God will never say sin is okay nor does he ask us to. God does not downplay sin. He does not excuse sin. God deals with sin. Because He is loving and just, every person must be held accountable for everything ever done. This includes your abuser. This includes a negligent father. This includes you. Has someone else's sin affected your life in a painful or devastating way? How can we forgive? You can forgive, because forgiveness is not saying that wrongs done against you do not matter. The only reason we can forgive is because God is the true judge and not us. He sees all and He knows the exact payment needed for each sin. He will demand payment in full.

But!

God is also a loving, gracious, and forgiving God. He sees how you have been wronged and He hates it with more hatred than you can imagine. If your abuser does not submit to God's forgiveness, given in Christ, then your abuser will experience the full weight of their sin.

WEEK 1........ WEEK 2........ WEEK 3........ WEEK 4........ WEEK 5........ **WEEK 6**........ WEEK 7........ WEEK 8........ WEEK 9........ WEEK 10........ WEEK 11........ WEEK 12

DAY 5

If your abuser is a child of God, however, the sin against you will still be paid in full. In fact, it already has. God still has that same hatred toward the way you were treated. It grieves Him that not only were you hurt, but one of His own hurt you. Jesus stands before you, grieving over the way you have been hurt while also standing in the gap, taking on the shame and the punishment for what was done to you. We sometimes shake our fist at God asking where He was when things happened to us. We have no idea how invested God is with our lives. He cares more than we can imagine.

Out of love, He doesn't look away. No matter how painful it is to watch, He stands with us. Jesus understands the gravity of sin so much more than we do. The shame of molestation, rape, pornography, pride, anger, orgies, slander, deceit, bitterness, and so on was placed on His shoulders. He experienced the judgment of God for each one of these things. He knows the extent of this evil and how painful it was to experience the sin of the world.

But, Jesus conquered sin and death. He drank the full cup of God's wrath, taking on the full judgment of each sin to its end. God did not hold back on the fullness of His justice. God did not let anything slide.

So when God is asking you to forgive, He is not asking you to excuse sin, He is asking you to let Him be judge. Romans 12:19 (ESV) says "'vengeance is mine; I will repay,' says the Lord." When we do not forgive, we are either saying that we have not seen the meaning of God's justice fulfilled on the cross, or that God's justice is not enough. When we do not forgive someone who is a Christ follower, we are saying, "I know Jesus paid for his sin on the cross, but that is not enough, he owes me too."

We know we have forgiven an unbeliever when we are willing to genuinely pray for their salvation.

Why don't we forgive? What are we hoping to gain from not offering forgiveness?

I think we want someone to stand with us and agree that what happened was wrong and should have never happened. We want someone to be our advocate and to say that we did not deserve to experience what was done to us. The wonderful thing is that God does all of

WEEK 1......... WEEK 2......... WEEK 3......... WEEK 4......... WEEK 5......... **WEEK 6**......... WEEK 7......... WEEK 8......... WEEK 9......... WEEK 10......... WEEK 11......... WEEK 12

DAY 5

these things for us. He is our advocate and judge. He validates our worth by saying, "You should not have been wronged."

Forgiveness is letting go. We often feel that if we let go, we are losing part of our dignity. But this is a lie. Picture a balloon in your hand. Letting go is allowing it to float up to heaven and placing it into the hands of him who is the true judge, the One who gave you your dignity and cares even more than you do that you were wronged. If we don't let go, the balloon becomes a heavy stone that weighs us down. It becomes our weight to carry. It does not affect the one who sinned against us. We cling to it with white knuckles, not knowing that forgiveness is the very thing that will give us our life back.

READ THE BIBLE

Read Romans 12, Matthew 18, and Proverbs 4:23. Write down any thoughts that come to mind.

_____

_____

_____

_____

_____

_____

_____

WEEK 1......... WEEK 2......... WEEK 3......... WEEK 4......... WEEK 5......... WEEK 6......... WEEK 7......... WEEK 8......... WEEK 9......... WEEK 10 .... WEEK 11......... WEEK 12

DAY 5

HEARTWORK

How does it affect you to hear that God stands with you as your advocate?

_____

_____

_____

_____

Is there any bitterness you are still harboring?

_____

_____

_____

Bitterness feels like a protective wall guarding your heart from pain. And in some ways, you are right. Bitterness keeps the pain at bay for a while. However, it is not protective. In fact, it destroys instead. God calls our heart the wellspring of life. Bitterness builds walls around it that shuts down our heart. When there is bitterness, we withhold love and shut out love. Letting go may bring on some fresh pain, and God will be there to comfort you in the midst of it. He will bring healing and make your heart new again so that you can be free to love Him and others.

WEEK 1 ...... WEEK 2 ...... WEEK 3 ...... WEEK 4 ...... WEEK 5 ...... **WEEK 6** ...... WEEK 7 ...... WEEK 8 ...... WEEK 9 ...... WEEK 10 ...... WEEK 11 ...... WEEK 12

DAY 5

PRAY

Spend time opening up to God about any bitterness that you have been harboring. Ask God to help you fully understand what it means that He stands alongside you as your advocate. Ask God to show you how destructive bitterness is in your relationship between you and Him. Spend time thanking Him for His presence in your life. Praise Him for many of His attributes that you have seen in your life lately.

Record your prayers below.

_____

_____

_____

_____

_____

_____

_____

_____

WEEK 1 .... WEEK 2 .... WEEK 3 .... WEEK 4 .... WEEK 5 .... WEEK 6 .... WEEK 7 .... WEEK 8 .... WEEK 9 .... WEEK 10 .... WEEK 11 .... WEEK 12

DAY 5

_____

_____

_____

_____

_____

_____

_____

_____

_____

_____

SPECIAL NOTE:

If there has been abuse in your life, I highly recommend counseling. This book is not meant to replace counseling. Traumatic events can have a huge impact on the mind. Some of the tendencies you have may be a result of experiencing trauma. Please be willing to look into counseling if there has been abuse in your life. Seeking counseling does not mean that you are not trusting God. He created the mind, and there are many Christians who have studied the mind and know how to walk alongside people toward healing. Some individuals will not be able to create healthy mental roads without clinical counseling. I highly recommend Christian counseling because its ultimate goal is to bring about transformation into the mind of Christ. Praying for your journey, dear sisters.

PW

WEEK SEVEN

TESTIMONY

"I was down one time because of my recurring tendency to sin against purity. It was such a time when I had repeatedly done it that my shame was overwhelming but my pride seemed to get the best of me. Then I just randomly checked the internet for help sites for my problem, and I clicked your site. It was such a blessing for me to have done that. I read through the site and found myself crying and realizing the things written there were all true. I thank God for that encounter and would just like to thank you guys for showing me the real way out of sin. You will never know how much it helped me."

Passionate for God,
Repentant in spirit,
Open and honest,
Victorious in living,
Eternal in perspective, and
Networking with other *PROVEN Women.*

MEMORY VERSE

Philippians 4:8 (ESV): "Finally, brothers, whatever is true, whatever is honorable, whatever is just, whatever is pure, whatever is lovely, whatever is commendable, if there is any excellence, if there is anything worthy of praise, think about these things."

WEEK 7 DAY 1 (MONDAY)

KEY THOUGHT: Satan's voice condemns, but God's voice is kind.

This week, we will talk about what to do in times of failure or a setback.

DAILY READING

We have been spending a lot of time dealing with the heart and mind. It is important that we take responsibility and partner with God to transform our mind and our desires. Even after you chart a course of earnestly seeking the Lord, you will probably experience moments of failures and setbacks. Although God does not grant us a license to sin, He instructs us on how to respond and be fully restored when we stumble. Failures often occur when we slip back into old routines. Perhaps you had an argument with someone or are tired or lonely and caved. Or perhaps you were doing so well that you thought you could put your guard down and a temptation snuck up on you. Instead of turning immediately to God in the midst of temptation, it is easy to allow old patterns to return and trigger a relapse.

Some people even stumble when they get frustrated over the length of time it seems to be taking to be free, so they "help God out." They may try to do things in their own strength or rely on self-help techniques rather than relying on God. Self-effort fails, however, because it attempts to take back permission from the Lord to work in your life. God won't force His help on you, and He won't make you live a holy life. Instead, He waits until you grasp that He alone heals and transforms. Don't misunderstand: God does this for your own good. We were made to know Him, and only relationship with Him can mend our damaged souls.

WEEK 1 .... WEEK 2 .... WEEK 3 .... WEEK 4 .... WEEK 5 .... WEEK 6 .... **WEEK 7** .... WEEK 8 .... WEEK 9 .... WEEK 10 .... WEEK 11 .... WEEK 12

DAY 1

In a relapse, self-condemnation often follows soon after. You may want to hide from God, but God wants to forgive and renew you. One of the first steps in the PROVEN Model in response to a setback, whether it is a sexual or other pride-based sin, is to put on an eternal perspective. God is in a lifelong process of healing you, changing you, and preparing you for divine intimacy now and forever. Perhaps the most important concept to understand is that the Lord loves you unconditionally. That's right! You cannot earn (Ephesians 2:8–9) or lose (Romans 8:35) God's great love for you. It's this complete and available love that draws people to Christ. Will you ask God to open the eyes of your soul to see Him and permit His love to penetrate your heart? To position yourself to experience His love, you must seek the Lord and truly yield your life to Him. Resolve to put the Lord first.

A victorious life does not just happen. It may take longer than you hope or expect for healing to occur. Remember, you're involved in a battle that requires more than self-will; you must have God-sized strength. This battle actually takes place in the spiritual world. Spiritual warfare is real, and if you're not actively engaged in the battle, you can expect to experience regular setbacks.

Later in this study, you'll learn more about spiritual warfare. For now, practice learning to tell the difference between the voice of God, who wants you to succeed, and the voice of Satan, who wants you to be ashamed and turn inward or toward the world. The Lord's voice is always gently calling you into His presence. He is not forceful or hurried, but soft. By contrast, Satan's voice is rushed and immediate. Under his plan, you feel pressured to act quickly and must always remain busy. Consider the difference between two parents teaching a child to ride a bike. The first parent is gentle yet strong. He tells his daughter how much he loves her. He tells her not to be afraid as he removes the training wheels. "I'll be right here with you." His strong arms hold her upright for as long as she needs him. He runs slowly by her, giving encouraging instructions: "That's right. You're doing great! Keep pedaling." The second parent is rushed: "I only have a few minutes, so you better be ready to ride this bike. I worked hard to buy this for you, so you'd better be appreciative and work hard."

When the child tips and falls, the first father is nurturing. He scoops her up into his arms and soothes her as she cries on his shoulder. He holds her as long as she needs. He knows she will eventually ride the bike and succeed; however, he doesn't rush her to get back on. As the tears subside, he encourages her again, helping her to feel confident to get back on the bike. The second parent makes the child feel like a failure for falling. She becomes as

WEEK 1 ...... WEEK 2 ...... WEEK 3 ...... WEEK 4 ...... WEEK 5 ...... WEEK 6 ...... **WEEK 7** ...... WEEK 8 ...... WEEK 9 ...... WEEK 10 ...... WEEK 11 ...... WEEK 12

DAY 1

fearful of disappointing her dad as she does of the pain of falling. She feels like she cannot do anything right because her dad is never pleased with her. He always finds something that she is doing wrong and continually points it out to her.

Are you seeing the connection? God is the gentle, loving Father. He's patient and kind, offering grace and encouragement. Because of Jesus' work on the cross, there is no condemnation in God's voice as He speaks to His children. Satan, however, is condemning and loud. He wants you to chase instant pleasures and to feel badly about yourself. All he really cares about is that you don't turn to the Lord. The more he can convince you to look to your circumstances, rights, or needs, the easier it is to get you to look to the world for empty healing. By contrast, when you fail, God remains kind and forgiving. He gently encourages you to return to Him right away. Satan would have you believe that you are no good and not worth the bother to God. He feeds the feeling, "I may as well give over completely to sin."

In contrast to the lies of Satan, the Lord has good instructions for you to succeed. Will you slow down and listen to God? Will you draw close to hear His gentle voice? Reject Satan's lies. Get to know your loving Father by immersing yourself in His truth, being part of God's family, spending daily time worshiping the only truly perfect being, and talking openly to the Lord as a friend. The more you do these things, the easier it'll be to hear and discern God's voice and to know that you're truly forgiven, reconciled to God, and deeply loved. You'll also begin to recognize when Satan is trying to tear you down with lies and steer you toward any of the wide roads leading away from God.

What struck you from today's reading?

_____

_____

Have you recently experienced any failures or setbacks? List them.

_____

_____

WEEK 1...... WEEK 2...... WEEK 3...... WEEK 4...... WEEK 5...... WEEK 6...... **WEEK 7** ...... WEEK 8...... WEEK 9...... WEEK 10 ...... WEEK 11...... WEEK 12

DAY 1

How did you feel when you had a setback? Did you feel abandoned by God? Did you wonder if He really cares whether you overcome or fail? Explain.

_____

_____

_____

_____

HEARTWORK

Consider this verse: "Therefore, there is now no condemnation for those who are in Christ Jesus, because through Christ Jesus the law of the spirit of life set me free from the law of sin and death" (Romans 8:1–2, NIV). Do you believe that God loves you unconditionally, even when you sin, and that He wants you to be healed? Don't confuse God's discipline with rejection.

Stop trying to succeed in your own efforts. Make a permanent decision to trust God, no matter the circumstances. Even after a fall, you'll be riding your bike again in no time, carried along by your loving Father. The Lord will pick you up when you stumble and fully restore you, so turn to Him and completely trust Him.

READ THE BIBLE

Read Hebrews 12:1–13 and record your insights.

_____

_____

Do you believe that God fully forgives you when you repent and turn to Him? Consider again 1 John 1:9 (ESV) that says, "If we confess our sins, He is faithful and just and will forgive us our sins and purify us from all unrighteousness."

WEEK 1 .... WEEK 2 .... WEEK 3 .... WEEK 4 .... WEEK 5 .... WEEK 6 .... **WEEK 7** .... WEEK 8 .... WEEK 9 .... WEEK 10 .... WEEK 11 .... WEEK 12

DAY 1

Trust that God is not a liar. He not only forgives your sin, but He also replaces it with His own righteousness. Your feelings or emotions, on the other hand, can give you a false impression. Confess any unbelief and turn to God.

Before we pray, read John 10:27–28.

PRAY

Set a timer if you have to, but pray for at least ten minutes. Evil wants to distract you and keep you from meeting with God. Try writing a list of the things that you need God to provide (e.g., soft heart, clean hands, pure mind) and then ask Him. Pray through John 10. Keep asking God to make you a needy, dependent servant who is hungry for His holiness. Talk to God about learning His voice. Talk to God about transforming you into a person who is grateful and content. Be sure to spend the bulk of your time praying for others.

Record your prayers below.

_____

_____

_____

_____

_____

_____

_____

_____

WEEK 1........ WEEK 2........ WEEK 3........ WEEK 4........ WEEK 5........ WEEK 6........ **WEEK 7** .... WEEK 8........ WEEK 9........ WEEK 10 .... WEEK 11........ WEEK 12

DAY 1

SPECIAL NOTE:

R is for Repentant in Spirit. Do you make it a practice to confess sin immediately and seek forgiveness, or do you beat yourself up instead and withdraw from God? If you delay in seeking forgiveness and restoration with God, you'll grow increasingly distant from the Lord and other people. Break the cycle. For instance, be diligent that each time you allow an impure thought to linger, confess it as sin, repent, and accept God's immediate forgiveness. Draw near to God; He promises to draw near to you (James 4:8).

In the past, you may have wallowed in guilt or sought to distance yourself from the Lord and others. Arm yourself now with the truth about His unconditional love, and live in freedom as His dearly loved daughter. Your first reaction to sin should be to recognize it for what it is: A desire to control life or hide from reality.

Carefully consider this: It is your turning from God that makes your thoughts and conduct sinful. The cure is to race back to the Lord immediately without giving Satan time to smother you in guilt and shame that perpetuates feelings of unworthiness. By running to the Lord, you'll be restored right away and will be able to worship and fellowship with God in openness.

In your own words, write out the things you will do the next time you see sin, then give it over to God.

_____

_____

_____

_____

_____

_____

MEMORY VERSE

Philippians 4:8 (ESV): "Finally, brothers, whatever is true, whatever is honorable, whatever is just, whatever is pure, whatever is lovely, whatever is commendable, if there is any excellence, if there is anything worthy of praise, think about these things."

WEEK 7 DAY 2 (TUESDAY)

KEY THOUGHT: God is faithful to deliver His people.

Today we are going to continue talking about setbacks. When we experience setbacks, it can be so easy to long to move backward in progress and cave in completely. We can get exhausted with fighting the battle toward purity. During these times, we can get tunnel vision and only see how difficult the process of moving toward freedom is. Throwing in the towel can become pretty attractive. But it is only attractive if we have forgotten how enslaving pornography and masturbation are.

READ THE BIBLE

Read Exodus 16—this passage takes place right after the Israelites have crossed the Red Sea. Is there anything that sticks out to you?

_____

_____

_____

_____

_____

WEEK 1........ WEEK 2........ WEEK 3........ WEEK 4........ WEEK 5........ WEEK 6........ **WEEK 7**........ WEEK 8........ WEEK 9........ WEEK 10........ WEEK 11........ WEEK 12

DAY 2

_____

_____

_____

_____

 ## DAILY READING

In the book of Exodus, the children of Israel go through a very similar situation. They had been slaves in Egypt for 400 years. They had cruel taskmasters and were treated terribly. It was a very harsh and demeaning life of captivity. They called out to God for deliverance and He heard their cries. He sent Moses and his brother Aaron to Egypt to rescue them out of slavery. The Israelites watched as God devastated Egypt with the ten plagues, revealing His power and might to the Egyptians. God even protected the Israelites from several of the plagues so that He could make a distinction between His people and the Egyptians. The Lord orchestrated things in such a way that the Egyptians were even begging the Israelites to leave and giving them their belongings.

Israel walked out of Egypt full hope for a new land that God had promised them. They stepped out without a backward glance, confident that they would not return to their captivity. God led them toward the Red Sea, a situation which looked impossible, because He once again wanted to show them His glory. He demonstrated to them how He can rescue them.

Picture yourself in that scene. In front of you is the Red Sea and behind you is an army of chariots coming to destroy you. There is absolutely nothing you can do to fix your situation. You are 100 percent at the mercy of the Lord your God. Either He acts, or you are destroyed. In an amazing display of power, God parted the Red Sea, allowing the Israelites to walk through it on dry land. After they were all safely on the other side, God allowed the Egyptian army to pursue them into the sea, but then He let the sea return to its normal place, crushing the Israelites' enemies.

Put yourself in the Israelites' shoes for a moment. You felt so burdened and hopeless for several years. But then, as promised, God showed up and delivered you out of captivity.

WEEK 1 ..... WEEK 2 ..... WEEK 3 ..... WEEK 4 ..... WEEK 5 ..... WEEK 6 ..... **WEEK 7** ..... WEEK 8 ..... WEEK 9 ..... WEEK 10 ..... WEEK 11 ..... WEEK 12

DAY 2

You see Him do crazy, miraculous things. You look at the tall walls of water around you as you walk through the Red Sea. You would not have believed it if this story had simply been told to you, but you are actually the one experiencing it. It has been an amazing several weeks of watching the impossible take place, and you are beginning to cling to the freedom that is waiting for you once you reach the Promised Land.

Read verse 3 again. How do the Israelites describe their situation in Egypt? What is wrong with their way of thinking?

_____

_____

_____

They had been in captivity. They had to work so hard for the food they had in slavery, yet when they experienced hunger and hard times as they journeyed toward freedom, they looked back with rose-colored glasses. They exaggerated the simplicity of their previous life while also exaggerating their current hard circumstances.

"Lord, have You made me give up something that was so fulfilling only to bring me to a place where I am going to die of sexual starvation?" This may be a little bit of an exaggeration, but haven't you heard people or even yourself talk like this?

When you think back to the time when you were not fighting against your fleshly desires, what are some positive things you may mention? What lies do you tell yourself? What is your version of "sat by meat pots and full of bread?"

_____

_____

_____

_____

WEEK 1 ...... WEEK 2 ...... WEEK 3 ...... WEEK 4 ...... WEEK 5 ...... WEEK 6 ...... **WEEK 7** ...... WEEK 8 ...... WEEK 9 ...... WEEK 10 ...... WEEK 11 ...... WEEK 12

DAY 2

Now spend some time remembering why you wanted freedom in the first place. Why are pornography and masturbation shackles that held you in captivity? What made that place so dark?

_____

_____

_____

_____

Please do not buy into the lie that your life was better when you were free to do whatever you wanted, including pornography and masturbation. You were not free to do these things, they ruled over you. They enslave! They also lead us toward destruction and death. No good thing will come from these things.

When the children of Israel complained to Moses, how did God respond?

_____

_____

God showed Israel that He would provide them with exactly what they needed day by day so that they would not go hungry. God is doing the same for you. There are going to be tough days and lonely days, but each day, God is going to give you enough to get you through that day. He will bring peace, joy, courage, love, and much more.

HEARTWORK

So much of this fight is a battle of the mind. If Satan can distort your perspective to get you to believe that you were better off with pornography and masturbation, then he will keep you in captivity.

WEEK 1........ WEEK 2........ WEEK 3........ WEEK 4........ WEEK 5........ WEEK 6........ **WEEK 7**........ WEEK 8........ WEEK 9........ WEEK 10 ....11........ WEEK 12

DAY 2

Is there anything that you think pornography and masturbation can bring to you that God cannot bring?

_____

_____

_____

_____

Do you believe that God will provide you everything you need today in order to finish out the day victoriously?

_____

_____

Why do you think it is important to trust Him on a day-by-day basis?

_____

_____

 ## PRAY

After you write out these answers, talk to God about them. Do not be ashamed to be honest with God about the deepest thoughts of your heart. The most effective prayers are the most honest prayers. He cares to know what you are thinking. But as you are praying, also ask God to help you trust that His way is best. Ask Him to help you crave the daily manna that He is going to bring rather than the things you received while you were in the bondage of pornography. He longs to transform your heart. This transformation begins by honestly opening up to Him, being repentant in spirit so that He can cleanse you.

Spend some time praying for others as well. Remember to petition for other people's needs with confidence that God cares about the details. He is at work in their lives. Pray through anything else that God puts on your heart. Trust Him to meet with you during this time...

MEMORY VERSE

Philippians 4:8 (ESV): "Finally, brothers, whatever is true, whatever is honorable, whatever is just, whatever is pure, whatever is lovely, whatever is commendable, if there is any excellence, if there is anything worthy of praise, think about these things."

WEEK 7 DAY 3 (WEDNESDAY)

KEY THOUGHT: Transformation is a lifelong process.

DAILY READING

Have you accepted that God's timing is perfect? This applies to all areas of your life (e.g., getting married, finding a job, healing old wounds, and becoming free from certain sins). God has a purpose behind everything. In fact, sexual healing is often slow because the Lord takes you at a pace that you can handle. Just as a loving father would not send his child down a steep hill when she was learning to ride a bike, God will not bring you through the healing process at a faster pace than you can learn, appreciate, and accept. God provides lasting healing, not merely a Band-Aid. Therefore, healing is a process with a purpose, and the process of healing lasts a lifetime. Still, there will be moments of significant progress along the way.

Let's continue to put on the mind of Christ and confront the tactics of Satan. Surrendering to the enemy is not an option in this battle. In order to deceive you into complacency or into setting aside God's armor, the devil will try to fill your mind with thoughts of self-effort and the need to earn God's love or approval. When your guard is down, Satan seeks to turn your thoughts inward and turn them towards your circumstances and rights. The devil also floods your mind with tempting thoughts of chasing after the momentary pleasures of the world while shielding you from the true nature and cost of such things. Life's "little" sins, such as gossip or anger, will seem too insignificant to bother with; but if you give Satan

WEEK 1........ WEEK 2........ WEEK 3........ WEEK 4........ WEEK 5........ WEEK 6........ **WEEK 7**........ WEEK 8........ WEEK 9........ WEEK 10........ WEEK 11........ WEEK 12

DAY 3

a foothold in small areas, he can gain more overall control in your life. Satan frequently fosters a "stair step" bondage approach, which looks something like this:

– Temptation to lust or fantasize
   – Acting out
      – Feeling guilty
         – Experiencing shame or self-condemnation
            – Turning inward (shutting out friends and community)
               – Desiring to escape
                  – Temptation to lust or fantasize

This seemingly never-ending downward cycle can and must be completely destroyed by the power of God. Leave no root remaining to spring up again later. Confess to the Lord that you turned away from Him and were consumed with your circumstances, allowing Satan to lead you astray. Set your mind and heart on living by God's Spirit and under His direction and control. Each time, at the moment of temptation, reject the so-called "escape" route that Satan offers and recognize it as a lie. Lust and fantasy breed discontentment, because they can never truly satisfy or fulfill. Engage in the spiritual battle and choose to take your place on God's winning side!

To allow God to lead, you must give Him total control. Tell the Lord that He not only has permission to run your thought life, but also has ownership of your mind. Keep your eyes fixed upon Christ in humility and chase after a real relationship with Him. Replace the thoughts that Satan would have you dwell upon with praise and thanksgiving to the Lord.

Replace self-condemnation with worshiping the Lord for His goodness. Accept His righteousness into your life. Preach the truth to yourself. Reject any thoughts that stand opposed to God's Word and replace them with God's promises and statements about His love for you and His purpose for your life. This can only happen as you saturate your mind with God's Word. That is why we read the Bible every day in this study. It is important that you can recognize when your thoughts contain lies about God's love. God's love is unconditional and cannot be earned. You simply receive it. He showers His love upon you whether you are aware of it or not. He does not stop loving you when you struggle or fall. So get back on the bike right away each time you fall by repenting with confidence that God forgives and lifts you back up. Then listen for and follow God's instructions.

WEEK 1 .... WEEK 2 .... WEEK 3 .... WEEK 4 .... WEEK 5 .... WEEK 6 .... **WEEK 7** .... WEEK 8 .... WEEK 9 .... WEEK 10 .... WEEK 11 .... WEEK 12

DAY 3

Write down your thoughts about this section.

_____

_____

_____

_____

Consider how the downward spiral works. Guilt and shame lead to hopelessness, which sets you up for using sex as a coping mechanism, which leads to temptation and a fall, which leads to more guilt and shame, which again leads to hopelessness, and on and on. God can break this cycle. His love is unconditional (Romans 8:35–39), He freely forgives and does not condemn (Romans 8:1), and He gives hope (Psalm 62:5, Romans 15:13). God does not tempt, but empowers you to walk through the temptation victoriously. He empowers you to remain steadfast in the midst of the struggle. (James 1:12–13). Satan wants you to think in those dark moments that caving is your only option. Stop turning away from God in those moments. Run to Him and accept His healing and power. Reject Satan and hate sin!

List some of the lies Satan uses to deceive you.

_____

_____

_____

_____

HEARTWORK

As we move forward in healing, we still need to be careful of what we are filling our mind with. Are you sometimes careless in what you allow in your field of vision—taking a second look at men at the gym, scanning your surroundings for opportunities to lust, laughing at

WEEK 1 ...... WEEK 2 ...... WEEK 3 ...... WEEK 4 ...... WEEK 5 ...... WEEK 6 ...... **WEEK 7** ...... WEEK 8 ...... WEEK 9 ...... WEEK 10 ...... WEEK 11 ...... WEEK 12

DAY 3

a dirty joke, watching a TV show that glorifies sex, or scrolling through social media and pausing on pictures that lure and entice? List areas where you know that you are somewhat careless in guarding your mind, then commit to stopping these inputs. Where are you allowing your mind to dwell? Are you allowing yourself to enjoy the attention of a married man at work, dwelling on what it would have been like to be with him? Are you allowing your mind to move into areas of self-pity, what ifs, or complaining that things are not fair? When we focus on what we think we deserve, our mind moves away from worshiping God and becomes very inwardly focused. This steals our joy, peace, and contentment.

What are some things you have been dwelling on lately, good or bad?

_____

_____

_____

_____

How can you be more intentional in taking your thoughts captive?

_____

_____

_____

Although healing is a lifelong process, you'll experience great victories along the way. Sure, you'll still have struggles and some occasional failures, but you can walk in victory as you continually repent of any sin and daily turn and rely upon God. Keep the E in PROVEN (Eternal in Perspective) always before you.

Don't be consumed with how long it takes to see the results. In Matthew 6:33–34 (ESV), Jesus says, "But seek first the kingdom of God and his righteousness, and all these things will be added to you. Therefore do not be anxious about tomorrow, for tomorrow will be anxious for itself. Sufficient for the day is its own trouble."

WEEK 1........ WEEK 2........ WEEK 3........ WEEK 4........ WEEK 5........ WEEK 6........ **WEEK 7** .... WEEK 8........ WEEK 9........ WEEK 10........ WEEK 11........ WEEK 12

DAY 3

I have talked with many girls who feel so discouraged while fighting for transformation. They feel like they are supposed to flip a switch and all of a sudden have the strength to not struggle again. The future seems so long and hard. How in the world will they persevere for so long?

But God does not call us to have enough strength to resist for the rest of our lives. He only calls us to persevere for today. This is a daily walk with the Lord. God doesn't ask you to know how you will continue to stand steadfast tomorrow. Each day, you get a fresh start and an opportunity to walk with God that day. Today, make the choice to seek God and His righteousness, expecting that He will provide for you along the way. Don't worry about how you will continue to do this tomorrow, next week, or next year. Know that each of those times, you will also need to rely on His strength for that day. We are doing this one day at a time. Walk step-by-step with your loving Father who is transforming your mind as you spend time with Him.

Participate with God. Don't take back control or think you can do this on your own. Rather, truly desire to be transformed. If you secretly want to enjoy the sensual pleasures of pornography or lust, God's transformation process will be thwarted. If the desire for pornography is still there, don't hide it or bury it. Confess it to the Lord and ask Him to continue to transform the desires of your heart. Ask God to help you dig into your heart to find what you are really desiring. Are you desiring to be noticed? Adored? Valued? Fully known by someone? Desiring a deeper connection and intimacy that seems impossible? Remember, God has given us the pure version of every one of these desires. He has designed us to fulfill these longings through Him and through His family.

READ THE BIBLE

Keep reading in order to get to know God. Read and meditate on Romans 7:7–25 and 13:11–14.

_____

_____

_____

_____

WEEK 1........ WEEK 2........ WEEK 3........ WEEK 4........ WEEK 5........ WEEK 6........ **WEEK 7**........ WEEK 8........ WEEK 9........ WEEK 10........ WEEK 11........ WEEK 12

DAY 3

_____

_____

_____

_____

_____

PRAY

List the people you want to pray for, but don't just think about them. Instead, petition the Lord to work in their lives. Your role in prayer is to communicate with God, not to merely think about others. Write out each prayer point.

- Ask the Holy Spirit to bring to mind anyone whom He wants you to pray for today.

- Ask God to guard your thoughts and heart, and then rely on His armor.

- Ask God to give you His power to carry out your commitment to eliminate worldly inputs and to replace them with the things of God.

- Ask God to make you a needy, dependent servant. Keep praying for others, especially other Proven Women and your family.

- Spend some time talking to God about your relationship with Him. Reflect on His love for you.

- Spend some time talking to God about the other relationships in your life. How are you loving and serving others? Are there any relationships you are avoiding? Are there any ways that selfishness and pride are getting in the way of these relationships?

_____

_____

_____

_____

WEEK 1 .... WEEK 2 .... WEEK 3 .... WEEK 4 .... WEEK 5 .... WEEK 6 .... WEEK 7 .... WEEK 8 .... WEEK 9 .... WEEK 10 .... WEEK 11 .... WEEK 12

DAY 3

MEMORY VERSE

Philippians 4:8 (ESV): "Finally, brothers, whatever is true, whatever is honorable, whatever is just, whatever is pure, whatever is lovely, whatever is commendable, if there is any excellence, if there is anything worthy of praise, think about these things."

WEEK 7 DAY 4 (THURSDAY)

KEY THOUGHT: God can recreate us into something remarkably beautiful.

Are you willing to be molded by God? He will not begin to work until you are ready. He waits for you to realize that you cannot do it on your own and that you must depend on Him. Will you look to Him alone for life? Read Jeremiah 18:1–4 (NIV).

This is the word that came to Jeremiah from the Lord: ²"Arise, and go down to the potter's house, and there I will let you hear my words." ³So I went down to the potter's house, and there he was working at his wheel. ⁴And the vessel he was making of clay was spoiled in the potter's hand, and he reworked it into another vessel, as it seemed good to the potter to do.

This picture shows us that God can take something "spoiled" and work it into something truly valuable.

You are ready for the potter's wheel when you're willing to have the Lord create in you these six elements:

Passion for God. Without passion for God, your soul will never find freedom and receive healing. It begins with humility—knowing in your inner being that the Lord is the One who created you and that apart from Him, you can do nothing. Deep love and thanksgiving will pour out from you as you begin experiencing His great love.

Repentant in Spirit. Pride is the greatest barrier to knowing and experiencing God. It blocks out intimate relationships with others. True repentance lays down self-interests and rights. It teaches you to freely forgive others. In humility, you realize that your greatest sin is departing from God as you go your own way to carry out your selfish desires. Then you race back to the Lord to be near Him again.

WEEK 1 ... WEEK 2 ... WEEK 3 ... WEEK 4 ... WEEK 5 ... WEEK 6 ... WEEK 7 ... WEEK 8 ... WEEK 9 ... WEEK 10 ... WEEK 11 ... WEEK 12

DAY 4

Openness in Communication with God and Others. Talk to the Lord as a friend, telling Him of your struggles and listening when He speaks. Purpose to build relationships with others and allow yourself to have feelings, which are intended for good and can help to signal when you stray from the Lord.

Victorious Living Under His Authority. Each moment you live by the Spirit, you'll be able to master each desire that enters your mind (Galatians 5:16). God wants you to draw near to Him so He can give you His righteousness and power to live in holiness and be united in spirit. Stop striving in your own strength and receive the Lord Himself. Then you will be transformed.

Eternal Perspective. When you look for meaning beyond your circumstances, the sin of selfishness is conquered. As you understand that your home is in heaven, your work on earth takes on new meaning. You look to and rely upon the Lord for strength to fulfill your purpose in life. You no longer need to control life, but gladly submit your will to the Lord and ask Him to carry out His plan as you seek after Him with all your heart.

Neediness for Others. You will never be stamped Proven by standing alone. The Lord uses others in your life to encourage you. Work to develop relationships (networking) with other women who are diligently seeking the Lord and, just like you, are finished with pretending or trying to go it alone.

DAILY READING

Do you want to know the key to victory—the antidote for lust and impurity? It is spending more time communing with God and becoming a lover of people!

Read the last paragraph again. Now commit to it. Write down how you will increasingly open yourself up to God while getting to know more of who He is. If you don't take steps now to incorporate worship into your daily life, you'll remain merely a listener and not a doer of the Word—a person self-deceived and trapped in bondage to sin (see James 1:22).

A good first step is living out Romans 12:1–2 (ESV), which says: "I appeal to you therefore, brothers, by the mercies of God, to present your bodies as a living sacrifice, holy and acceptable to God, which is your spiritual worship. 2Do not be conformed to this world, but be transformed by the renewal of your mind, that by testing you may discern what is the will of God, what is good and acceptable and perfect."

WEEK 1 .... WEEK 2 .... WEEK 3 .... WEEK 4 .... WEEK 5 .... WEEK 6 .... **WEEK 7** .... WEEK 8 .... WEEK 9 .... WEEK 10 .... WEEK 11 .... WEEK 12

DAY 4

Describe some of the patterns of this world to which you still conform (for example, TV shows which glorify sex, a desire for overshadowing other women in appearance or skill, selfishly seeking pleasures, materialism, boastfulness, judgmental attitudes, or jealousy). These things lure and entice us. Initially it hurts and feels like a sacrifice to cut these things out of our life, but it is necessary and worth it.

DECISION TIME

It is time to switch masters. Matthew 6:24 (NIV): "No one can serve two masters, for either he will hate the one and love the other, or he will be devoted to the one and despise the other." We cannot be devoted to both God and to the patterns of this world at the same time. We have to make a choice. God's pattern is for you to be gentle, humble, kind, forgiving, grateful, content, thankful, and at peace. Read this sentence again, asking the Lord to give you a desire for these things. Can you imagine what all of your relationships would look like if these characteristics were always present? This is God's will for our lives. But pride and selfishness become primary obstacles. Fortunately, God has given us the gift of conviction. Conviction draws us to God. Repentance is the road that ushers us straight into God's presence. And within God's presence, temptation has no power.

Right now, make a conscious decision to yield your life fully to God and to allow Him to fill you with the fruit of the Spirit. Let's return to Galatians 5:16–25 (ESV):

"But I say, walk by the Spirit, and you will not gratify the desires of the flesh. [17]For the desires of the flesh are against the Spirit, and the desires of the Spirit are against the flesh, for these are opposed to each other, to keep you from doing the things you want to do. [18]But if you are led by the Spirit, you are not under the law. [19]Now the works of the flesh are evident: sexual immorality, impurity, sensuality, [20]idolatry, sorcery, enmity, strife, jealousy, fits of anger, rivalries, dissensions, divisions, envy, drunkenness, orgies, and things like these. I warn you, as I warned you before, that those who do such things will not inherit the kingdom of God. But the fruit of the Spirit is love, joy, peace, patience, kindness, goodness, faithfulness, gentleness, self-control; against such things there is no law. And those who belong to Christ Jesus have crucified the flesh with its passions and desires.

If we live by the Spirit, let us also keep in step with the Spirit. Let us not become conceited, provoking one another, envying one another."

WEEK 1 ...... WEEK 2 ...... WEEK 3 ...... WEEK 4 ...... WEEK 5 ...... WEEK 6 ...... **WEEK 7** ...... WEEK 8 ...... WEEK 9 ...... WEEK 10 ...... WEEK 11 ...... WEEK 12

DAY 4

Another necessary ingredient for lasting victory is found in Ephesians 4:19–24, particularly verse 23: "...be made new in the attitude of your minds." Romans 12:1–2 similarly commands us to renew our mind so that we can know God's will. Ladies, there are no shortcuts to the renewal of your mind, which once dwelt upon lust and fantasy. You must replace the backward thinking of the world with the truth of God. Reading the Bible and openly talking to God will help forge a new imagination and new patterns of thought.

HEARTWORK

God wants you to think about things that are true, noble, right, pure, lovely, admirable, excellent, or praiseworthy (Philippians 4:8). Are you replacing worldly thoughts (fantasies of lust, of being in the spotlight, or of getting revenge) with godly thoughts? Are you also taking captive every thought and making it obedient to Christ (2 Corinthians 10:5)?

READ THE BIBLE

Open your Bible to Romans 8:5–17. As you read and meditate upon this passage, ask God to reveal His truth about living by the Holy Spirit. Won't you allow the Holy Spirit to move into your heart and melt it as wax as you read this Biblical passage? It is written for you! Open your heart and soul to the Lord.

PRAY

Describe how well you are doing in these areas, and list anything you intend to start or stop doing, then pray through it.

_____

_____

_____

_____

WEEK 1 .... WEEK 2 .... WEEK 3 .... WEEK 4 .... WEEK 5 .... WEEK 6 .... **WEEK 7** .... WEEK 8 .... WEEK 9 .... WEEK 10 .... WEEK 11 .... WEEK 12

DAY 4

MEMORY VERSE

Philippians 4:8 (ESV): "Finally, brothers, whatever is true, whatever is honorable, whatever is just, whatever is pure, whatever is lovely, whatever is commendable, if there is any excellence, if there is anything worthy of praise, think about these things."

WEEK 7 DAY 5 (FRIDAY)

KEY THOUGHT: More than anything else, God's very presence is what changes our hearts and sets us free.

All of today is going to be Heartwork. We are going to finish out the week meditating on certain verses and evaluating our heart.

HEARTWORK

Don't rush through the following meditation, but turn your attention toward meeting with God.

- Begin by allowing your spirit to be overwhelmed by God and His great love, mercy, and grace. Open your heart to God and allow Him to transform your will to His.

- Picture yourself fixing your eyes on Jesus, who perfects your faith. Picture Him on the cross with a look of love as He hangs there looking for you. Then picture Him walking out of the grave.

- Contemplate the Lord deeply in your heart right now, what He has gone through to know you and all that He has done for you.

- Read 2 Corinthians 3:18. Ask God to illuminate your face with the glory of the Lord—the glory that dims as you drift away from Him. Pray that your countenance becomes more radiant as you draw nearer to Jesus and experience more of the likeness of Christ. Purpose to be grateful, thankful, and content.

WEEK 1........ WEEK 2........ WEEK 3........ WEEK 4........ WEEK 5........ WEEK 6........ WEEK 7........ WEEK 8........ WEEK 9........ WEEK 10........ WEEK 11........ WEEK 12

DAY 5

- Change the way you see and act out love. Choose not to conform to the pattern of this world any longer (Romans 12:2). Make it your goal in life to pursue Jesus and get to know Him and His perfect love. As you do, you will gladly and gratefully accept His unearned and unconditional love, and you will start truly loving others.

- Your fixation on sex and the view of love as sex will also change, replaced by an appropriate view of the sexual intimacy God designed for marriage. Single women, too, will cherish real love that is not dependent upon sex or even a spouse, but is birthed in spirit and is fulfilling.

- Right now, confess any sin you have committed this week and ask for healing.

- Confess ways that you have been withholding love from others or have not been a friend.

- Confess ways you have been avoiding or ignoring God.

- Ask the Lord to instill in you a deep desire to worship and praise Him. Commit to spending specific times for meeting with God with zeal and passion.

- Ask the Holy Spirit to reveal any areas where you treat God like a vending machine, demanding what you think you deserve or need.

- Ask God to show you ways in which you do not fully turn and trust in Him.

- Openly discuss with the Lord whether you see Him as good. Keep going to God in prayer and petition, asking Him to open your eyes to His faithfulness, forgiveness, and unconditional love. Soak in the promise that if you seek Him with all of your heart, He will make Himself known to you. Tell God that you are no longer pretending to trust in Him or simply going through the motions of trying to get to know Him.

- Ask the Lord to cause you to truly believe that His Word is trustworthy and true and that it has daily application for your life. Also, keep reading the Bible to know God, meeting with Him in your heart and soul, not merely to gain knowledge about Him.

- Ask God to change your inner desires so that you make pursuing the Lord your number one priority in life.

- Desire absolute purity across the board in your life. Spend time talking to God about purity and renew your commitment to sexual integrity.

- Be still and listen to whatever else the Lord presses upon your heart.

WEEK 1........ WEEK 2........ WEEK 3........ WEEK 4........ WEEK 5........ WEEK 6........ **WEEK 7** .... WEEK 8........ WEEK 9........ WEEK 10 .... WEEK 11 .... WEEK 12

DAY 5

PRAY

Prayerfully read Ephesians 1:15–21, asking God to give other Proven Women the same wonderful gifts in this passage. As you pray this passage of Scripture, replace the pronouns "you" and "your" with the names of others. Keep the focus off of yourself, except to ask to become a willing and obedient servant who is humble, content, and grateful.

Record your prayers below:

_____

_____

_____

_____

_____

_____

_____

_____

_____

_____

_____

WEEK 1 .... WEEK 2 .... WEEK 3 .... WEEK 4 .... WEEK 5 .... WEEK 6 .... **WEEK 7** .... WEEK 8 .... WEEK 9 .... WEEK 10 .... WEEK 11 .... WEEK 12

DAY 5

SPECIAL NOTE:

A word of caution: As you begin to experience victory, pride will seek to return. You'll be tempted to think that you're now in good enough shape to continue the battle in your own strength. That's Satan's goal—to turn you away from the one and only real God. As you willingly walk in your own steps outside of God's camp, you'll be ripe for capture. Instead, cling to the Lord. Stay close to Him by living out your greatest purpose in life: to love the Lord with all your heart and to know Him as a friend. Allow God to set your feet on sure ground and heal your wounds. You'll become whole and complete, not lacking anything (James 1:2–4). Imagine having true peace and contentment. Even greater than that, the Lord Himself is being offered to you! Don't just pursue Jesus so that He can fix you, pursue Him to know Him.

PW

WEEK EIGHT

TESTIMONY

"I am currently working on the study and it is making some unbelievable changes in my life! Well actually, God is making the changes but the devotional is helping me right my relationship with Him! THANK YOU VERY MUCH for following God's leading to do this!"

Passionate for God,
Repentant in spirit,
Open and honest,
Victorious in living,
Eternal in perspective, and
Networking with other ***PROVEN Women.***

MEMORY VERSE

Psalm 19:13–14 (ESV): "Keep back your servant also from presumptuous sins; let them not have dominion over me! Then I shall be blameless, and innocent of great transgression. Let the words of my mouth and the meditation of my heart be acceptable in your sight, O Lord, my rock and my redeemer."

WEEK 8 DAY 1 (MONDAY)

KEY THOUGHT: Fasting kills our false passion and grows our affection in Christ.

DAILY READING

FASTING

This week can be a giant step forward if you are committed to doing whatever it takes to be healed and to living a Proven life. Make this decision now. Ask God to reveal truth to you about sexual sin, its roots, and its cure. Have you made a decision to do "whatever it takes" to be free and receive God's healing? This week, we are going to take these steps together. We are going to rely even more heavily on God by implementing the following steps:

1. If you are physically able, do a mini-fast every day this week by skipping lunch. Go ahead and eat a normal (or light) breakfast and a normal (or light) dinner, and then only liquids for lunch. Each time you feel hungry, pray and ask God to transform your passions and affections. Isaiah 58:6 (NIV) says, "Is not this the kind of fasting I have chosen: to loosen the chains of injustice and untie the cords of the yoke, to set the oppressed free and break every yoke."

   During the day, frequently contemplate how you are recommitting and solidifying decisions to prioritize loving and pursuing God above everything else in your life. (Note: A fast isn't a magic formula. It won't remove sin. It can, however, help you focus and learn to become more dependent upon God.)

WEEK 1........ WEEK 2........ WEEK 3........ WEEK 4........ WEEK 5........ WEEK 6........ WEEK 7........ WEEK 8 .... WEEK 9........ WEEK 10....... WEEK 11........ WEEK 12

DAY 1

2. Give up all television and social media this week. Use this time to listen to praise music, go for walks, and do other activities with family or friends. Devote the week to prayer and spending time with Jesus.

3. Don't let any unresolved anger remain in you. Make a decision to be at peace through the gift of reconciliation.

4. Freely forgive each and every transgression you have suffered, no matter what.

5. Practice being content and grateful for everything.

HIDING OR SURRENDERING?

For many people, turning to sex or other things is a way to escape the present, whether that is present pain, present stress, or present relationships or a lack thereof. However, these escapes never end up bringing about the desired result. In order to attempt to reach the desired result, many keep increasing the practice of the activity in a vain attempt at trying to force it to work. Some will eventually spend hours a day viewing pornography and further increasing the amount of masturbation.

Regardless of what you turn to, you'll always be on a constant hunt for more, for newer and better ways to feed your desires with a moment of pleasure. Although you think that you receive temporary relief from the issues that you are hiding from, you're ultimately left feeling empty. Guilt and shame lurk beneath the surface. You often lack any real sense of contentment and purpose. Your double life also creates loneliness because you are seeking intimacy through these false forms of satisfaction rather than healthy, vulnerable relationships.

So many ladies are struggling in the dark, afraid to talk to others about these struggles and issues. The secrets feel suffocating, yet women are too afraid to open up about the dark corners of their heart. It is easier to continue in sin than to be vulnerable. But this is a vicious cycle.

Sin never satisfies. How true, and yet often we believe the opposite. Just knowing in your head that fantasy, pornography, and other sexual sins cannot truly satisfy your needs brings little relief. This is especially true if you still do not clearly see the real source of your hidden pain. Instead, you remain caught in a flight from real intimacy. Some don't see any need to revisit old painful memories or look for the deep roots; yet to obtain healing, you need

WEEK 1 ...... WEEK 2 ...... WEEK 3 ...... WEEK 4 ...... WEEK 5 ...... WEEK 6 ...... WEEK 7 ...... **WEEK 8** ...... WEEK 9 ...... WEEK 10 ...... WEEK 11 ...... WEEK 12

DAY 1

to confront these underlying issues and the source of pain. For instance, if your hand feels numb and you refuse to look for the cause, how can it be treated or healed? Perhaps you have a thorn under the flesh from an old accident or injury. How long will you pretend all is well? When will you surrender and allow the doctor to remove it?

As hard as it is to accept, you have deep wounds in your spirit. The intense pain gives way to escape and coping methods, but when your shots of Novocain wear off, you keep going back to the same numbing activities. Now is the time to stop claiming the pretense that you are okay. Admit that you are hurting inside, that the pain of prior relationships hasn't simply gone away, and that you fear intimacy. There is no shame in admitting these things. God is already aware of the condition of your heart, and He brings healing rather than ridicule. Your escapes to fantasy, masturbation, pornography, or other anesthesia prove that you are not okay. Stop hiding your true condition from yourself. Tell God about your fear of real intimacy, and that you're afraid to let others get close to you. Ask Him to show you how you've equated sex with love and therefore are trying to live without vulnerable and intimate love.

You may have experienced horrible abuse or neglect as a child. Maybe harsh teasing by others left scars. The memories may be painful, yet the Lord asks you to open up to Him and to others. Part of the healing process is (re)developing open and honest communication with others. Seek out a trusted confidant, such as another Proven Woman, with whom you can talk about your pain without fear of rejection or condemnation. Even if some people fail you, don't give up. The Lord will supply you with someone else to talk to if you're willing to do whatever it takes to be healed and fully restored in your relationships with God and others. Also, if after many attempts, you simply cannot locate someone with whom you can openly share, it doesn't mean that God cannot or will not heal you. It just may take longer and require even more time spent in open communication with the Lord. Once you establish a networking partner, tell her about your pain. Admit that you have a hard time showing or receiving love or trusting others. Diligently build relationships with her and with several other women. Earnestly ask God to give you someone that you can befriend.

Live out a Proven life and purpose:

• Recognize the painful loss of a relationship with a loved one.

• Forgive the abuser of all harm.

• Form new relationships with other Christians.

• Purpose to see God as good.

WEEK 1........ WEEK 2........ WEEK 3........ WEEK 4........ WEEK 5........ WEEK 6........ WEEK 7........ **WEEK 8** .... WEEK 9........ WEEK 10........ WEEK 11........ WEEK 12

DAY 1

- Pursue the Lord with all your heart.

- Trust the Lord completely.

Stop acting out of what you don't know about God and begin seeing how the Lord has proven His love. It is easy to question God's love for us. I don't know why, but even though God's love is the most consistent, reliable truth in this world, we have a tendency to question it. Anytime we doubt His love, we need to train our mind to remember the cross. The cross is the proof and the display of God's love for us. When I remember what Jesus endured in order to bring you and me into a relationship with Him, confidence in His love begins to return. We should be seeking to get to know this God who gives Himself freely to us. Record any insights, prayers, or commitments.

_____

_____

_____

_____

HEARTWORK

Pride and selfishness are the root causes of a lack of intimacy and are the reasons we turn towards sexual immorality.

In your own words, describe how pride and selfishness keep sexual sins alive in your life. Don't brush this off, but ask God to open your eyes.

_____

_____

_____

_____

WEEK 1........ WEEK 2........ WEEK 3........ WEEK 4........ WEEK 5........ WEEK 6........ WEEK 7........ **WEEK 8**........ WEEK 9........ WEEK 10 .... WEEK 11........ WEEK 12

DAY 1

Make sure you grasp that sexual addiction involves relational sins and meditate on the remedy of turning to God in zeal, repentance, and openness. Rebellious anger must be dealt with before healing occurs because these sins cause a flight from real intimacy. Meditate on how to pursue true intimacy with God and others, and record any commitments.

_____

_____

_____

_____

Don't forget to fast over lunch. Spend some time in prayer, asking God to change you and mold you as He sees fit. All day long, keep telling the Lord that you are His and that He now has control over all areas of your life. It's very liberating to let go of control and allow God to be in charge. Fasting may be very hard at first, but just like any discipline, you will grow strong in it over time and practice.

As you also fast from television and social media, you may have more time on your hands, and you may not know what to do with yourself. You may discover that going to television and social media is a mindless way to escape. Is there anything that you need to face this week that you have been putting off? Is there anything you need to do that you have been avoiding? Without the distractions of television and social media, determine to accomplish something this week you have been putting off.

Write down a list of issues you need to face, conversations you need to have, or things you need to do. Make sure prayer and rest are on that list.

_____

_____

_____

_____

WEEK 1........ WEEK 2........ WEEK 3........ WEEK 4........ WEEK 5........ WEEK 6........ WEEK 7..... **WEEK 8** .... WEEK 9........ WEEK 10........ WEEK 11........ WEEK 12

DAY 1

READ THE BIBLE

Are you hungry for the things of God? Keep reading to get to know God and apply His truths in your life. Read Psalm 22. Jesus quoted from this psalm while on the cross. The next time you feel overwhelmed, recall that your risen Savior can empathize with you and is ready and able to comfort you. No matter what type of pain you are experiencing, you are entering into a place where Jesus has been. He understands pain so much more than we realize. He grieves with you.

_____

_____

_____

_____

_____

_____

PRAY

With a soft heart, meet with the Lord.

- Ask God to reveal how you are afraid, in rebellion, or angry with Him.

- Ask God to cause you to believe that He is perfect and totally good.

- Ask God to forgive you for not trusting Him with all areas of your life.

- Ask God to open your heart to Him and to others.

- Ask God to heal your wounds.

- Accept God's healing and unconditional love.

- Forgive those who have hurt or abused you.

WEEK 1........ WEEK 2........ WEEK 3........ WEEK 4........ WEEK 5........ WEEK 6........ WEEK 7........ **WEEK 8**........ WEEK 9........ WEEK 10........ WEEK 11........ WEEK 12

DAY 1

- Pray for others. (List them.)

_____

_____

_____

_____

_____

_____

SPECIAL NOTE:

Sexual addiction involves relational sins. Perhaps you choose not to engage in vulnerable relationships because the wounds of your past lead you to fear future wounds if you let anyone get close again. Therefore, you hide in sexual activities and fantasy. Although you include others in parts of your life, you do so only up to a point that you determine, and you put up walls that others cannot see over or penetrate. On the other hand, the essence of healing from sexual addiction is developing relationships, starting first with God and moving toward others.

O is for Open and Honest. Use discussions with others to aid in the healing process of renewing relationships. Try telling a trusted friend about the rejection and abuse you have suffered and about your fears. Ask them to listen without offering fixes, and ask them to affirm you. Some who are deeply wounded may find it useful to talk to a Christian counselor, but it is important to guard against becoming overly dependent upon him/her for hope or healing, which comes only from God. Allow the counselor to help uncover the root issues so that you can move toward freedom expressed through forgiving others. Look for ways in which you have learned to back away from intimate relationships. Then seek to be open and honest in your real relationships

MEMORY VERSE

Psalm 19:13–14 (ESV): "Keep back your servant also from presumptuous sins; let them not have dominion over me! Then I shall be blameless, and innocent of great transgression. Let the words of my mouth and the meditation of my heart be acceptable in your sight, O Lord, my rock and my redeemer."

WEEK 8 DAY 2 (TUESDAY)

KEY THOUGHT: Lean on God to be your stability. We change like the wind, but He remains the same.

DAILY READING

The biggest battle that a person trapped in sexual bondage faces is turning the focus away from herself and toward God.[6] Read that last sentence again. Will you engage in that battle? You must rely upon God's strength to do this!

Powerlessness or a lack of control can be uncomfortable or even scary because you're at the mercy of others. Unfortunately, people sometimes abuse authority and can inflict serious pain on others, such as child abuse. List ways in which you are powerless today (e.g., addiction, controlling boss or spouse, debt, deadlines, overwhelming fear).

_____

_____

Describe how you have felt in times of powerlessness.

_____

_____

WEEK 1 ...... WEEK 2 ...... WEEK 3 ...... WEEK 4 ...... WEEK 5 ...... WEEK 6 ...... WEEK 7 ...... **WEEK 8** ...... WEEK 9 ...... WEEK 10 ...... WEEK 11 ...... WEEK 12

DAY 2

Most people don't like being out of control. Some worry about this to the extent that they build unhealthy walls in order to gain control in every area of their life. How about you? Do you hate powerlessness or a lack of control? List what unhealthy walls you may have built for self-protection.

_____

_____

Some women seek rock-solid control over emotions as a way of coping with a sense of powerlessness. They attempt to not need or expect anything from others in order to avoid pain. They shut down their heart and may even be proud of feeling nothing (e.g., no fear, no pain, no exuberance—nothing). However, God made us emotional beings with feelings. Suppressing those feelings becomes a full-time job. It's time to change course. Start recognizing your feelings and sharing them with others.

Pornography and fantasizing are tempting substitutes for your need for intimacy, but they are a false intimacy that never satisfy. The addiction grows deeper and leads to places you never imagined. Also, anger and defensiveness are often just around the corner since you never truly gain the control you seek.

One of the most common characteristics of people who turn to pornography, masturbation, or other sexual escape is that they want to control their lives. You subconsciously rely upon a chosen form of sexual activity to avoid the pain of open, vulnerable relationships. While you cannot fully control others or cause them to love you, you can control your fantasies, what you watch in pornography, and your own body.

You also control how much of your life you open up to others. For instance, you can have sex with someone but not allow them to know your spirit. You can run from real relationships, or at least those at a certain level of vulnerability, because relationships are a source of pain. It seems better to squeeze any pleasure you can from self-focused sexual activities, even enduring the resulting guilt and shame, than to risk the hurt or rejection associated with real intimacy. You end up dehumanizing the object of your lust and thus turn sex, which is a valid aspect of intimacy with a spouse, and you turn it into an inward, self-serving form of phantom relationship.[7] Frequently, even a spouse is treated as an object of pleasure to the point where you become single-minded in heart, rather than being treated as a spiritual partner with whom you can grow in deepest intimacy and vulnerability.

WEEK 1........ WEEK 2........ WEEK 3........ WEEK 4........ WEEK 5........ WEEK 6........ WEEK 7..... WEEK 8 .... WEEK 9........ WEEK 10 .... WEEK 11........ WEEK 12

DAY 2

Consider the following passages from the recommended book *False Intimacy: Understanding the Struggle of Sexual Addiction* by Dr. Harry Schaumburg:

"Sex addicts think and plan their lives around sex... A sexually addicted person becomes fully absorbed with sex, for it becomes the greatest need—not the greatest desire. Sex is wanted, demanded, and will be pursued at any cost.[8]

"The truth is, however, that when we try to bury the core reality of emptiness, the result is false intimacy, not genuine. When we insist that our needs for intimacy be fulfilled and ignore the reality that loneliness is always present, we get the very opposite of what we're demanding: We're left alone to stare with open eyes at the harsh reality of nakedness.[9]

"But at its core, sexual fantasy is a worship of self, a devotion to the ability of people to fabricate in their minds the solution to what they know is a need and believe they deserve.[10]

"Simple recognition of addictive behavior is not on its own enough to accomplish healing. Sex addicts who stop living in denial and recognize that they have hurt others and turned away from God may not always have an urgent desire to change. Their tears of sorrow over their addictive behaviors may spring more from the fear of being rejected and feelings of ridicule than from genuine brokenness and repentance.[11]

"You must pursue God on His terms, in brokenness and humility, facing the sinful condition of your heart and inviting God to begin healing you. A sex addict truly changes when his or her relationship with God changes."[12]

Record your thoughts:

_____

_____

_____

_____

_____

WEEK 1........ WEEK 2........ WEEK 3........ WEEK 4........ WEEK 5........ WEEK 6........ WEEK 7........ **WEEK 8**........ WEEK 9........ WEEK 10 .... WEEK 11........ WEEK 12

DAY 2

_____

_____

_____

The fundamental underlying problems that sex addicts face include:

• A reluctance to be in a passionate, dependent relationship with God.

• The use of sex (like pornography, fantasy, or masturbation) as a method of avoiding pain.

• A longing for love but without intimacy.

These, and the other problems associated with sex addiction, are hard to swallow. Right now, are you beginning to shut down your emotions rather than facing these difficult issues? Instead, will you accept truth revealed by God and seek change? Real change will only come through an intimate relationship with God. Your other relationships thereafter can be healed and restored.

It's worth repeating that fantasy is, in essence, serving yourself. It's time to switch masters.

 ## HEARTWORK

God is perfect, and His mercy is real and available to you. He offers love and forgiveness when we do not deserve it and lavishes His favor onto us based on Jesus' righteousness. God can be trusted. We were talking earlier about being out of control. However, when we relinquish control, we place ourselves under God's control, which is the best place to be. It's a lot safer to be under the control of God than to be under your own control. Read that sentence again. It's only scary to be out of control if you cannot trust the parameters that you are in. For instance, when I was in high school, I rode a zip line several times. The first time I went down it, it was exhilarating to jump off the platform, but I still gripped the harness with all of my might even though it would hold me up whether I clung to it or not. After a few jumps, I realized the harness was safe and began to have more fun, even flipping upside down. On my last trip down, the zip line workers talked me into standing on the edge of the platform and just free falling backwards. It was one of the scariest things I ever did, but I absolutely knew the zip line would catch me. And you know what, I did it!! It is so freeing to let go when you know that something else is your stability.

WEEK 1 .... WEEK 2 .... WEEK 3 .... WEEK 4 .... WEEK 5 .... WEEK 6 .... WEEK 7 ...... **WEEK 8** ...... WEEK 9 .... WEEK 10 .... WEEK 11 .... WEEK 12

DAY 2

This is just a silly illustration compared to the stability of God. You do not need to grip your heart so tightly. You do not need to build walls. I guarantee you, there will be pain at times in your life—at times, more pain than you think you can bear. But I also know that the God of all comfort will be there for you in those moments. There will be peace that transcends your understanding. Some of you are not experiencing this peace and comfort because you stiff-arm God and numb your pain through sexual sin.

Sexually addictive behavior is an attempt to control your life. Explain what this means to you and how it is true in your life.

_____

_____

_____

Can you see ways that God has brought comfort into your life?

_____

_____

Do you believe He can continue to comfort you?

_____

_____

READ THE BIBLE

Read Psalm 36. Don't rush, but meet with God.

WEEK 1........ WEEK 2........ WEEK 3........ WEEK 4........ WEEK 5........ WEEK 6........ WEEK 7........ **WEEK 8**........ WEEK 9........ WEEK 10........ WEEK 11........ WEEK 12

DAY 2

PRAY

Turn your attention to God in prayer.

Review the memory verse.

- Admit and repent over how you have sought to control your life instead of giving control to the Lord.

- Ask the Lord to gift you with brokenness and humility so that you can offer your life to God as a pleasing sacrifice (Romans 12:1–2).

- Ask God to give you a heart that loves Him and hates your sin.

- Ask the Lord to soften your heart so that you can hear His voice and follow His commands.

- Confess any anger or ambivalence (numbness or competing emotions) toward God or a family member, and then repent and turn away from it.

- Ask the Lord for His strength and grace to forgive others completely.

- Meditate on the goodness of God and praise Him for being holy and just.

- Seek first the kingdom of God and His righteousness (Matthew 6:33). Pour out your heart in worship.

- List others to pray for and earnestly ask the Lord to open their spiritual eyes to His rich mercy.

Don't forget to fast over lunch. Spend time in prayer, asking God to change and fashion you as He sees fit. Continue to keep telling the Lord that you are His and that He now has total control over your life. Perhaps kneel in your workspace (if you have privacy) to be more reverent and focused on God.

_____

_____

_____

_____

WEEK 1 ..... WEEK 2 ..... WEEK 3 ..... WEEK 4 ..... WEEK 5 ..... WEEK 6 ..... WEEK 7 ..... WEEK 8 ..... WEEK 9 ..... WEEK 10 ..... WEEK 11 ..... WEEK 12

DAY 2

_____

_____

_____

_____

_____

_____

_____

_____

SPECIAL NOTE:

O in PROVEN is for Open and Honest. You're supposed to have feelings. Don't confuse suppressing anger with resolving anger. Suppressed anger leads to unrest and even violent explosions. Resolved anger leads to restored relationships and unrestricted hearts. Anytime there is division, there is always an enemy, but the enemy is never the person on the other side of the divide. Satan is always the enemy, and he utilizes schemes to cause division. Ephesians 6:12 says, "For we do not wrestle against flesh and blood, but against the rulers, against the authorities, against the cosmic powers over this present darkness, against the spiritual forces of evil in the heavenly places."

You'll see that at times you feel angry, hateful, bitter, and enraged. If you lock up these feelings, you won't be free to love God or love others. Admit these emotions to God. Share with God why you have these feelings and listen for His response. As He calls you to forgive, release these emotions to Him. Releasing your thoughts and feelings upward to God is so much better than burying them. But, in order to release them, you have to trust in God's goodness, love, and forgiveness.

MEMORY VERSE

Psalm 19:13–14 (ESV): "Keep back your servant also from presumptuous sins; let them not have dominion over me! Then I shall be blameless, and innocent of great transgression. Let the words of my mouth and the meditation of my heart be acceptable in your sight, O Lord, my rock and my redeemer."

WEEK 8 DAY 3 (WEDNESDAY)

KEY THOUGHT: We don't grow by leaving God's love, we grow by realizing God's love.

Once again, we want to remind you to reject the idea of performance-based victory. We definitely need this reminder during a week of fasting. Legalism focuses on controlling our behavior in an attempt to earn God's favor and love. We can think that we are earning God's favor by making sacrifices. These sacrifices, such as fasting, do not earn anything though. Instead, they teach you how reliant you are on God.

You already have God's love, which is unconditional. You also have His favor, because Christ's righteousness covers you. Legalism, however, is conforming to a code or system of deeds and observances in the energy of the flesh, hoping to gain the blessing and favor of God and man. Legalism invariably denies the principle of grace and exalts the pride of man. For example, if you set aside 10 percent of your income so that you can feel like a good Christian, then you are just practicing legalism. However, truly desiring to give God your first fruits honors Him. (Of course, there are times that you simply must be obedient and ask God to give you the desire to obey Him.)

A warning bell should ring in your mind anytime you catch yourself checking off this series as homework instead of performing Heartwork. Being legalistic or performance-based quickly saps the life and passion out of your relationship with God.

List ways in which you have been legalistic or performance-based.

_____

_____

_____

WEEK 1........ WEEK 2........ WEEK 3........ WEEK 4........ WEEK 5........ WEEK 6........ WEEK 7........ **WEEK 8** .... WEEK 9........ WEEK 10 .... WEEK 11........ WEEK 12

DAY 3

P is for Passionate for God. One good way to keep a check on legalism is to stay passionate for God. Make knowing and loving God (instead of following rules) your goal. Obedience to God necessarily flows from a heart that longs for Him. Is there anything you can be doing to stir your affection for the Lord? When is the last time you got out in nature and simply enjoyed being with God? Make your favorite dessert or hot beverage, put on some great worship music, put your phone away, and be with God. What are some other things that you enjoy doing? If these are good, honorable things, then God has wired you to enjoy them. Spend time doing these things while worshiping Him.

DAILY READING

Which is a solid foundation, sand or rock? No one should build a house upon sand. How about your spiritual foundation? Is it built upon self or God? The only sure foundation for a life free from the grip of sin is to stand upon the Rock of Christ (1 Corinthians 10:4).

Read Matthew 7:24–29 (ESV): "'Everyone then who hears these words of mine and does them will be like a wise man who built his house on the rock. And the rain fell, and the floods came, and the winds blew and beat on that house, but it did not fall, because it had been founded on the rock. And everyone who hears these words of mine and does not do them will be like a foolish man who built his house on the sand. And the rain fell, and the floods came, and the winds blew and beat against that house, and it fell, and great was the fall of it.' And when Jesus finished these sayings, the crowds were astonished at his teaching, for he was teaching them as one who had authority, and not as their scribes."

These are Jesus' closing remarks in the Sermon on the Mount. Matthew 5–7 is a sermon that Jesus gives to a large group of people toward the beginning of His ministry. He shares many wonderful truths in this sermon and ends it with these words. He compares a foolish man and a wise man. Read verses 24 and 26. What is the difference between the wise man and the foolish man?

_____

_____

_____

_____

WEEK 1........ WEEK 2........ WEEK 3........ WEEK 4........ WEEK 5........ WEEK 6........ WEEK 7........ **WEEK 8**........ WEEK 9........ WEEK 10........ WEEK 11........ WEEK 12

DAY 3

Growing up, I was always taught that the wise man builds His house on the rock and the foolish man on the sand. While this is true, this is merely the illustration that Jesus uses. Do you see the real difference? The context of this passage is key to understanding it in greater depth. Jesus is basically saying, "All of you have just heard this great sermon. Those of you who don't just listen but also put these words into practice are wise and will withstand the storms of life. However, if you merely listen to these words of mine but do not put them into practice, you will collapse in those same storms."

How are you doing? We are in the eighth week of this study. It has asked a lot of you. Are you putting these things into practice? Or are you merely reading this and agreeing with it? This study is calling you to walk in a deeper, more intimate relationship with Jesus. Are you trusting Him? Are you desiring to know and love the Lord? It's a choice. You must choose to accept Him, because He won't force Himself upon you. You cannot have two masters (Matthew 6:24). Either you are acting apart from God, or He is Lord of your life. The more you see God's perfection, power, and might, the more you'll know that He is capable of guiding and protecting your life. The more you see His real and unconditional love, mercy, and grace, the more you'll understand that He always has you in mind and He can be trusted as the Builder.

Intimacy with God occurs and grows when you spend time with Him in worship and praise. This is more than an opportunity to receive an emotional high. Our selfishness holds us back from experiencing true joy and union with God. When we go into worship to experience an emotional high or to seek what the Lord can do for us, we are missing out on truly experiencing God. Sometimes we go into worship with apprehension, wondering if God truly accepts us in that moment. Being wrapped up in ourselves steals the joy of truly worshiping and experiencing the presence of God.

The same can be true of sexual encounters with your spouse. God designed sex to be an intimate experience between a husband and a wife in which they are fully with one another, delighting in one another while experiencing great pleasure. Sex is meant to be a display of one's love to the other. It is a time of giving. Yet, when both are giving, they are also receiving and becoming united in a powerfully beautiful display of love. However, when either the wife or the husband goes into sex with the expectation of getting his or her needs met rather than connecting intimately, this sacred act becomes a self-centered venture.

WEEK 1...... WEEK 2...... WEEK 3...... WEEK 4...... WEEK 5...... WEEK 6...... WEEK 7...... WEEK 8 ...... WEEK 9...... WEEK 10 ...... WEEK 11...... WEEK 12

DAY 3

Selfishness and pride hinder complete intimacy with God. They also hinder intimacy with a spouse. Selflessness and humility are necessary to foster true intimacy. Intimacy between a husband and a wife is symbolic of the relationship between Christ and the church.

When you meet with the Lord to give of yourself in times of worship and praise, He fills your heart and feeds your soul. Your intimate knowledge of the Lord is also fed by reading His Word daily with a mind-set of experiencing Him. Your relationships with both God and others blossom while serving others and seeing them as dearly loved souls and children of your heavenly Father. While serving others, you step outside of self-centeredness and learn to give without expecting to receive anything other than an opportunity to live out worship.

Choose to network with other Proven Women, where acceptance and encouragement are received. When pain knocks at your door, make a choice to turn to the Lord (standing beside other Proven Women), rather than retreating inward and toward sexual behavior. Stop treating the world as a mirror in which you only look at yourself. Quit focusing on and agonizing over your circumstances. It may be true that you are going through tough circumstances, but having tunnel vision on your situation can send you into a downward spiral. Focusing on yourself is like sticking your head into a barrel. It blocks out the reality and beauty of God and all He created. Rather, open the eternal eyes of your soul and look upward to your precious Lord in heaven. You'll realize that joy doesn't depend upon circumstances.

As you look to God for purpose and fulfillment, you'll soon discover that He has a plan for you. You won't know or achieve it when your eyes don't look beyond your selfish interests. You must lose your life—not control it—to become joined with God (Matthew 10:39). Repent over your death grip on the need to control and yield completely to the Lord. You cannot rescue yourself or turn your own life around. Embrace being a daughter of God and commit to being an obedient servant of an all-powerful yet all-loving, good God. He is the One who handcrafted you in His very image, and He has prepared wonderful experiences for you (Ephesians 2).

Let this speak to your heart. Write down your thoughts.

_____

_____

_____

WEEK 1........ WEEK 2........ WEEK 3........ WEEK 4........ WEEK 5........ WEEK 6........ WEEK 7........ **WEEK 8** .... WEEK 9........ WEEK 10........ WEEK 11........ WEEK 12

DAY 3

HEARTWORK

The actions of a Proven Woman clearly set her apart because she is continually dying to selfishness and pride. You must carry your title of being Proven humbly, boasting only in the Lord. You're no longer ruled by laws or burdened by commands, heavy laden with rules. You are set free! God fulfilled the law so that you could live. Therefore, stop striving in your own strength to be perfect (or seen as perfect); instead, live an honest life before a God who truly cares for you. Start becoming so filled with His Spirit that you're now starting to desire what God desires. Your mind is renewed and transformed. You no longer act on your own. In fact, even passion for God is not obtained by striving, but by yielding to Him. Dear friend, long to yield to the Lord, making it your highest calling. Knowing God as the true Lord and a true friend is the joy of our lives.

God is calling you to yield your life so you may unite with Him.

- Will you commit to declaring your dependency on God? It's important to realize that you will suffer setbacks during times you act independently from God, but you can trust Him to be your strength.

- Will you commit to abiding in Christ? Rely on His strength rather than your own.

- Will you commit to totally and completely yielding to Christ's will for your life? God doesn't force Himself on you but eagerly awaits your surrender to Him.

- Will you make a decision to believe the truth that God is good and perfect regardless of your feelings or circumstances? Ask God to give you a correct view of Him.

- Commit to knowing God as a friend.

Make an intentional decision to live by the Spirit. Record your commitments.

_____

_____

_____

WEEK 1........ WEEK 2........ WEEK 3........ WEEK 4........ WEEK 5........ WEEK 6........ WEEK 7........ **WEEK 8**........ WEEK 9........ WEEK 10........ WEEK 11........ WEEK 12

DAY 3

READ THE BIBLE

Read Psalms 14, 15 and 19:12–14. Keep going to God's Word daily and applying it in your life.

PRAY

Spend five or ten minutes with the Lord. Some suggestions include:

Confess where you are striving in your own strength and ask God to help you trust Him to transform your heart.

- Ask God, where are you still holding back from him?

- Commit to approaching God with worship rather than seeking an emotional high.

- Be passionate in telling God how much you love Him.

- Ponder His names (see Appendix A).

- Brag about God's might and wonders.

- Seek a broken and contrite heart (Psalm 51:17).

- Ask God to melt your proud spirit.

- Ask the Lord to give you a heart that loves Him.

- Pray for others. (List them as you do.)

If you are fasting, instead of having lunch, consider reading the Bible at that time. Be sure to keep asking God to change you and fashion you as He sees fit. Keep telling the Lord that you have yielded completely to Him, that you are like a lump of clay for the master Potter to form, and that you will accept and be content with whatever role He chooses for you.

_____

_____

_____

_____

WEEK 1........ WEEK 2........ WEEK 3........ WEEK 4........ WEEK 5........ WEEK 6........ WEEK 7........ WEEK 8 .... WEEK 9........ WEEK 10 .... WEEK 11........ WEEK 12

DAY 3

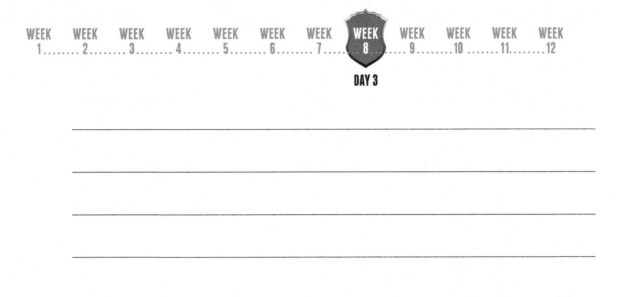

_____

_____

_____

_____

_____

SPECIAL NOTE:

Whenever you doubt the Lord's love, return to the cross. Consider what love it took for Jesus to leave heaven and all His glory to take the form of a human like you. He was tempted in every way and experienced sufferings in order to become a perfect sacrifice and substitute for your sin. He willingly took the punishment rightfully due you in order to give you life. Do you think a God of such love wants you to remain in the misery of despair or that He will reject you? No! His perfect love, not the piercing nails, held Him to the cross. He gave you His name and has a place in heaven prepared for you. Even now, He gives you the choice to refuse His gifts. You can keep living independently from Him in agony and despair, but He longs for you to run to Him. He will not withhold His forgiveness or love. Choose Him this day; He's already chosen to love you.

MEMORY VERSE

Psalm 19:13–14 (ESV): "Keep back your servant also from presumptuous sins; let them not have dominion over me! Then I shall be blameless, and innocent of great transgression. Let the words of my mouth and the meditation of my heart be acceptable in your sight, O Lord, my rock and my redeemer."

WEEK 8 DAY 4 (THURSDAY)

KEY THOUGHT: Healing doesn't come by performing harder, healing comes by knowing Him.

DAILY READING

God designed you for relationships. Decide today that you'll be a friend to others. Get to know other Proven Women. The Lord uses the words and actions of other Christian women for the purpose of encouragement. Choose to talk to other people about spiritual matters, and share your hopes and goals with them. Discuss your roles in life. Stay connected with these women. I have heard many girls say they do not get along with other women easily. This is because we are often each other's competition when we allow pride and selfishness to get in the way. Do not let that be an excuse. God actually guides us by giving us relational advice. He doesn't want us to endure difficult relationships to punish us. He knows we need relationships, He calls us to love because we are designed to do so. As much as we might hate to admit it, we need relationships.

The Lord is also calling you into His service. This is the opposite of selfishness and pride, which feed worldly passions. Make a decision to live by God's standards and to forsake the world. Stop striving to gain what the world offers. To God, your life isn't measured by positions, looks, or possessions. Real joy isn't based upon sex, fantasy, or other momentary pleasures. When you adopt an eternal perspective you will experience fulfillment and lasting peace. Remember, service should flow out of a heart that loves God and is confident in His love for you and others. We do not serve to gain God's affection. He's already poured out all of His affection for us. Being Jesus' disciples means growing in our identity to live with His affection.

WEEK 1 .... WEEK 2 .... WEEK 3 .... WEEK 4 .... WEEK 5 .... WEEK 6 .... WEEK 7 .... **WEEK 8** .... WEEK 9 .... WEEK 10 .... WEEK 11 .... WEEK 12

DAY 4

Have you taken notice how double-minded people often are? Perhaps they claim to want to bring glory to the Lord while still imagining how they can obtain something for themselves on the side. Sometimes they are unaware of much of a dual-thought life they have. This can be true of any one of us. It's time to live single-mindedly for God. Be attentive to double-mindedness, and trust that you'll only be truly satisfied when you seek the Lord with all of your heart. Allow the Holy Spirit to be your guide. Test every thought. Dwell and act upon only that which is holy, pure, and pleasing to God. In the end, your new eternal perspective will radically change the way you think and act. You will no longer remain solely focused on the moment, but you'll be living out your true purpose in the reality of the presence of your Lord, Savior and Friend.

Until you understand and live by God's grace, you will remain subject to a shame-based lifestyle. Many use shame to control others and get them to do what they want. For instance, they say, "Why did you do this?" or "You're wrong" to manipulate others. Even failing to complete all of your daily Heartwork study can catch you in this self-shame trap. Do you beat yourself up or think yourself unworthy? If they are not careful, other Proven Women can resort to shaming each other as a way of trying to help each other overcome. Someone might say in a group, "Who did not finish all of the study? Raise your hand."

Each time you're shamed into acting, you place a greater emphasis on performance-based living. You think you can earn love or respect based on your actions and not because of who you are in Christ. When you view yourself based on your performance, you incorrectly focus on acting in your own power and attempt to overcome sin so that God sees you and loves you. Over time, performance-based people are unable to accept unconditional love. They are uncomfortable receiving a gift or a favor. They feel the need to repay it. They must earn love. How often have you thought, "If they only knew me, they would not like me"? Therefore, you strive all the more to seem worthy while a battle rages deep in your heart because you never really measure up.

To put it simply, a shame-based emotional structure measures your worth based upon what you've worked to earn. It refuses God's grace and healing. But you will never be perfect. Fortunately, you can stop allowing shame to tear you down by making a choice to live under God's affection. In Scripture, this action is called grace. It's a gift to yield to God and remember that you are covered by Christ's righteousness. You are no longer a slave to feelings of inadequacy. When you see yourself as the Lord does, as a wonderfully created and dearly loved child of God, healing from a shame-based framework occurs.

WEEK 1........ WEEK 2........ WEEK 3........ WEEK 4........ WEEK 5........ WEEK 6........ WEEK 7........ **WEEK 8**.... WEEK 9........ WEEK 10........ WEEK 11........ WEEK 12

DAY 4

The transformation process begins by meditating on the truth of God's perfect nature and who you are in Him. As you begin to know and experience God as He is, rather than how you once incorrectly viewed Him, a shift in your thinking and internal framework begins. You finally see that God alone is good and perfect and that He has given the entirety of Himself to us. He is truly worthy of praise and worship. Your heart becomes refreshed, no longer needing to be perfect in the strength of your own hands. Instead, you begin by taking on Christ Himself, including His righteousness and power. You desire what He desires as you fall deeply in love with Him.

By no longer worrying about failing to measure up, you accept God's unconditional love. You become humble and dependent upon the Lord to lovingly guide you and meet your needs. Through faith, you rely upon God. Real and vulnerable relationships are forged. You're free to be open and to be real because His love is not dependent upon how good or in control you appear to be. Rather, it's based upon a real and intimate relationship with Jesus. You finally live in the freedom that there is no condemnation for those who live in and through Christ (Romans 8:1). Who you are in Christ supersedes what others think. God will never reject you.

Many who turn to fantasy have internalized this shame-based emotional framework. Shame leads to broken relationships and avoidance of intimacy. For instance, some people are afraid to accept love, and some fear telling others about themselves—about their dreams, emotions, fears, or longings—because they think that people won't like them if they really knew them. Perhaps you're horrified that someone someday might learn that you looked at pornography or masturbated. To compensate for a damaged self-image, some women strive to excel at other activities to try to win the approval of others. Although these outward or merit-based achievements may win compliments, they never truly satisfy or replace what is missing in one's life. Under the surface, deep feelings of unworthiness of love exist.

We don't have to live this way anymore! There is One who sees our absolute worst and has embraced us. That's what the cross is: Jesus embracing our worst. The resurrection is Jesus giving us His best.

HEARTWORK

God says that no one is holy or righteous (Romans 3:10; 3:23; 6:23; Ephesians 2:8–9). You cannot earn God's love. That's where mercy and grace fit in (Romans 5:8; 10:9–13). To

WEEK 1........ WEEK 2........ WEEK 3........ WEEK 4........ WEEK 5........ WEEK 6........ WEEK 7........ **WEEK 8** .... WEEK 9........ WEEK 10........ WEEK 11........ WEEK 12

DAY 4

reject grace requires perfection, which is beyond your reach. Surrender and accept God's unfathomable grace and pursuing love.

Pay close attention to the process of healing from a shame-based life. This begins with viewing God as perfect and accepting that you are not. Your identity in Christ—an adopted, deeply cherished, and unconditionally loved daughter—is what really matters. You do not need to be perfect. In fact, you cannot! That's why you always remain frustrated when you live a life based on performance. You're aiming at an unattainable target. Start correcting your backward thinking. What the Lord wants is a relationship with you. Healing occurs as you yield to Him and turn over all areas of your life, including the desire for control.

Your thought life must be brought before God; you must take every thought captive and redirect it to things pure and holy, not selfish in nature. Make time each day to spend in worship and praise. Embrace the truth that humility and dependence mark the road to real freedom.

Write out some of your performance and shame-based thinking.

_____

_____

_____

READ THE BIBLE

Keep reading to know and love God. Read Psalm 27 out loud.

PRAY

Be still. Spend five or ten minutes with the Lord.

- Meditate on how much God loves you.

- Meditate on how much Jesus gave up for you.

- Keep up the fasting and heartfelt prayers, asking earnestly for God to change your heart.

WEEK 1........ WEEK 2........ WEEK 3........ WEEK 4........ WEEK 5........ WEEK 6........ WEEK 7........ **WEEK 8**........ WEEK 9........ WEEK 10 .... WEEK 11........ WEEK 12

DAY 4

- Pray for Passion for God.

- Pray for Repentance. Ask for a teachable, non-judgmental heart.

- Pray for Open relationships and the ability to express feelings.

- Pray for Victory over pornography, lust, pride, and greed. Be willing to follow the promptings of the Spirit.

- Pray for an Eternal perspective. Stop trying to earn love and respect.

- Pray for Networking opportunities with godly women. (List other prayer requests.)

_____

_____

_____

_____

SPECIAL NOTE:

The cure to doubt and lack of faith is immersing yourself in the Word of God. Read it to impart life. Stop reading the Bible to solely learn about God, but accept that it is God's living Word, written to penetrate your very bones, refresh your mind, and nourish your soul (Hebrews 4:12). When you humbly seek the Lord, the Holy Spirit lights up Scripture and opens your eyes to eternal truths. God's truth and the working of the Holy Spirit will set you free. Test everything by God's Word and seek His wisdom and understanding.

MEMORY VERSE

Psalm 19:13–14 (ESV): "Keep back your servant also from presumptuous sins; let them not have dominion over me! Then I shall be blameless, and innocent of great transgression. Let the words of my mouth and the meditation of my heart be acceptable in your sight, O Lord, my rock and my redeemer."

WEEK 8 DAY 5 (FRIDAY)

KEY THOUGHT: Sin is not just wrong action, it is wrong relationship.

DAILY READING

We stated earlier that the biggest battle you will face in life is taking the focus off yourself and shifting it onto God. This is especially true for those who have turned to sexual behaviors as substitutes for other needs. Regardless of the precise reasons you have looked to fantasy, masturbation, pornography, or other self-focused sex-based activities, these practices all are fueled by selfishness and pride. Your priority is your need to control your circumstances and your entitlement to pleasure.

Even your relationship with God can be selfish. God points this out by saying that you don't receive what you ask for when you ask to spend it upon yourself (James 4:3). With respect to sexual healing, some think that it is noble to ask God to take away sexual temptations just so that they will not sin. In reality, this shallow prayer only reveals a hatred for the feelings of guilt, shame, or hopelessness, rather than a true desire to be a "living sacrifice" for God (Romans 12:1). At its core, sin is a lack of relationship with God. Taking the "ask and you shall receive" portions of Scripture out of context treats God as a vending machine and ignores the need to give of oneself in a mutual relationship with Him.

Even when a spouse is involved, so many times we can become focused on how we think he is meant to meet our needs. And sometimes, when he falls short, the woman feels justified in filling these emotional voids with sexual sin.

WEEK 1........ WEEK 2........ WEEK 3........ WEEK 4........ WEEK 5........ WEEK 6........ WEEK 7........ **WEEK 8**........ WEEK 9........ WEEK 10........ WEEK 11........ WEEK 12

DAY 5

Oh, how our thinking is so backwards and self-focused! We miss out on the real meaning in life and often fight against our purpose for living. It's time to surrender your heart to the Lord.

Record your reflections.

_____

_____

_____

_____

HEARTWORK

Spend a few moments asking God to show you any areas that are blocking repentance, such as:

What pleasure do I still gain from my sin?

_____

_____

Why don't I think that God's ways are better than my own?

_____

_____

Do I doubt that God can really change me?

_____

_____

DAY 5

Have you been fasting this week? Fasting develops a spiritual hunger for the Lord. Spiritual breakthroughs can really take place when we demonstrate our dependence on the Lord in this way. I want to encourage you to continue in this fast. Do not give up. If you haven't started, determine to begin the fast today.

Admit your utter powerlessness and inability to be renewed apart from God, and humbly ask the Lord of the universe for His undeserved mercy and grace. Then, act upon the power and strength God provides.

Set your heart toward repentance. Ask God to open your heart to the need to repent as you examine His definition of repentance:

1. Recognize all of your sins as sins against a loving God, which break you apart from Him;
2. Confess and turn away from each sin the moment it occurs; (If this is difficult, what holds you back from confessing right away? Is it a desire to continue in the sin? Feelings of shame and embarrassment? Forgetfulness?)
3. Answer God's call back to Himself, turn to God right away, and accept His forgiveness;
4. Allow and trust God to do the work to cleanse and heal you; and
5. Produce fruit by relying upon God's power and direction.

1) WILL YOU REPENT BY RECOGNIZING YOUR SINS AND NOT MAKING EXCUSES OR BLAMING OTHERS?

- "After I strayed, I repented; after I came to understand, I beat my breast. I was ashamed and humiliated because I bore the disgrace of my youth" (Jeremiah 31:19, NIV).

- "If we confess our sins, he is faithful and just to forgive us and cleanse us of all unrighteousness" (1 John 1:9, ESV).

2) WILL YOU REPENT BY TURNING AWAY FROM YOUR SINS?

- "Put on sackcloth, you priests, and mourn; wail, you who minister before the altar. Come, spend the night in sackcloth" (Joel 1:13, NIV).

3) WILL YOU REPENT BY TURNING TO GOD?

- "Repent, then, and turn to God, so that your sins may be wiped out, that times of refreshing may come from the Lord" (Acts 3:19, NIV).

WEEK 1...... WEEK 2...... WEEK 3...... WEEK 4...... WEEK 5...... WEEK 6...... WEEK 7...... WEEK 8 ...... WEEK 9...... WEEK 10...... WEEK 11...... WEEK 12

DAY 5

4) WILL YOU REPENT BY ALLOWING AND TRUSTING GOD TO DO THE WORK?

- "God's kindness is meant to lead you toward repentance" (Romans 2:4, ESV).

- "Godly sorrow brings repentance that leads to salvation and leaves no regret, but worldly sorrow brings death" (2 Corinthians 7:10, NIV).

READ THE BIBLE

Read Psalm 51 slowly. This is your daily Bible reading. Ask God to speak to you. Read it twice and meditate on it as you do.

The letter **R is for Repentant in Spirit.** Will you adopt the heart of Psalm 51? In the space below, write your own Psalm 51 to God.

_____

_____

_____

_____

PRAY

As part of your prayer today, you'll write out a prayer of repentance. Go to the Lord right now, asking Him to give you repentance.

- Confess how you have depersonalized people and lusted after them for selfish pleasure.

- Confess how you have objectified yourself and sought value from your body rather than your identity as a beloved daughter.

- Confess times you have committed adultery in your heart.

- Confess that you have not really wanted to be dependent upon God.

- Admit that you cannot overcome sin in your own strength.

- Turn away from your attempts to live apart from an intimate relationship with God.

WEEK 1 ...... WEEK 2 ...... WEEK 3 ...... WEEK 4 ...... WEEK 5 ...... WEEK 6 ...... WEEK 7 ...... **WEEK 8** ...... WEEK 9 ...... WEEK 10 ...... WEEK 11 ...... WEEK 12

DAY 5

- Cry out to God to restore you and give you a new and intimate relationship with Jesus.

_____

_____

_____

_____

_____

_____

_____

_____

_____

_____

_____

TESTIMONY

"One of the biggest lies' girls struggling with sexual impurities believe is that they are the only ones who have these desires. The devil continues to work in this isolation, to pull women deeper and deeper into their sin. Maybe this isn't the case for everyone, but it sure was for me before I began this study. Proven Women has not only shown me that I am not alone in this fight but has also voiced feelings that I never knew how to express. I've learned that my struggle with masturbation is not because I have more of a sex drive than the average girl, but rather it is a result of a much deeper heart issue of pride and selfishness. Now knowing the root of this issue, I can talk honestly about it with God and have seen him transform my heart through it all. The Proven Women bible study and group has helped me to be more outspoken and vulnerable with my struggle. Through this, God has taken the sin that used to hold me captive in shame and guilt and turned it into a story of redemption and grace."

Passionate for God,
Repentant in spirit,
Open and honest,
Victorious in living,
Eternal in perspective, and
Networking with other ***PROVEN Women.***

PW

WEEK NINE

TESTIMONY

"I had no clue how selfish and prideful I was in my life. This may be a 12-week study, but I'll be reviewing and praying with this material for a long time afterward."

Passionate for God,
Repentant in spirit,
Open and honest,
Victorious in living,
Eternal in perspective, and
Networking with other *PROVEN Women.*

MEMORY VERSE

2 Corinthians 10:5 (ESV): "We destroy arguments and every lofty opinion raised against the knowledge of God, and take every thought captive to obey Christ."

WEEK 9 **DAY 1 (MONDAY)**

KEY THOUGHT: What does it look like for you to remove temptation?

It's been eight weeks, which, when work is done every day, is about the time it takes to begin breaking old habits or establishing new ones. Have you been consistent in doing your daily *Heartwork?* If you've been devoting yourself to the Lord, then it may be getting a bit easier for you now. If not, begin again. God grants you a new "today" to set your sail toward Him. Describe how your heart is changing and softening toward God.

_____

_____

_____

_____

Earlier in this series you asked yourself:

- Do I believe that God is good?

- Do I trust God with total control over all areas of my life?

Believing God is good means to trust Him. It doesn't mean you act perfectly. So don't rob yourself of joy by holding back. Make a choice today that God is good and to trust Him. Keep being *open and honest* in your discussions with the Lord. It's time to give up all of your so-called rights and follow the Lord with passion.

WEEK 1 ...... WEEK 2 ...... WEEK 3 ...... WEEK 4 ...... WEEK 5 ...... WEEK 6 ...... WEEK 7 ...... WEEK 8 ..... WEEK 9 ..... WEEK 10 ...... WEEK 11 ...... WEEK 12

DAY 1

DAILY READING

One reason so many people remain in bondage to pornography is that they don't really see it as evil. As a result, it's difficult to hate or turn from it. A person doesn't truly repent of a behavior that he fails to consider wrong. How about you? Do you still refuse to see pornography as idolatry and wicked?

Sadly, our society actually condones and promotes subtle forms of pornography. Hardly any television shows or advertisements pass up the opportunity to use sex to entice. Most grocery stores have racks filled with magazines displaying scantily dressed women. In short, our entire society is given over to idolizing the human body and receiving instant gratification.

Even though you're tempted at every corner, you don't need to join the masses. The will of man doesn't prove itself right merely because others enroll. God is jealous for your love. He knows that when you lust after the ways of the world, you're left empty. Telling you to turn from the world is for your own good!

Who is the commander of your life, and which master do you want to serve? God instructs you to guard your eyes and heart and to go against the flow of the world. How about it? Are you careful about what you allow your eyes to see or your mind to dwell upon? Just as a good soldier doesn't involve himself in the affairs of the world, you must not play with sin (2 Timothy 2:4). The proof of your dedication and devotion to God is in your eyes. They are a doorway to your heart and soul. Do they scan the horizon for someone to lust after, or are they fixed upon God? Don't let your eyes master you, but be the master over them!

What will it take for you to turn from evil and cling to good? Ask God to reveal to you the evil of pornography and to cause you to hate it because it blocks you from enjoying the Lord. Hate it for the harm it causes others. Each time you use pornography, it leads someone else into sin. You're the market that lures others to exchange their self-respect for money or attention. You indirectly cause them to blind their eyes from seeing God as they uncover their bodies for the insatiable lust of others. Innocence is taken from those who want to be desired and loved when they trade it away for a lie. Even their so-called consent doesn't justify your participation in what kills their souls and leads them into an ever-degrading path of destruction.

WEEK 1........ WEEK 2........ WEEK 3........ WEEK 4........ WEEK 5........ WEEK 6........ WEEK 7........ WEEK 8........ **WEEK 9**........ WEEK 10 .... WEEK 11........ WEEK 12

DAY 1

Dear friend, repent, because God warns that it's better for a huge rock to be tied around your neck and thrown into the sea than for you to participate in another person's fall (Luke 17:1–2). Hating sexual sin is not easy. There is something very enticing about it. But you can hate how evil and destructive it is. You can hate that it is Satan's way of distorting a sacred, God honoring creation of intimacy.

Many don't like the shame and guilt afterwards, but have to admit that they secretly enjoy the moment of sin. If that is the case for you, you have to retrain your way of thinking and living. From now on, focus on how sin grieves God, and how you don't want to grieve Him any longer. Keep reminding yourself: "Pornography and masturbation are sins, and God hates sin; therefore, I hate pornography." Continually go to the Lord and place yourself in a position to receive true repentance in order to want to turn from pornography, masturbation, and any other things you place ahead of your relationships with the Lord. Until you see pornography, lust, and fantasy as wrong and damaging to relationships, you will only pretend to stop. Even if you must ask God every day for weeks, don't stop petitioning the Lord in earnest for a heart that hates chasing after pornography.

The healing path for addiction to pornography (or other forms of impurity) looks like this:

o   Admit that you have a problem.

o   Understand your root reasons for turning to pornography.

o   Recognize impurity as wrong, inhibiting your relationships with God and others.

o   Repent (grieve and turn from sin, and seek God's grace) the moment your mind lusts.

o   Accept God's forgiveness and unconditional love and return home to Him.

o   Stop self-efforts (no longer relying upon your own strength) and die to self-interests.

o   Ask and allow God to heal your wounds and fill your heart.

o   Live for a larger purpose and keep an eternal perspective.

o   Spend your time in praising and worshiping God.

o   Live victoriously in God's power every day.

o   Purposefully live out real love and real intimacy with openness, honesty, and vulnerability.

o   Stay connected with other Proven Women who are earnestly seeking the Lord.

WEEK 1........ WEEK 2........ WEEK 3........ WEEK 4........ WEEK 5........ WEEK 6........ WEEK 7........ WEEK 8........ **WEEK 9**........ WEEK 10........ WEEK 11........ WEEK 12

DAY 1

HEARTWORK

You can only serve one master. Tonight, destroy anything in your house that's remotely pornographic or tempting you toward sexual sin. Pray through the following list and ask God to convict you of any changes you need to make.

- Discard novels, magazines, DVDs.

- Clear out music that tempts or entices you.

- Remove phone apps and accounts that make you struggle.

- Throw away sexy underwear that tempts you toward men (if you are not married).

- Delete contacts from your phone that lure and entice you toward sexting, one-night stands, and hook-ups.

- Destroy anything else you've been holding on to or things that block real intimacy with God (or your husband, such as love notes from prior boyfriends and other memorabilia).

- Commit to placing a filter on your computer or cell phone, removing the internet function from your cell phone, cutting up credit cards that you have used to buy sinful items, or even changing jobs, friends, or activities that continue to lead you downward.

Are you still lusting after men in TV shows or commercials? Are you allowing shows that feed your fantasy sex life? If you still are, after eight weeks, you must now know that the TV has to go. Stop watching all TV for a season. At first, it will be hard to figure out what to do with the time. Choose to get out of the house and plan relational activities to take the place of TV. You'll get to know others better, which is a great by-product! The same goes for the internet. You don't need to be spending time on it. Don't deceive yourself: You can live without checking social media or bingeing on TV shows.

We need to always be on guard. Because of our past brokenness, we will always be vulnerable to attack.

PRAY

Spend time using the above-stated healing path statements as a tool for prayer.

- Ask God for His strength for replacing self-seeking with God-seeking.

- Participate with the Lord in choosing to hate evil and seeing pornography as evil.

WEEK 1........ WEEK 2........ WEEK 3........ WEEK 4........ WEEK 5........ WEEK 6........ WEEK 7........ WEEK 8........ **WEEK 9** .... WEEK 10 .... WEEK 11........ WEEK 12

DAY 1

- Stay focused in prayer; keep talking to God.

- Ask God to renew your mind, and to allow you to see things through His eyes.

- Pray for others, especially other Proven Women.

_____

_____

_____

_____

_____

_____

_____

_____

_____

_____

_____

_____

_____

_____

_____

_____

WEEK 1........ WEEK 2........ WEEK 3........ WEEK 4........ WEEK 5........ WEEK 6........ WEEK 7........ WEEK 8........ **WEEK 9** .... WEEK 10 .... WEEK 11........ WEEK 12

DAY 1

READ THE BIBLE

Are you reading the Bible daily? There's no substitute for hearing from God. Romans 6:21 says: "What benefit did you reap at that time from the things you are now ashamed of? Those things result in death!" Settle in your mind that any so-called benefits from pornography, masturbation, or fantasy are short-lived, unfulfilling, sinful, and lead to the death of relationships. Right now, read and meditate on 1 Peter 1.

SPECIAL NOTE:

When you're living by the Spirit of God, temptations take on a new meaning. In the past, your stomach may have churned, knowing that if you were not strong enough, you would end up giving in to lust. The times you fell were many. Now, however, temptations are an opportunity to grow and judge the level of your true commitment to the Lord. Armed with an eternal perspective and relying upon God's power, begin to view temptations as an invitation to turn to the Lord, giving Him control. Your role is to desire absolute purity and to earnestly seek God's face. *The Lord will turn your weakness into His victory!*

MEMORY VERSE

2 Corinthians 10:5 (ESV): "We destroy arguments and every lofty opinion raised against the knowledge of God, and take every thought captive to obey Christ."

WEEK 9 DAY 2 (TUESDAY)

KEY THOUGHT: Whatever we pursue is what we worship.

DAILY READING

The Lord grants victory to His children as they seek Him with all of their hearts and live according to the working of the Holy Spirit in their lives (Galatians 5:16). Which master will you serve? Will you see pornography for what it is: evil? Confess that you have turned from God, hunting after some pleasure you thought He was withholding. Acknowledge that your idolatry, self-centeredness, and pride have actually torn others down while you were pursuing pleasure. Your thoughts and actions were tarnishing the beauty of God's children. Now, as you receive a heart of repentance from God, accept His forgiveness. The Lord doesn't demand that you sit in isolation as payment for your sin. Instead, He immediately forgives and purifies you from the stain of sin (1 John 1:9). He wants you to enter His courts (Psalm 100:4).

The next time you're tempted, choose whom you'll serve and meditate upon who is Lord of your life.[13] As you make the decision to live under the power of Christ, accept all of Him. Stop pretending that He is Lord and actually make Him your Lord. Give up the reins of your life. He will supply the power to overcome sin. He wants you to succeed. In fact, each time you unite with someone sexually, whether in body or heart, you drag God with you since He permanently indwells all who believe (1 Corinthians 6:16–17, 2 Timothy 1:14). Know that He doesn't want you to sin. The Lord will be your help. Turn to Him at the moment of temptation. Don't allow thoughts to linger.

WEEK 1........ WEEK 2........ WEEK 3........ WEEK 4........ WEEK 5........ WEEK 6........ WEEK 7........ WEEK 8........ WEEK 9 ....10 ....11........12

DAY 2

Have you committed to set your heart against pornography? Have you made an irrevocable commitment to never turn to it again? Do so now. Consider this analogy. If you committed to stop eating chocolate, would you leave a candy bar easily accessible on the counter? Would you dwell upon the pleasure you could have from it? No. Well, it's time to stop thinking and dwelling upon pornography. Unlike the candy bar, pornography is a forbidden fruit that causes tremendous harm to all who eat of it, as well as their families. Don't torture yourself by constantly dwelling upon some temporary pleasure that might be found in pornography. Stop accepting the lie that no one gets harmed and giving in "just this one time." Instead, think about the love of God and consider how He alone can fill the real needs and voids in your life without your feeling empty or dirty afterward.

Constantly remind yourself of God's truths and promises. Regularly meditate upon and visualize the cross of Christ—the greatest proof of His unconditional love for you. Respond to the Lord with thanksgiving and appreciation. Married women, accept that the man you married is now God's chosen husband for you. Choose to value him above all others. Single women, wait upon the Lord. God has not forgotten about you. Each should be mindful not to scorn God's gifts by wanting something else or by lusting after other things. Purpose to have a grateful heart and a content spirit. Finally, do as God wants when He says, "Hate what is evil; cling to what is good" (Romans 12:9, NIV). God will empower you to fulfill your commitment to hate and to forever forsake pornography.

What's on your heart? Are you trusting that God is good today? Why or why not?

_____

_____

_____

_____

An idol is anything you greatly admire or pursue instead of the Lord. God tells us not to have idols—He is jealous for our attention and affection (Exodus 34:14).

WEEK 1 .... WEEK 2 .... WEEK 3 .... WEEK 4 .... WEEK 5 .... WEEK 6 .... WEEK 7 .... WEEK 8 ..... **WEEK 9** ..... WEEK 10 .... WEEK 11 .... WEEK 12

DAY 2

Consider these verses about idolatry, allowing God to speak to you:

- "For rebellion is like the sin of divination [witchcraft], and arrogance like the evil of idolatry" (1 Samuel 15:23, NIV).

- "Put to death, therefore, whatever belongs to your earthly nature: Sexual immorality, impurity, lust, evil desires and greed, which is idolatry. Because of these, the wrath of God is coming" (Colossians 3:5–6).

Describe how looking at pornography or looking at another person with lust in your heart is the same thing as making pornography or self-gratification an idol in your life. Put it into your own words.

_____

_____

_____

_____

Given what God says about idols, how do you expect that He will react to your having an idol (pornography, greed, pride, lust) in your life? Seeking after idols also interferes with your prayer life. You ask the Lord for gifts and blessings, but you worship false gods! Does this help you see why, with this double-minded lifestyle, you're still in bondage to sin? Repent and turn away from evil. You must join one team and not the other. Therefore, choose to hate sin and live by the Spirit.

Explain in your own words why spending more time with God and worshiping Him are the antidotes for lust and impurity.

_____

_____

_____

_____

WEEK 1........ WEEK 2........ WEEK 3........ WEEK 4........ WEEK 5........ WEEK 6........ WEEK 7........ WEEK 8........ **WEEK 9**........ WEEK 10........ WEEK 11........ WEEK 12

DAY 2

The next time you're tempted to lust after a person or an image of a person, turn away or close your eyes and ask God to bless that person. That's right, pray for them. Expect that you'll be tempted to focus on them in a sexual way while praying. Choose to engage in a spiritual battle. Pray for them as a person rather than longing for them to bring you some type of pleasure. This is putting their interests above your own. Pray that God will pursue them and guide them. Pray for God to transform them the way God is transforming you. Ask God to help you see them as an image bearer of God. If the person is a woman and you are longing to look like her, pray that God will help her not find worth in her image. Then thank God for the way He designed you. Gratitude is a great antidote for covetousness. If it is a man, pray for his wife (current or future), then pray for your current or future husband.

With practice and reliance upon the Lord, you'll be able to take every lustful thought captive and even view women as sisters and men as brothers. What victory you'll experience as God entrusts you to protect and bless others instead of taking from them!

HEARTWORK

Have you made an irrevocable decision that you will never watch pornography again? It's not enough to say "I will try" or "I will do my best." That leaves the door open for failure. Make that decision right now. This is not an option. Then ask God to give you His power to carry out your commitment. Trust that He will. Now, be willing to do whatever it takes. Write out your commitment to receive Jesus' grace and gentleness along with any other commitments you're making.

_____

_____

_____

_____

_____

WEEK 1........ WEEK 2........ WEEK 3........ WEEK 4........ WEEK 5........ WEEK 6........ WEEK 7........ WEEK 8........ **WEEK 9**........ WEEK 10 .... WEEK 11........ WEEK 12

DAY 2

READ THE BIBLE

Read and meditate upon 1 Peter 2:11–12. Ask God to speak to you. If you have time, read Matthew 5:27–28 and James 1:13–15.

PRAY

Seek God first. Healing will follow.

- Ask the Lord to draw near to you as you draw near to Him (James 4:8).

- Tell God about your commitment to pursuing Christ and seeking Him with all your heart.

- Pray for others (your family, other Proven Women, co-workers, and other people in your life).

_____

_____

_____

_____

_____

_____

_____

WEEK 1 .... WEEK 2 .... WEEK 3 .... WEEK 4 .... WEEK 5 .... WEEK 6 .... WEEK 7 .... WEEK 8 .... **WEEK 9** .... WEEK 10 .... WEEK 11 .... WEEK 12

DAY 2

SPECIAL NOTE:

No matter how often temptations tug at you, immediately turn each and every time to God. As you faithfully tighten your grip on God, instead of seeking to control the temptation yourself, Satan will tire of battling God. Don't misunderstand, Satan doesn't want to leave you alone. However, if the more he tempts you, the more you cherish and rely upon Christ, he will see his plan backfire. He will visit you another time, hoping to find you acting in your own strength.

P *is for Passionate for God.* The spirit and flesh wage war against each other. Sinful desires seek to capture your soul (1 Peter 2:11). God says that if you live by His Spirit, you won't gratify sinful desires (Galatians 5:16–26). Therefore, turn your passion toward God.

MEMORY VERSE

2 Corinthians 10:5 (ESV): "We destroy arguments and every lofty opinion raised against the knowledge of God, and take every thought captive to obey Christ."

WEEK 9 DAY 3 (WEDNESDAY)

KEY THOUGHT: Lust robs intimacy.

Have you set a bouncer at the door of your mind? Do you take every thought captive?[14] Throughout the day, practice rejecting all sexual thoughts immediately. Refuse to take any bit of pleasure from them. Some people follow a three-second rule to determine if they sin when looking at a someone. That's ridiculous! Don't look for three seconds and then turn away. Turn away immediately. Be aggressive in attacking such thoughts. You'll begin to experience victory when you mean business (God's business) and continue to go to the Lord for His strength.

Look at this week's memory verse, 2 Corinthians 10:5. Write out in your own words what it means to:

"take captive every thought"

_____

_____

"make it obedient to Christ"

_____

_____

Describe what thoughts you struggle with and need to take captive (sexual and other) and think through how to take them captive. Not all of these thoughts will be sexual. Some of the thoughts are "woe is me." When we get into a funk thinking that our life is missing things and that God is holding out on us, we

WEEK 1........ WEEK 2........ WEEK 3........ WEEK 4........ WEEK 5........ WEEK 6........ WEEK 7........ WEEK 8........ WEEK 9........ WEEK 10 .... WEEK 11........ WEEK 12

DAY 3

become easy prey for Satan to attack. Your thoughts may be stirring on complaints about your husband and kids. Or stirring about the fact that you are single and once again didn't have plans this past Friday night. Perhaps you feel like people are not appreciative enough of you and everything you are doing. Even these non-sexual thoughts can become a breeding ground for evil which will eventually turn toward pornography, masturbation, or fantasy as a quick fix. Do you see why it is so important to take these negative thoughts captive as well?

When prior sexual images or unclean thoughts enter your mind, make it a practice to actually think or say out loud, "I take no pleasure from you." Cut off the thought mid-stream. Don't let it finish. Then confess the thought as sinful and ask for forgiveness. Keep asking God for His power, and rely on it. Repeat this same process every single time, even if it's every minute as you first get started.

We are each being challenged to change the way we see people. For instance, a proud person may think that God loves her more than others. She somehow deceives herself into thinking that she's better than others and that she deserves God's love and blessings. At the same time, however, she may treat herself and other women as objects, trying to outshine them to receive the attention of other men. Perhaps she sees the men around her as a means to pleasure rather than as a brother in Christ. How about you? Do you often compare yourself to others? Are you quick to see faults in others? Do you complain when others disagree or don't go along with your ideas or desires? Take a moment to think through how you view others.

 ## DAILY READING

Although there's not a program to purity, there is a Proven path or outline for growing with Christ, which leads to freedom from pornography and other compulsive activities. The following six principles should help clarify your new direction in life and dependency upon the Lord:

Passionately seek God. Take the focus off yourself and put it onto God. Turn your desire toward the Lord. Stop concentrating on your circumstances or your cravings for selfish pleasures. There is only One true, perfect, and holy God. He alone deserves worship and praise. Your refusal to release your passion for God robs you of the riches He intends for you. Run to the Lord, who loves you unconditionally and is the only Source of true life and healing. During times of worship, the Lord imparts Himself to you, which burns away apathy, anger, self-pity, self-condemnation, and pride. Ask for and receive God's forgiveness and enter into a passionate and restored relationship with Him. Make time to simply praise the Lord.

WEEK 1........ WEEK 2........ WEEK 3........ WEEK 4........ WEEK 5........ WEEK 6........ WEEK 7........ WEEK 8........ **WEEK 9**........ WEEK 10........ WEEK 11........ WEEK 12

DAY 3

Repent from your sin of turning from God. You must see pornography as evil, a sin that grieves God because it: (1) treats others as objects for degradation; (2) makes you discontent with what God provides; and (3) keeps you from seeking intimacy with the Lord. Confess your idolatry, which is acted out through pornography, lust, and fantasy. Your selfishness and pride attempt to place you on a throne above God. Without truly repenting, you'll remain at a distance from God, and all of your relationships will be shallow and unfulfilling. Nothing will satisfy an appetite for self-pleasure. Therefore, weep and mourn. Cry out to God to break your stubborn, hard heart. Practice repenting after each impure thought.

Openly communicate with God and others. End the pretense. No longer say that you hate sin while secretly enjoying it. Turn away from false intimacy and be willing to accept the pain that goes along with deep relationships. Begin with the single greatest relationship you can and must have, unity with God. Will you openly talk with the Lord? In fact, what kind of a relationship exists if you don't communicate? Stop praying *at* God, instead of praying *to* Him relationally. Tell the Lord of your hurts and what troubles you. Ask questions and listen for answers. Be real. Be vulnerable. Purpose to get to know God on a personal level. Spend time on your knees in respectful but open conversations. Ask God to expose any underlying issues in your life or sources of pain that keep you from turning to Him and fleeing from intimacy. Talk about your desire for absolute purity and your need for the Lord to carry out your commitments. Allow yourself to have and experience feelings, rather than stuffing them away. However, don't let your feelings become your master. You need not give into anger or lust.

Victoriously live the life God has given you. God grants you a way of escape. Rely on it. As you live by His Spirit, which prompts you, you will live in victory (Galatians 5:16). It's only when you take back control that you sin. When tempted, take captive the thought and cut it to shreds. Don't take pleasure in any lustful thoughts. Each and every time you stumble, return to God immediately in confession and seek His forgiveness. You'll be restored. Reject performance-based thinking and self-condemnation. As you accept the Lord's mercy and unconditional love, you'll remain in His camp and under His wing, wearing the name of God on your sleeve. Put away self-effort and become dependent upon Christ.

Keep an Eternal perspective. Human thinking is futile and leads to sin. As you focus upon your circumstances, you become consumed with yourself. What rights do you protect so desperately that you would rather live apart from God than be His dependent servant? Fifty years from now, what will matter? Read and dwell on God's promises in Scripture. Ask God to give you His perspective. Begin seeing trials as opportunities to grow. Accept that God

WEEK 1........ WEEK 2........ WEEK 3........ WEEK 4........ WEEK 5........ WEEK 6........ WEEK 7........ WEEK 8........ WEEK 9 .... WEEK 10 .... WEEK 11........ WEEK 12

DAY 3

won't give you a temptation greater than you can bear and that He provides a way of escape, then look for and rely upon it (1 Corinthians 10:13). Keep your center based upon your home and citizenship in heaven. Set out to be grateful and content in all circumstances.

Network with other Proven Women. The Lord sent out His disciples two by two (Luke 10:1). Don't go it alone. Because you were created for relationships, you won't have rest in your soul by holing yourself up in a room and reading a self-help book or by allowing others to only see the exterior of your life. As iron sharpens iron, so do two godly women sharpen each other (Proverbs 27:17). Engage with other women in open and vulnerable relationships (see Appendix H). Attend church because you want to obey the Lord and fill your innate need to engage in corporate worship. Join a women's Bible study or group in order to encourage and be encouraged in living a Christian life. Purpose to connect with Network Partners for the rest of your life.

Memorize the PROVEN acronym, testing your life daily by each letter.

HEARTWORK

Today, settle in your heart that pornography and unbridled lust are evil. Recognize that they will destroy your relationships or any hope of real intimacy and that they will keep you distanced from God. Ask the Lord to reveal the truth about pornography and fantasy to you. Did you irrevocably commit that pornography and sexual immorality are no longer options in your life? Restate your promises here. Ask God to honor your commitments, and then rely upon His strength to carry them out.

READ THE BIBLE

Be sure to fill your mind daily with God's Word. You have a lot of backward thinking to undo. Read and meditate on 1 Peter 3. Write down a few thoughts.

_____

_____

WEEK 1 ...... WEEK 2 ...... WEEK 3 ...... WEEK 4 ...... WEEK 5 ...... WEEK 6 ...... WEEK 7 ...... WEEK 8 ...... WEEK 9 ...... WEEK 10 ...... WEEK 11 ...... WEEK 12

DAY 3

_____

_____

_____

PRAY

Take time to hurt and be honest with Him. Share yourself with Him as you would to a best friend. Spend a few minutes praying for others. Be earnest in asking God to bless them. Some suggestions include praying for your family, missionaries, other women in your church, co-workers, and neighbors.

_____

_____

_____

_____

_____

_____

_____

_____

MEMORY VERSE

2 Corinthians 10:5 (ESV): "We destroy arguments and every lofty opinion raised against the knowledge of God, and take every thought captive to obey Christ."

WEEK 9 DAY 4 (THURSDAY)

KEY THOUGHT: God makes it possible to be free and feel free.

Masturbation (and a fantasy life) is something you try to keep a secret and private thing, and it's something you do by yourself for yourself. Many women make vows to go to the grave never admitting to someone that they masturbated. This sexual sin is like a noose around their necks, and Satan wants them to try to keep it a hidden sin so that they feel alone. *The letter O in PROVEN is for Open and Honest.* God wants you to walk in the light and not to keep things hidden in darkness.

Describe how you feel after you masturbate.

God wants to free you from guilt, shame, and self-condemnation (Romans 4:7–8). Decide now to accept His love and forgiveness and to rely on His power to stop the downward cycle.

DAILY READING

Even in a world where self-indulgence is flaunted, there remains one thing that is secret and shameful: Masturbation. For many, it's the single greatest source of self-condemnation. Although some advocate that it's always a harmless activity, inside we know otherwise.

Those gripped in the bondage of this sin feel the pain and aren't easily consoled when others claim that it's not harmful. For most of us, the only way to continue masturbating is to shut off our conscience and lock out God, both of which are destructive.

Despite the fact that this word doesn't appear in the Bible, we know that masturbation is almost always sinful. Jesus told us that to even look at someone with sexual lust is the same

WEEK 1........ WEEK 2........ WEEK 3........ WEEK 4........ WEEK 5........ WEEK 6........ WEEK 7........ WEEK 8........ WEEK 9 .... WEEK 10 .... WEEK 11........ WEEK 12

DAY 4

as adultery (Matthew 5:28). It's hard to imagine not having lustful thoughts as a prelude to or an instrument of masturbation. In any event, anything that turns you inward and selfish in focus opposes God. Masturbation is an inward activity which blocks out real intimacy with God and others.

Why does God want to keep you from lusting or turning to masturbation? As an initial matter, it feeds a self-centered lifestyle. It also confirms the mind-set that sex is about personal pleasure more so than it is about intimacy with a spouse. Praise God that He created sex as such a pleasurable thing. God is so good: He designed sex in such a way that such delight occurs when husband and wife are intimately giving of themselves to each other. That connection is so good, and it is both enjoyable and holy. Masturbation moves completely away from the purpose of intimacy and makes sexual activity only about a self-centered desire, pleasure, or need. When masturbation becomes a common practice, with the expectation that someday sex within marriage will be its replacement, then sex with your husband will have that same purpose—fixing your selfish desire, pleasure, or need. I have heard many say they have a hard time viewing sex within marriage as good because they felt so dirty doing other sexual things outside of marriage.

Realize that sex within marriage has a different purpose than selfish gain and making sure our own needs are met. We need to evaluate our heart toward our husband throughout our marriage. Are you being intimate with your husband in other ways? Are you opening up to him and being vulnerable? Are you sharing your fears, or struggles, or even your dreams and hopes with your husband? Are you allowing him into your life? Building intimacy with your husband emotionally and spiritually will bring intimacy to your sexual life as well. Also asking about his hopes and dreams will affirm him to create emotional intimacy.

Masturbation does not help at all with intimacy. In fact, it does the opposite. Intimacy with God is about the furthest thing from your mind when you are hunting for sex or escaping into a fantasy world culminating in masturbation. Please note, the Lord wants you to be fulfilled, not left empty. He knows how lonely masturbation is and how it cannot bring peace or lasting joy. Only true intimacy with God feeds and frees your soul. In addition, masturbation ushers in many other problems beyond guilt and shame. It fosters treating others as objects and idolizes sex over intimacy.

Years of masturbating can actually so fine-tune your response to sexual stimulus that you may experience difficulties in permissive sexual relations with a spouse. For example, a spouse cannot measure up to a fantasy, which causes frustration and discontentment.

WEEK WEEK WEEK WEEK WEEK WEEK WEEK WEEK **WEEK** WEEK WEEK WEEK
1........2........3........4........5........6........7........8........**9**........10........11........12

DAY 4

Masturbation can feed a lustful fire that cannot be extinguished. You'll end up charting a course of seeking new and increased thrills to make up for the fulfillment lacking in masturbation. Eventually, you may add pornography to your rituals. The door often opens to practices that you could never imagine, such as affairs, one-night stands, and unhealthy relationships.

What's the solution? It isn't getting married. A wedding ring doesn't quench the fire you stoke. You'll carry over rituals and selfish practices into your marriage. Although you might seek alternative solutions, such as expecting your husband to live up to the fantasies you had created, the root problems and dysfunctions don't just disappear.

You won't find lasting healing through self-help because human efforts always fail. The good news is that the Lord can and will heal you and change your improper desires. The letter **V in PROVEN** stands for *Victorious in Living.* God wants you to live a holy and pure life, but it's so much more than just living a good life free from masturbation or another sin. It revolves around living out a relationship in holiness because our God is holy. The Lord has the power to change you into His likeness to foster that relationship in order to stamp you Proven. Each moment you allow the Holy Spirit to be your guide, you'll live in victory (Galatians 5:16).

What keeps a person locked into rituals of sexual selfishness? The root that feeds such a desire is pride and the accompanying sin of selfishness. Self-focus naturally turns to self-pleasure. Ask the Lord to reveal your pride. It exists no matter how much you have condemned or belittled yourself. Your pride either minimizes the problem or wants you to rely upon self-effort to overcome it. Pride also keeps you from talking about secret sins because you're worried about what others may think of you.

A good question to ask yourself is whether the main reason you want to stop masturbating is because you hate the consequences. That reason never produces lasting change. A proud heart pays less attention to the fact that you made masturbation an idol in place of intimacy with God. Pride also blocks you from deeply worshiping and praising the Lord or humbly considering others to be more important than yourself (Philippians 2:3). Pride acts to stop you from freely giving of yourself to others. It also prevents you from yielding control to God and becoming dependent upon Him.

Although the reasons people turn to masturbation are many, the cure is the same: a deep abiding relationship with the Lord. The bondage of masturbation can be broken only

WEEK 1 ...... WEEK 2 ...... WEEK 3 ...... WEEK 4 ...... WEEK 5 ...... WEEK 6 ...... WEEK 7 ...... WEEK 8 ...... **WEEK 9** ...... WEEK 10 ...... WEEK 11 ...... WEEK 12

DAY 4

when you are broken over your flight from intimacy with God. You must develop a daily, dependent relationship with the Lord. As you earnestly seek Him, the Lord opens your eyes to the pain in your life that causes you to keep going back to destructive practices. God will provide healing and give you an appetite for things holy and pure. No longer will you unwisely repeat your folly like a dog that returns to its vomit (Proverbs 26:11).

Write down your insights.

_____

_____

_____

_____

HEARTWORK

Are you ready to receive God's healing? Do you want purity more than instant pleasure? Will you love the Lord more than you love your own life? As long as you keep the focus upon yourself or your circumstances and rights, you'll never fully yield your life to God. You'll remain a fringe Christian or perhaps a "polished cup" on the outside (Matthew 23:27–28), but you will still be filled with greed and lust on the inside.

The way out of hidden sexual sin is to pursue that which:

- Nourishes your soul instead of staining it.

- Fosters relationships instead of weakening them.

- Encourages you to give of yourself to others instead of taking for yourself.

Meditate for a moment upon James 1:13–15 (ESV): "When tempted, no one should say, 'God is tempting me.' For God cannot be tempted by evil, nor does he tempt anyone; but each one is tempted when, by his own evil desire, he is dragged away and enticed. Then, after desire has conceived, it gives birth to sin; and sin, when it is full-grown, gives birth to death."

WEEK 1........ WEEK 2........ WEEK 3........ WEEK 4........ WEEK 5........ WEEK 6........ WEEK 7........ WEEK 8........ **WEEK 9**........ WEEK 10........ WEEK 11........ WEEK 12

DAY 4

Do you see that temptations arise out of your own selfish desires, and that when you are enticed by the world, you literally have to drag yourself away from God? Once you're away from God, your own desires grow until you can stand it no more and give in to sin. Because sin never satisfies, you seek even more self-love, allowing masturbation to be your idol. In the end, you squeeze God out. That's why you must always wear the armor of God (Ephesians 6) and take captive every thought before being enticed to sneak out of God's camp. Adultery and other sexual sins don't just happen. You are first enticed by your selfish desires, and over time, you put God aside.

READ THE BIBLE

Keep reading the living and active Word of God (Hebrews 4:12). If you read it to get to know God, it will change you. However, if you read the Bible just to acquire knowledge about God or to check off homework, you'll be a legalistic Pharisee, and you won't experience the divine power needed to overcome. Right now, read 1 Peter 4.

PRAY

Spend five or ten minutes with the Lord in prayer.

- Tell God you really want to be free from self-obsession, lust, and masturbation and to be dependent on Him.

- Tell God that you will not secretly enjoy fantasies or sexual sins anymore.

- Tell God that you now believe and trust that He is good and able and willing to set you free as you yield to Him.

- Commit to getting to know and love God as the top priority in your life.

- Be real and open and honest with God. If you are hurting, cry in prayer as you talk to Him; if you are filled with joy, sing Him a song; if you have sinned, repent and accept His forgiveness.

WEEK 1 ...... WEEK 2 ...... WEEK 3 ...... WEEK 4 ...... WEEK 5 ...... WEEK 6 ...... WEEK 7 ...... WEEK 8 ...... **WEEK 9** .... WEEK 10 ...... WEEK 11 ...... WEEK 12

DAY 4

- Pray for others. (List them as you do.)

_____

_____

_____

_____

SPECIAL NOTE:

Often, self-pity or self-condemnation keep you in bondage. Maybe you think you need an escape from pain or drudgery in life. Some have a deathly fear of closeness to others. Whatever the lure, masturbation can be as addictive as drugs. In fact, just like a runner's high, the body produces certain chemicals in the brain during an orgasm. This feeling psychologically deadens pain for a moment. Also, rituals have an addictive, habit-forming quality. In short, you can become chemically and psychologically programmed to "need" the relief of masturbation. However, the relief is temporary and unfulfilling. Masturbation can never meet the actual needs you have for real relationships with God and others.

MEMORY VERSE

2 Corinthians 10:5 (ESV): "We destroy arguments and every lofty opinion raised against the knowledge of God, and take every thought captive to obey Christ."

WEEK 9 DAY 5 (FRIDAY)

KEY THOUGHT: Healing comes from rest.

What are your plans for Friday night? Keep it a holy night dedicated to resting and being with God.

_____

_____

DAILY READING

Do you want victory over masturbation or other sexual sins? Begin disciplining your mind and body as instruments of holiness. This includes fiercely attacking every evil or impure thought. It also means putting an end to the rituals you once followed as a prelude to masturbation or other sexual sin. Next, solidify your decision that masturbation is not an option in your life. Make that decision now. In addition, make a covenant not to look at others with lust (Job 31:1) or view people as sexual objects.

Don't rush—it is your pride and selfishness that make demands for a quick fix. The Lord isn't in a hurry, and He speaks in a gentle, soft voice. To hear Him, you must slow down and wait upon Him. You won't find God by racing through portions of Scripture or rushing through your daily Heartwork study. In all things, purpose to meet with the Lord and hear from Him.

WEEK 1........ WEEK 2........ WEEK 3........ WEEK 4........ WEEK 5........ WEEK 6........ WEEK 7........ WEEK 8........ **WEEK 9** ....WEEK 10 ....WEEK 11........WEEK 12

DAY 5

At times, sit still in a room, quietly asking God to open your heart. Don't present a list of requests but ask Him what He wants you to know. As the Holy Spirit speaks to you, carefully weigh His words. When He moves you to act, immediately obey. If God reveals sin, admit it without excuse and repent. If you don't understand something, tell Him. The Lord permits open and honest communication—even to ask Him why. For instance, if the Holy Spirit prompts you to forgive an abuser, you might be angry because you don't want to release this person. Tell God of your hurts, but do so respectfully. In time, your heart will open and change as you want to experience the fullness of God instead of retreating into your self-protected world where sin abounds and you harbor hatred.

Keep passionately turning to the Lord and obeying His commands. It is during times of worship and praise that God heals and renews your heart. Have you truly repented over masturbation and other selfish sexual acts? Guard against confusing self-pity or self-condemnation with repentance. Even tears are not proof of repentance (Matthew 27:3–5). True repentance requires humility. Godly sorrow is a recognition that you have grieved God by turning away from Him and attempting to live without Him. Beating yourself up because you disappointed God is nothing more than pride-driven self-scolding because you failed to measure up. Real repentance, on the other hand, involves desiring intimacy with God more than self-efforts to fix what's broken in your life. Learn to recognize when you engage in the false humility of shame-based self-condemnation or self-efforts. Admit that your pride fuels selfish thoughts which block out the Lord and thwart real repentance. In fact, without genuine repentance over sin, you won't experience complete reconciliation and restoration. True humility is the doorway to divine intimacy and the healing of wounds. The humble won't fall because they're carried by the Lord.

In addition, your prayers and communication with the Lord must be open and honest. Allow the Lord to reveal and then heal the deep roots of your emotional pain. Reject the sinful response of simply blocking out relationships and intimacy. Trust that God is good and that He can and will heal you as you turn to Him. Then act upon God's strength and promises.

What struck you from this reading?

_____

_____

WEEK 1........ WEEK 2........ WEEK 3........ WEEK 4........ WEEK 5........ WEEK 6........ WEEK 7........ WEEK 8........ **WEEK 9**........ WEEK 10........ WEEK 11........ WEEK 12

DAY 5

Write out a brief prayer thanking God for His gentleness.

_____

_____

_____

_____

❤ HEARTWORK

To have victory, you need to invite God into your weakness and failures, not just when you feel good and happy. Write out a prayer inviting God to know all of you.

_____

_____

_____

_____

Expect a battle. There is a line drawn in the sand. On one side is Satan with his deception and false intimacy. Here, pornography, masturbation, degradation, destruction, and sexual addiction exist. On the other side stands God with His unconditional love and unlimited grace. Here await the gifts of peace, joy, love, and true intimacy. Here is the privilege to stand in worshipful awe of your Creator while joyfully experiencing the life He has for you.

O is for Open and Honest. Give up secret sins (pornography, masturbation, and all fantasies) and turn to God. He will never leave you or forsake you (Hebrews 13:5). Because God already knows what sins you commit, there's no need to pretend. God forgives you for imperfection, but you have to draw near to Him in your imperfection. Be open and honest with Him and yourself. The Lord is pleased by a heart that seeks after Him with passion. He will reward you with His righteousness.

WEEK 1........ WEEK 2........ WEEK 3........ WEEK 4........ WEEK 5........ WEEK 6........ WEEK 7........ WEEK 8........ WEEK 9........ WEEK 10........ WEEK 11........ WEEK 12

DAY 5

ADDRESSING LUSTFUL DREAMS:

What about sexual dreams? Are they sinful or beyond your control? When you make a decision for purity, you can expect increased temptations and even lustful dreams. What can you do about them? No part of your life should be off-limits to God. Continue to invite Him to be Lord of your dreams. During the midst of healing from masturbation or pornography, you may find that sexual dreams pop up on occasion. This is not an area that you should ignore or brush off as something that just happens.

If you have a sexual dream, as soon as you wake up confess it to the Lord. Don't let shame beat you up. Many people feel like a dream is a setback and think this means they have backslidden. But that is your pride saying this, not God. But don't go to the other extreme and see dreams as an excuse to enjoy the moment. Confess immediately and accept that God cleanses us from all unrighteousness. After confessing, move forward and don't give it another thoughts. If the content keeps popping into your mind, intentionally turn your mind to Scripture you are memorizing. Replace the thought with something good. Or simply slow down, sit on the floor, and talk to Jesus about how you feel.

Consider Galatians 2:20 (NIV): "I have been crucified with Christ and I no longer live, but Christ lives in me. The life I live in the body, I live by faith in the Son of God, who loved me and gave himself for me." Give Christ the total control and authority over your life that He desires. He will guide you to a victorious life. When you wake up and realize that you had a sexual dream, immediately confess it as sinful. Even if you had no control over the dream, recognize that the content was evil and ask God to cleanse it from your mind. Forcefully remove all evil and impurity from every part of your mind. The key is not to accept even a moment of pleasure from a sexual dream. In other words, don't keep replaying it in your mind. Rather, take it captive, rejecting any pleasure from it. The same is true for any sexual thought during the day. Destroy and ruin the moment. Condition your dream life, as you do your daily thought life, to consider all impure thoughts as something to ruthlessly exterminate. Keep turning your entire life over to Christ and give Him authority to evict the intruder. Bend your will more completely to die to self. Reject fantasy and all impure thoughts so that you may live through Christ. Cling even harder to God in living out a Proven life.

WEEK 1........ WEEK 2........ WEEK 3........ WEEK 4........ WEEK 5........ WEEK 6........ WEEK 7........ WEEK 8........ **WEEK 9** .... WEEK 10 .... WEEK 11 .... WEEK 12

DAY 5

READ THE BIBLE

Read 1 Peter 5. If you have done all of the daily reading this week, then you have read all of 1 Peter. Write out something that stands out to you from the reading.

_____

_____

_____

_____

PRAY

Ask God to reveal to you and cause you to accept that lust, pornography, and other sexual sins are evil and ugly. Talk with God about your weaknesses. It cannot be overemphasized that change comes from God and that God answers prayer. So pray.

- Ask God for the things that He delights in giving.

- Spend time meeting with God in heartfelt prayer for others.

- Pray for other women striving for purity.

- Pray for your family.

SPECIAL NOTE:

Do you truly want to end the charade and pretense? Are you willing to do whatever it takes to stop seeking selfish sex and other sins that flow from pride? What blocks you from experiencing complete freedom from masturbation, pornography, or lustful fantasies? It may be that your pride is so deep that if you were healed, you would take all the credit for overcoming it. God knows that such pride will only lead you on to another selfish activity. Perhaps you don't really want to stop. Maybe you doubt that God can give you real strength to overcome pride and certain sexually addictive behaviors. You cannot yet see God-sized power because you still see yourself as the source of life or strength. It's time to yield your entire life to the Lord and allow Him to renew you.

PW

WEEK TEN

TESTIMONY

We are always looking for testimonies of life change. If you would like to share your story and testimony with us please email us at info@provenwomen.org.

Passionate for God,
Repentant in spirit,
Open and honest,
Victorious in living,
Eternal in perspective, and
Networking with other ***PROVEN Women.***

MEMORY VERSE

Ephesians 6:12 (ESV): "For we do not wrestle against flesh and blood, but against the rulers, against the authorities, against the cosmic powers over this present darkness, against the spiritual forces of evil in the heavenly places."

WEEK 10 DAY 1 (MONDAY)

KEY THOUGHT: Knowing God is the most liberating pursuit that there is.

DAILY READING

One reason people remain trapped in bondage to sexual sin is that they have never truly made a decision to strive for absolute purity or holiness. Obviously, none of us will reach perfection; but when we make **holiness** our goal, we are willing to partner with God to see His victory in our life. We will quickly turn to Christ for forgiveness and strength in the moments we fall. We will run to God for strength in our weak moments when we are tempted. However, when we do not make holiness our goal, we are quick to cave. We often give in and opt that we will try harder tomorrow, but tomorrow never comes. We keep caving in "this one time," but that one time takes place over and over and over again.

God always stands with us ready to help, but He isn't just going to snap His fingers and remove temptation when we ask out of selfishness. The Lord wants a personal and complete relationship with you, His adopted daughter. In fact, God already fused Himself to you. The moment you trusted Jesus as Lord of your life and asked Him into your heart, He entered; the Holy Spirit permanently indwells your soul. It's time to give God total control.

Arrogance and double-mindedness also rear their ugly head when we claim we don't want to look at pornography, yet we hold onto other sins such as bitterness, greed, jealousy, and self-indulgence. Understand this: The Lord wants you to live in intimacy with Him and experience holiness across the board. Every sin you harbor grieves the Lord and signifies your self-reliant and prideful spirit. A real relationship with God is 24/7. It's an all-out unity of two becoming one.

WEEK 1........ WEEK 2........ WEEK 3........ WEEK 4........ WEEK 5........ WEEK 6........ WEEK 7........ WEEK 8........ WEEK 9..... **WEEK 10** .....11........12

DAY 1

Once again, we are not asking anyone to attempt to perform for God or carry the weight of trying to be perfect for God. The important part is to be willing to call anything that God calls "sin," sin, and to allow Him into all areas of our heart and life. Let Him convict you of lust, jealousy, bitterness, selfishness, and pride. If we excuse certain sins in our life, they become strongholds that Satan can use to keep us down.

Recall once again this familiar verse: "I have been crucified with Christ and I no longer live, but Christ lives in me. The life I live in the body, I live by faith in the Son of God, who loved me and gave himself for me" (Galatians 2:20, NIV).

Don't gloss over this passage. Each time you read this verse ask God to melt your heart. Learn to delight in His love for you, knowing you pursue a God who gladly laid down His life for you.

Right now, tell the Lord that starting today you want to know Him for who He is, not how you've wanted Him to be. Search for Him like you would search for a hidden treasure so that you'll see His beautiful, wonderful, and perfect nature more clearly. Ask God to give you passion to live for and through Him. Ask Him for a soft and repentant heart that openly communicates with the Lord as a true and loyal friend. Commit to becoming a needy and dependent servant of the only true and worthy God. Desire to seek sexual integrity as a way of giving glory to the Lord in real worship and to be holy in all areas of your life, because He is holy and because you never want to leave His side again.

 ## HEARTWORK

Here's a helpful question to determine whether and why a person is still in bondage to sexual sins: "Am I willing to do whatever it takes to receive God's healing?" Can you honestly say, "No matter what the cost, Lord, I am willing"? Notice that you're asking to receive God's healing rather than to stop lusting. Do you understand the difference? Until you do, real freedom may escape you. Are you pursing God because He is your Father who delights in you, or for what you can get from Him?

Have you allowed non-sexual sins to stay in your life because they were just not important enough to address (selective living), or did you think you could handle these little sins on

WEEK 1........ WEEK 2........ WEEK 3........ WEEK 4........ WEEK 5........ WEEK 6........ WEEK 7........ WEEK 8........ WEEK 9..... WEEK 10 ....WEEK 11........ WEEK 12

DAY 1

your own (self-reliant living)? God wants you to be holy in all things, which comes only from depending upon Him in everything. God is so big that He wants to know us, even in the smallest areas of our lives. Learning to trust and know Him in the small struggles will allow us to hear Him with the big ones.

This is why it is important for us to be in God's Word daily. We cannot just make a checklist of things to do and not do and expect to follow all of them. When we spend time in His Word daily, however, He allows His word to transform us. Then, opening up to God and talking to Him about the things we are learning allows His Word to sift our thoughts and desires. We invite God in to cleanse and transform these areas in our life. We realize that His grace covers us and frees us. He empowers us to walk away from the ugly parts of our heart and to begin seeing His fruit of love, joy, peace, patience, kindness, and more in our life (Galatians 5:22–23).

Do you think God only wants His children to be free from sexual sins but not to be free from lies or other unfaithful acts? Similarly, if you seek to use your own strength to overcome smaller sins, why would you turn to God for overcoming larger sins? Do you see the big picture now? Be dependent upon God in all things and seek to really know Him intimately; be His friend and His obedient child.

God doesn't want you to just live a life free from sexual sins; He wants a relationship with you. He is absolutely holy in all areas, and He wants you to be like Him. Friends share things in common. Consider this familiar verse: "Be holy, for I am holy" (1 Peter 1:16, NIV). Even if you once overlooked this command or merely dismissed it as an impossible statement, try to view it in a new way as you view God differently. Close your eyes and imagine God gently calling your name, whispering to you, and inviting you to enter His court: "My daughter, be holy as I am holy; draw near to Me so we can be close" (see 1 Peter 1:16; James 4:8).

READ THE BIBLE

Read Ephesians 1. Let your heart sing as you absorb God's Word.

WEEK 1........ WEEK 2........ WEEK 3........ WEEK 4........ WEEK 5........ WEEK 6........ WEEK 7........ WEEK 8........ WEEK 9...... WEEK 10 .....11........12

DAY 1

PRAY

Answer God's calling by meeting with Him in intimacy right now.

_____

_____

_____

SPECIAL NOTE:

Meeting with the Lord in times of praise and earnest prayer is perhaps the greatest moment of receiving God Himself (and thus His healing, wisdom, and strength) into your life. It's then that you are lifted into His courts and His presence. The world and its lusts are purged and burned away, replaced by a passion for more of Him. The gifts of repentance and humility are poured into you during times when you long to be with the Lord. Your purity grows in direct proportion to the time you spend with the Lord in earnest prayer and devotion. During such times of intimacy, God imparts truth, life, and healing to you. This is the surgical room of the Great Physician. You'll live out a Proven life as you commit to living out absolute purity in total dependence upon and gratitude to God.

MEMORY VERSE

Ephesians 6:12 (ESV): "For we do not wrestle against flesh and blood, but against the rulers, against the authorities, against the cosmic powers over this present darkness, against the spiritual forces of evil in the heavenly places."

WEEK 10 DAY 2 (TUESDAY)

KEY THOUGHT: Pursue God for who He is.

We have mentioned many times in this study that all sin stems from selfishness and pride. The Bible also says that the love of money is the root of all kinds of evil (1 Timothy 6:10). Why is it vital to keep away from the love of money? One reason is that when you dwell on material things, you don't earnestly pray or seek after God; you forget His promises, and you forget about Him. Matthew 6:24 says that we cannot serve two masters. We will either serve the Lord or money. Our hearts cannot serve both at the same time. The Lord knows that the love of money (greed or pursuing material things) keeps you from being content with what He knows is best for you. Your desire for temporary selfish pleasures will only drag you away from God's camp and breed discontentment.

Being content with what you have means not seeking more pleasures, more wealth, or more of anything of this world. Reflect on why God's promise, "Never will I leave you; never will I forsake you" (Hebrews 13:5, NIV), leads to contentment.

_____

_____

Will you commit to trusting in the strength of the Lord alone? Ask God to reveal to you what He gives. Ask Him to show you that He is sufficient and that following Him is in your best interest and keeps you in a joyful and kingdom-minded mentality.

WEEK 1........ WEEK 2........ WEEK 3........ WEEK 4........ WEEK 5........ WEEK 6........ WEEK 7........ WEEK 8........ WEEK 9........ **WEEK 10**........ WEEK 11........ WEEK 12

DAY 2

DAILY READING

One of the biggest reasons people remain trapped in bondage to sexual sin is that they haven't fully embraced the true nature of God and their relation to Him. This plays itself out in many ways.

- Some refuse to turn completely to God because they love themselves and their sins too much. They remain ignorant of the fullness and beauty of God and how He offers Himself freely to us. They incorrectly trust in what they feel in their heart rather than what God says is true.

- Others incorrectly believe they are unworthy of God's love or grace and see their sins as too great a chasm for God to cover. They feel too dirty to be wiped clean.

- Others merely want temptations to be taken away. They ask God to spare them of all trials and temptations and to grant them happy lives without the necessary aspects of intimacy or dependency. They lose sight of the fact that trials develop perseverance and aid in making you whole and complete.

Do you want to be changed by God and live out a pure life? If anyone purposefully positions herself to see and meet with God, she will be transformed. She will find a completely loving God who eagerly desires to hold and protect her. She will know a God who so freely and perfectly forgives that it's as though each day she becomes a new creation. That's the great joy of the gospel.

To grow in Christ, you must humbly seek the Lord with all of your heart in order to passionately and openly worship the King of the universe, your Father and Friend. You must transition from wanting to control your own life to wanting what the Lord wants. His desires will become your desires when you see God as good and therefore trust Him. It's that simple.

God has a purposeful life planned for you. However, when you don't trust Him, you lag behind by taking side trips in whatever direction you think is best. Within His plan, some days will be hard, but He has all of the right equipment for the venture. As you continue to obey, you'll be able to handle difficulties with more ease. The trials merely prepare you for tomorrow. Your growing faith enables you to go to higher levels and new places. What a journey God has for you as you travel with Him as your personal guide! Don't you want to be guided by Him so that you can go wherever He leads? But God never intends for you to

WEEK 1........ WEEK 2........ WEEK 3........ WEEK 4........ WEEK 5........ WEEK 6........ WEEK 7........ WEEK 8........ WEEK 9..... WEEK 10 ....11........12

DAY 2

become strong enough that you can venture off without Him. The whole point is a journey with God. As women, we desire to share in an adventure with someone. God desires to venture every step of the way with you.

God transforms you by drawing you to Himself through the outpouring of His unconditional love. No whip is needed because His beauty and perfect nature are irresistible if you permit yourself to experience Him. As you yield control to God and trust in Him, He imparts perseverance, which must grow so that you can withstand the temptations and evil forces of the world and journey with Him to special places. Your obedience reflects your love for God and permits further refinement of your spirit and will. You become more than a worshiper of God: You unite as one with Him (1 Corinthians 6:17), experiencing His perfect holiness and righteousness. Your old nature of pride and self-focus is put away. Victorious living naturally follows.

What is something you especially love about God? Write it out.

_____

_____

_____

If you spend time with Jesus with the goal of getting to know Him, you'll fall in love with Him. Then, you'll want what Christ wants more than you will want sexually immoral activities. Your desires will change. They will become what they were initially intended to be at creation. You'll experience lasting freedom. Start the process now by meditating on the proof of God's love for you, beginning with the cross. Christ's willingness to take your punishment is positive proof.

Is the healing process going too slowly for you? It won't be if you focus on seeking God day by day rather than focusing on how much time has gone by. Don't get me wrong. At first, it's normal to be mindful of how many days since you last committed a sexual sin. For some, counting up these days provides a glimmer of hope. However, you cannot place your worth on this length of time or seek to rush the process. Otherwise you'll put more emphasis on behavior modification techniques than upon purposing to daily live out each element of a Proven life as part of the process of turning to the Lord.

WEEK 1........ WEEK 2........ WEEK 3........ WEEK 4........ WEEK 5........ WEEK 6........ WEEK 7........ WEEK 8........ WEEK 9........ WEEK 10 .... WEEK 11........ WEEK 12

DAY 2

Those living in lasting freedom no longer base their worth on how many days they have not masturbated or looked at pornography. They know that their true worth has already been established in Christ. Ultimately, Proven Women finally see that true freedom is living each day with Christ. You see, victory is not based upon or measured by the diminished presence of a certain sin. It is based on how you respond to setbacks. I rejoice each time someone shares what she has learned after she stumbles.

When we move into the truth that our worth (our value and significance) is not determined by what we do or don't do but instead by the unconditional love and acceptance of Jesus Christ, this wisdom renews us beyond our greatest expectations. As women, so many times our struggle with lust is connected with our desire to know our true worth. We long to be desired. This yearning can lure us into sexual sin. Then, shame over sin attacks the little value that we believe that we have. If we listen to shame, we think our sin has devalued us in God's eyes. But when we understand how valued we are by God, it helps us not run after finding our worth in other things. We can confidently carry our worth into the relationships that He has for us.

When we understand that God's grace through the cross protects our worth in His eyes, we will not allow shame to attack our worth. Satan wants to attack our view of our worth, but we need to stand steadfast on the truth that God sees us as we are and chooses to love us and accept us. He desires to free us from sin and transform us into His holiness, but the timing of this transformation does not measure our worth in His eyes. He transforms us because He already values us and wants to see us reach the potential that He has placed in us.

I received an email from a fellow Proven teammate that clarifies this wonderful point:

> As I am starting to see into the heart of Jesus—the source of pure love—I am finally beginning to understand that our sexual dysfunctions and the inordinate time we spend thinking about it take up only a very tiny corner of His heart. Indeed, there is so much light there that our little darkness is wiped totally clean. This shouts the great truth: Jesus is far more interested in having a progressively intimate relationship with us rather than emptying us of our inappropriate choices. It helps to know that Jesus is saying: "I'm crazy-nuts about you. I want all of you, brokenness, fears, failures, and

WEEK 1........ WEEK 2........ WEEK 3........ WEEK 4........ WEEK 5........ WEEK 6........ WEEK 7........ WEEK 8........ WEEK 9........ **WEEK 10** ..... WEEK 11........ WEEK 12

DAY 2

all the rest." It is when we love Him in return that nothing else will matter except pursuing Jesus.

There is so much "good news" in that paragraph. This type of eternal perspective helps to forge passion and openness with Christ that frees us from dwelling on setbacks. This gives us time to focus instead on our relationship with Jesus.

Be patient. God often heals slowly in the area of sexual impurity on purpose and for good reason. It requires time for you to get to know God intimately and to fall completely in love with Jesus. Once you do, you'll fulfill your purpose in life: To love God with all of your heart and to love others as yourself (Matthew 22:36–39). Peace is assured, and holiness follows.

HEARTWORK

A by-product of an intimate relationship with God is that it loosens the grip of sexual sins. Read this sentence again, contemplating its meaning and application in your life. The greater aim of knowing Jesus intimately is what brings about the holiness and purity you desire.[15] That's why you must not make your goal to merely stop masturbating or watching pornography. Don't misunderstand. A short-term goal can be to immediately stop masturbating while you are pursuing God. But the greater goal of knowing Jesus is the way to absolute purity.

R is for Repentant in Spirit. If you are still having a hard time seeing pornography, lust, or masturbation as idols in your life, continue to ask God to help you see them the way He sees them. Remember, because of the cross, God does not turn His back on you; however, you distance yourself from God when you choose sin. What good would it do if God just delivered you from something that you do not even see as evil? If you make seeking selfish pleasures your passion in life, what difference does it make if one item (e.g., masturbation) is removed? God wants to give you permanent freedom in all aspects of your life. Repent from your selfish desire to be instantly healed of one sin without becoming His daughter and living a life characterized by a relationship with Him. Right now, surrender your will to God and ask Him to transform your heart.

WEEK 1...... WEEK 2...... WEEK 3...... WEEK 4...... WEEK 5...... WEEK 6...... WEEK 7...... WEEK 8...... WEEK 9...... **WEEK 10** .... WEEK 11...... WEEK 12

DAY 2

READ THE BIBLE

Are you reading Scripture daily? Read Ephesians 2 and write out your thoughts or insights.

_____

_____

_____

PRAY

In true humility, talk to the Lord and spend five or ten minutes being with Him. Spend time telling God about the things you value and love about Him.

_____

_____

_____

_____

_____

_____

SPECIAL NOTE:

Earlier, the term "truth therapy" was introduced. Basically, it means immersing yourself in God's truth to counteract the lies of Satan and any incorrect thinking you have formed about yourself, about God, or about whether you will be healed. Because God is perfect and all-knowing, He is always right. He has given you a book that is totally reliable. The Bible is your source for promises and truths. When you read it to know God, you are transformed.

MEMORY VERSE

Ephesians 6:12 (ESV): "For we do not wrestle against flesh and blood, but against the rulers, against the authorities, against the cosmic powers over this present darkness, against the spiritual forces of evil in the heavenly places."

WEEK 10   DAY 3 (WEDNESDAY)

KEY THOUGHT: Intimacy with God redeems our broken intimacy.

DAILY READING

You were created to experience and enjoy intimacy, first with God and then with others. However, many tend to shy away from true intimacy due to the deep pain associated with prior relationships. They turn to false forms of intimacy that they think they can guard and control. Pornography, masturbation, and fantasy seem to be about the safest forms of "intimacy," especially when sex is incorrectly viewed as a replacement for love. Pornography and masturbation appear safe for those who do not want to rely on another person. Some want to be self-sufficient yet still have the perks of a relationship. God designed sexual pleasure to take place between a husband and wife, within the covenant of marriage. When we think we can be completely independent, we seek the pleasure that God designed for a specific context in the world.

This is an act of rebellion because we seek our own design rather than looking to God's design. This also demonstrates a lack of patience. God has asked us to wait to engage in sex if we are not yet under the covenant of marriage. We are also to depend on Him to bring about reconciliation in our marriage if there is not currently intimacy within it. Who are we to tell God how we can obtain pleasure? He is our Creator and Lord.

Do you fear aspects of intimacy like letting your guard down or being completely open with someone? Explain how and why.

WEEK 1....... WEEK 2....... WEEK 3....... WEEK 4....... WEEK 5....... WEEK 6....... WEEK 7....... WEEK 8....... WEEK 9....... **WEEK 10**.... WEEK 11....... WEEK 12

DAY 3

_____

_____

_____

Have you ever considered why pornography is the largest moneymaker industry in the world? The reason people end up spending billions of dollars a year to buy internet pornography is because it doesn't and cannot supply the real needs that are missing in life. In other words, people keep trying to force it to work by buying more and more. In fact, many websites offer free sneak previews or thumbnail pictures because they know that people won't be satisfied and will only crave greater thrills. Eventually, some turn to more hard-core and costly pornography in the vain hope that these more expensive fantasies will satisfy.

If you struggle with pornography, fantasy, or masturbation, chances are that you've closed off areas of your heart to God and others. For instance, a married woman may have sexual contact with her husband while withholding her innermost self. Similarly, single women often look to forms of sexual pleasure in place of intimate (non-sexual), open, and vulnerable relationships. Those turning to sexual activities to fill their lives are actually running away from real intimacy. It is not so surprising that the key ingredient to sexual healing is intimacy with God.

Because many of us have had poor success with some prior relationships, we doubt that intimacy with God or others is possible. We are afraid because we view this as giving control to someone who might hurt us or reject us. Chances are you have many barriers against trusting God. Perhaps you blame Him for your circumstances or you don't think He heard your cries for help in the past. Some would rather be in charge of their life at any cost, than risk being hurt again. The reasons are numerous, but the cure is the same: to see God as good and to trust Him.

What would occur if you really viewed God as totally good, as One who cares completely about the details of your life? What if you felt His great and rich love? Suppose you thought His peace could totally soothe your wounds. Well, these things are the true nature of God. No matter how painful your past relationships with others have been or how blurred your view of God is, you simply must allow God to join with you in spiritual intimacy. You might think, "But how can I? I don't really know God enough to turn to or trust in Him with my whole life." This concern is real to many, and yet the solution is quite simple. Devote yourself

WEEK 1........ WEEK 2........ WEEK 3........ WEEK 4........ WEEK 5........ WEEK 6........ WEEK 7........ WEEK 8........ WEEK 9..... WEEK 10 .....11........ WEEK 12

DAY 3

to discovering God's character. Spend time each day in His Word and ask God to open your eyes to see Him as He really is: perfect. Purpose to find God. To all who seek, they find; to all who knock, the door will be opened; and to all who thirst for righteousness, they will be filled (see Matthew 5:6; 7:7). Don't shrink away. There is nowhere else to go to receive lasting healing. The truth is that only God can mend your wounds. Only He can rescue you. Openly tell God of your fears and concerns. He won't reject you. He will never leave your side (Hebrews 13:5). He proved His love on the cross. Let Him carry your burden now.

Intimacy with God is available to you. God wants you to meet with Him. He paid a very high price for your freedom from sin and shame. You're of great value to God. It's now time for you to see God as good. It's time to embrace the love the Lord has for you. It's time to live out your purpose in life of worshiping a worthy God and experiencing Him in intimacy alongside others "who call upon the Lord from a pure heart" (2 Timothy 2:22).

Yes, intimacy with God is waiting for you. It's born through a lifestyle of worshiping the Lord from your heart and praising Him with your lips.[16] Expressing passion for God gives life to your soul and tears down walls around your heart because it draws you into the very presence of a holy, loving, and merciful God. While in the Lord's presence, you no longer need to cling to anything else. You're set free.

The key to developing intimacy with God is focusing on Christ, not on your circumstances. Begin by thanking the Lord throughout each day. Set out to make Him your closest confidant. He truly cares about the details of your life. He cares about the longings, the dreams, and the struggles. There's no other way to know your God than to spend time with Him. Reading books about God is not the same as being with Him. Won't you go to Him now? Open your heart to Him. Thank Him for each blessing during the day. Sing worship songs and write letters to Him. Read the Bible as though it was written to you—it was. Talk to God in prayer, not asking for selfish requests or babbling on with memorized words. Pour out your heart in open and vulnerable discussions and communications.

Without a growing, intimate relationship with God your Father, you won't know and experience His deep, abiding love, which heals past wounds and imparts great faith. Spending long periods of time in worship and open communication with God forges a mighty friendship that can be relied upon. You'll experience the character and nature of the Holy One as you meet with Him. Your mind and soul will be transformed, and your heart renewed. God promises that all who hunger and thirst after righteousness shall be satisfied (Matthew 5:6). It's time to hunger and thirst for God instead of the world.

WEEK 1 ...... WEEK 2 ...... WEEK 3 ...... WEEK 4 ...... WEEK 5 ...... WEEK 6 ...... WEEK 7 ...... WEEK 8 ...... WEEK 9 ...... WEEK 10 ...... WEEK 11 ...... WEEK 12

DAY 3

V is for Victorious in Living. Are you walking in victory? The remedy is to make a decision to love God with passion by spending lots of time meeting with Him. Give up TV and internet time and replace it with praying, reading Psalms, singing hymns, and writing love letters to Christ. Your family may think you're crazy to sing praise songs out loud at home, but why not celebrate God in this way?

Will you commit to establishing and maintaining a lifestyle of worship and praise?

Explain how you will put this into practice.

_____

_____

_____

_____

_____

Pride is a major stumbling block to becoming dependent upon God, because it leads to some of the following thoughts:

- "I can do it myself."

- "I don't need help."

- "My sins aren't that bad."

- "I don't need God."

Describe how you struggle with any of these types of self-sufficient thinking.

_____

_____

WEEK 1........ WEEK 2........ WEEK 3........ WEEK 4........ WEEK 5........ WEEK 6........ WEEK 7........ WEEK 8........ WEEK 9........ **WEEK 10**........ WEEK 11........ WEEK 12

DAY 3

Does pride still make you think things such as these?

- "I can change my heart."

- "I can overcome a sinful action."

- "I can be kind, good, and faithful in my own strength."

- "I only need a bit of help from God to overcome."

HEARTWORK

Write out ways you are struggling to see God's love for you.

_____

_____

_____

_____

READ THE BIBLE

Keep reading Scripture and asking God to reveal truth. Read Ephesians 3.

Write out some of the truths below.

_____

_____

_____

_____

WEEK 1........ WEEK 2........ WEEK 3........ WEEK 4........ WEEK 5........ WEEK 6........ WEEK 7........ WEEK 8........ WEEK 9........ **WEEK 10**........ WEEK 11........ WEEK 12

DAY 3

PRAY

Spend time actively imagining Jesus on the cross looking at you. Spend time looking over His naked and broken body. Look at His face, see the fierce love in His eyes as He looks back at you. Then be led to pray as He shows you these things.

Record your prayers below.

_____

_____

_____

_____

_____

_____

_____

_____

_____

Make a donation. It is our vision to provide life-transforming resources to every man and woman who wants to experience lasting victory from the strongholds of pornography and sexual addiction by partnering with local churches to offer our 12-week studies combined with accountability and ongoing discipleship; however, we can't do this without you! Visit our website *www.ProvenWomen.org* to learn more about how to becoming a ministry partner through ongoing financial support.

MEMORY VERSE

Ephesians 6:12 (ESV): "For we do not wrestle against flesh and blood, but against the rulers, against the authorities, against the cosmic powers over this present darkness, against the spiritual forces of evil in the heavenly places."

WEEK 10 DAY 4 (THURSDAY)

KEY THOUGHT: God has given us resources so that we can stand fast.

 ## DAILY READING

I don't know about you, but I consider myself to be a somewhat intelligent person. The game of chess, however, is beyond my way of thinking. I have been taught what the different pieces do, but besides that, I am clueless of the strategy needed to play the game. If I were to ever learn the game, I would need someone who would take the time to explain things to me, someone who would be patient with me while serving as my opponent and teaching me their strategies.

Unfortunately, when it comes to spiritual warfare, Satan is not an understanding opponent. If you don't know the rules or are unaware of the strategies of spiritual warfare, he will gladly use that against you! Satan is a real spiritual being, described by God as a roaring lion seeking to devour the spirit of man (1 Peter 5:8). Would you enter a lion's den unarmed and unprepared? Of course not! We do not have an option of staying out of Satan's den. He seeks opportunities to pounce on us; therefore, it is vital that we learn how to fight well in spiritual warfare. Just as a lion won't pass up an ostrich with its head buried in the sand, the devil won't pass you up simply because you didn't know he was harmful. An easy target is not overlooked.

Certainly, you know that there are spiritual forces that affect your life. You're quick to admit that your spirit is damaged by harsh words of a friend. How much more harm, though, is inflicted by a powerful spiritual being that considers you an enemy? Satan's tactics or weapons aren't as visible as a knife, but they cut just the same. Satan is pleased when you

WEEK 1........ WEEK 2........ WEEK 3........ WEEK 4........ WEEK 5........ WEEK 6........ WEEK 7........ WEEK 8........ WEEK 9........ **WEEK 10**........ WEEK 11........ WEEK 12

DAY 4

become a slave to lustful, judgmental, or self-centered thoughts. He is pleased by your ignorance and refusal to put on God's armor. You die a slow death without knowing that you're under attack.

Consider these descriptions of Satan:

- **Devil**—Matthew 4:1 (ESV) "Then Jesus was led up by the Spirit into the wilderness to be tempted by the devil."

- **Murderer and Liar**—John 8:44 (ESV) "You are of your father the devil, and your will is to do your father's desires. He was a murderer from the beginning, and does not stand in the truth, because there is no truth in him. When he lies, he speaks out of his own character, for he is a liar and the father of lies."

- **Lord of Darkness**—Ephesians 6:12 (ESV) "For we do not wrestle against flesh and blood, but against the rulers, against the authorities, against the cosmic powers over this present darkness, against the spiritual forces of evil in the heavenly places."

- **Evil one**—Matthew 13:19 (ESV) "When anyone hears the word of the kingdom and does not understand it, the evil one comes and snatches away what has been sown in his heart. This is what was sown along the path."

- **Ruler of the Earth**—John 12:31 (ESV) "Now is the judgment of this world; now will the ruler of this world be cast out."

- **Tempter**—Matthew 4:3 (ESV) "And the tempter came and said to him, 'If you are the Son of God, command these stones to become loaves of bread.'"

We have already discussed the fall of Satan, but here is a quick reminder. The story of the rise and fall of the devil goes like this: Before creating the earth and man, God made angels. The most beautiful and powerful angel was Lucifer. Sadly, Lucifer began focusing on himself, noting his own beauty. He became puffed up and proud. In rebellion, he sought equality with God. Therefore, God changed his name to Satan and cast him out of heaven, together with one-third of the angels who rebelled with him. On earth, Satan set out to pervert man, who was made in God's image and was designed to worship God and enjoy fellowship with Him. It pleases Satan when man refuses to praise and acknowledge God. Satan and the other fallen angels (called demons) want to destroy all that God considers precious, including you.

Although we don't understand why God permits Satan to rule the world until the end of this age, we do know that Satan is real. Scripture says that he held the power of death

WEEK 1 ...... WEEK 2 ...... WEEK 3 ...... WEEK 4 ...... WEEK 5 ...... WEEK 6 ...... WEEK 7 ...... WEEK 8 ...... WEEK 9 ...... **WEEK 10** .... WEEK 11 ...... WEEK 12

DAY 4

(Hebrews 2:14–15). Despite his great power, Satan cannot defeat God. He has no ability to live inside a Christian because God already has made each adopted child His temple. Nor can Satan ruin the work of the Lord. In fact, God has given man authority over Satan when acting through Christ (1 John 3:8; Luke 10:18–19). However, you'll always fail when you act in your own strength. You on your own are no match for this powerful spiritual being. But he is no match for Christ who is within you. When you stand in Christ's strength, you will win every time.

One way you grant Satan a foothold in your life is when you allow anger, pride, greed, lust, or other sins to fester and go unconfessed before God (Ephesians 4:27). The good news is that by the strength of Jesus Christ, you can repent and resist Satan (James 4:7). God has spiritual armor for you to wear and spiritual weapons to fight with against the forces of evil (Ephesians 6).

Don't be deceived—a spiritual battle takes place around and over you. Make a decision to take a stand for the kingdom of God and wear His armor. Join with Proven Men and Women in the army of God, taking your position as a loyal soldier who willingly obeys the Lord's commands.

Record your insights.

_____

_____

_____

HEARTWORK

Right now, commit to getting to know Jesus as the top priority in your life. Open your eyes and heart to His glory and grace. Seek Him with all of your heart. Indicate your decision below.

If you aren't accustomed to wearing and using God's armor daily, you won't know how to use it when Satan does attack—and he carefully plots his attacks! As you're becoming more

WEEK 1........ WEEK 2........ WEEK 3........ WEEK 4........ WEEK 5........ WEEK 6........ WEEK 7........ WEEK 8........ WEEK 9........ **WEEK 10**........ WEEK 11........ WEEK 12

DAY 4

proficient using the armor of God, you'll be able to rely upon God's strength when Satan attacks (like when you're tempted to lust).

Read Ephesians 6:10–18.

Why wear God's armor? (See verses 10–11.) Describe where and how the real struggle takes place in overcoming sexual sins. (See verse 12.)

_____

_____

_____

_____

_____

Read Appendix E. Describe how to put on and use each piece of the armor:

HELMET OF SALVATION:

_____

_____

BREASTPLATE OF RIGHTEOUSNESS:

_____

_____

SHIELD OF FAITH:

_____

_____

WEEK 1........ WEEK 2........ WEEK 3........ WEEK 4........ WEEK 5........ WEEK 6........ WEEK 7........ WEEK 8........ WEEK 9........ WEEK 10 .....11........ WEEK 12

DAY 4

SWORD OF THE SPIRIT (WORD OF GOD):

_____

_____

BELT OF TRUTH:

_____

_____

GOSPEL OF PEACE:

_____

_____

READ THE BIBLE

Read and mediate on Ephesians 4. Immerse yourself in God's Word—the only place where you will obtain eternal truth! Be sure to keep asking God to reveal truth to you.

PRAY

P is for Passionate for God. Spend five to ten minutes meeting with God. Keep the focus off yourself and your own circumstances and practice praying for others.

- Ask God to continue to change your heart so that you are passionate for Him.
- Ask God to show you how to wear His armor and how to live under His protection.
- Make a commitment to wear His armor daily.
- Commit to praying in the Spirit on all occasions and with all kinds of unselfish requests.
- Ask God to make you alert to spiritual warfare and the source of temptations.

WEEK 1........ WEEK 2........ WEEK 3........ WEEK 4........ WEEK 5........ WEEK 6........ WEEK 7........ WEEK 8........ WEEK 9......... WEEK 10 ......11........12

DAY 4

• Pray for other Proven Women.

_____

_____

_____

_____

_____

SPECIAL NOTE:

After this series is over, consider using the book, _Lord, Is It Warfare? Teach Me to Stand_ by Kay Arthur[17] as one of your next study aids. It's not too early to plan your next study. Don't drop the shield at the end of twelve weeks.

Will you embrace and wear the whole armor of God daily? Just like weapons of this world, using God's armor requires practice to be proficient.

MEMORY VERSE

Ephesians 6:12 (ESV): "For we do not wrestle against flesh and blood, but against the rulers, against the authorities, against the cosmic powers over this present darkness, against the spiritual forces of evil in the heavenly places."

WEEK 10 DAY 5 (FRIDAY)

KEY THOUGHT: We are free to rejoice in Jesus.

DAILY READING

Today's Daily Reading is largely a time of reflection and meditation. Use it to reaffirm your total dedication to the Lord. Go slowly through each reflection, making decisions and yielding to the Lord. Ask God to speak to you and listen to what He has to say.

- Commit to living out holiness in all areas of your life. What sins have you overlooked? Spend a moment listening to God. Picture what your life would look like free from these sins. God wants to cleanse you both for His glory and for your well-being. Confess each sin that the Holy Spirit brings to your mind.

- Turn complete control of your life over to Christ. Stop striving in your own strength and admit that you need God's help. Pray this as your own: I have been crucified with Christ and I no longer live, but Christ lives in me. The life I live in the flesh, I live by faith in the Son of God, who loved me and gave himself for me (based on Galatians 2:20).

- Meditate upon how you will turn to and rely upon Christ to resist temptations that you face each day.

- Tell the Lord about any struggle you're facing, whether it is sexual temptation, greed, anger, rivalry, jealousy, or something else.

- Ask God to reveal to you in greater depth who He is, how much He loves you, and who you are in Him. Ask God to make His unconditional love real to you and to use His unconditional love to draw you close and to heal your wounds. Picture this in your mind.

WEEK 1........ WEEK 2........ WEEK 3........ WEEK 4........ WEEK 5........ WEEK 6........ WEEK 7........ WEEK 8........ WEEK 9........ WEEK 10 .... WEEK 11........ WEEK 12

DAY 5

- Ask God to mend your broken relationships with parents, siblings, friends, or a spouse. Ask the Lord to show you ways in which you block out others, withhold love or forgiveness, or are being selfish. Ask the Lord to open the door and show you what to do to seek and pursue reconciliation with others.

- Ask God for passion, including a burning desire to read the Bible daily, pray, and praise Him.

- Ask the Lord to tell you what things He wants you to know. Be still and anticipate Him.

- Stay focused upon hearing from God without making any petitions or allowing your mind to wander.

God designed you to rejoice and delight in Him. Meditate upon the following verses:

"Let the righteous rejoice in the Lord and take refuge in him; let all the upright in heart praise him!" (Psalm 64:10).

"Once more the humble will rejoice in the Lord; the needy will rejoice in the Holy One of Israel" (Isaiah 29:19, NIV).

"May my meditation be pleasing to Him, as I rejoice in the Lord" (Psalm 104:34).

"Blessed is the man who does not walk in the counsel of the wicked... But his delight is in the law of the Lord, and on His law he meditates day and night" (Psalm 1:1–2).

"... my soul will rejoice in the Lord and delight in His salvation" (Psalm 35:9).

"Delight yourself in the Lord and He will give you the desires of your heart. Commit your way to the Lord; trust in Him and He will do this: He will make your righteousness shine like the dawn, the justice of your cause like the noonday sun. Be still before the Lord and wait patiently for Him; do not fret when men succeed in their ways, when they carry out their wicked schemes" (Psalm 37:4–7).

"Great are the works of the Lord; they are pondered by all who delight in them" (Psalm 111:2).

"They that wait upon the Lord shall renew their strength; they shall mount up with wings as eagles; they shall run, and not be weary; and they shall walk, and not faint" (Isaiah 40:31, KJV).

WEEK 1........ WEEK 2........ WEEK 3........ WEEK 4........ WEEK 5........ WEEK 6........ WEEK 7........ WEEK 8........ WEEK 9........ **WEEK 10** .....11........ WEEK 12

DAY 5

HEARTWORK

State how you will rejoice and delight in Christ and write down the exact times of the day you will dedicate to worship and prayer.

_____

_____

_____

_____

Have you made knowing God the greatest pursuit of your life? If not, will you do so now? Write out your prayers to do just that.

_____

_____

_____

READ THE BIBLE

Read Colossians 4. Read God's Word so that you can love God. Guard against only being an information gatherer. Soften your heart and do what God's Word says.

PRAY

Spend five or ten minutes meeting with God the Father. Pray to get to know Him as a living being. Seek to be intimate with God in times of prayer.

- Praise the Lord with all of your heart.

- Tell God of your love for Him.

- Sing a melody to Him, perhaps a favorite song or verse of Scripture.

WEEK 1........ WEEK 2........ WEEK 3........ WEEK 4........ WEEK 5........ WEEK 6........ WEEK 7........ WEEK 8........ WEEK 9..... WEEK 10 .... WEEK 11........ WEEK 12

DAY 5

- Ask God to give you His power and strength to carry out the commitments you make.

- Ask the Lord to make you a needy, dependent servant.

- Ask God to break all remaining pride in your heart.

- Pray for others, including church leaders, the country's leaders, and your family.

The fifth letter in a PROVEN life is **E, which means Eternal in Perspective.** Do you believe that the Word of God is truth? Do you want to apply it in your life? The things of today will all perish, and they don't satisfy. The Word of God, however, will never pass away (see Matthew 24:35).

PW

WEEK ELEVEN

TESTIMONY

"Sexual sin can trap our identity in the jaws of shame. What seemed charming and inviting turns out to be isolating and humiliating. This was the epitome of my struggle. I was enslaved by desire. But there was Someone seeking to rescue me—because I was designed to exist in love and freedom. Proven Women guided me into understanding the essence of sexual sin, forcing me to face what I was really pursuing and why? What did I believe sin could give me that God could not? The truths in this book pried open my heart and identified the root of my sin, it didn't just treat the symptoms. It taught me that Heaven doesn't operate out of shame and humiliation and spoke to the truth that there is a better way to live. This study taught me to humble myself before God and invite Him into all the areas of my life. He has always wanted me and because of this study I have been able to find healing and rest."

Passionate for God,
Repentant in spirit,
Open and honest,
Victorious in living,
Eternal in perspective, and
Networking with other *PROVEN Women.*

MEMORY VERSE

Ephesians 4:1–2 (ESV): "I therefore, a prisoner for the Lord, urge you to walk in a manner worthy of the calling to which you have been called, with all humility and gentleness, with patience, bearing with one another in love."

WEEK 11 DAY 1 (MONDAY)

KEY THOUGHT: God fights with us.

The primary lesson for you this week is to develop a humble heart of worship. You only have two more weeks left in this series. Do you have your next study picked out and the book(s) on order? Consider repeating this 12-week study. When going over it a second time, ask God to give you fresh eyes to see His character in greater depth.

Do you still have an insatiable hunger for earthly pleasures such as pornography, masturbation, fantasy, or greed? God says that to love the world or anything in the world is to hate Him (1 John 2:15–17 (NIV): "Do not love the world or anything in the world. If anyone loves the world, love for the Father is not in them. ¹⁶For everything in the world—the lust of the flesh, the lust of the eyes, and the pride of life—comes not from the Father but from the world. ¹⁷The world and its desires pass away, but whoever does the will of God lives forever.") These are very strong words. What is your initial response when you read this?

_____

_____

Is there anything that is keeping you from turning to God and trusting Him completely? Are you afraid He will withhold something good from you? God wants you to be filled (see Matthew 5:6). He wants to satisfy your real needs, deep in your soul. In fact, the Lord created you for real intimacy. Fantasy, however, is make-believe and robs you of joy and true satisfaction. It doesn't satisfy. The solution is found in seeking real intimacy with the Lord and others. As far as sexual intimacy goes, God did not hold back good things from you. He purposefully created you as a sexual being, capable of enjoying real and fulfilling intimacy, including sexual intimacy; but He knows that true sexual fulfillment without guilt and shame is available only in the context of a marriage based on vulnerability and sacrificial love.

WEEK 1........ WEEK 2........ WEEK 3........ WEEK 4........ WEEK 5........ WEEK 6........ WEEK 7........ WEEK 8........ WEEK 9........ WEEK 10.... **WEEK 11** 12

DAY 1

HEARTWORK

Hear the Word of God:

"As for you, you were dead in your transgressions and sins, in which you used to live when you followed the ways of this world and of the ruler of the kingdom of the air, the spirit who is now at work in those who are disobedient. All of us also lived among them at one time gratifying the cravings of our sinful nature and following its desires and thoughts. Like the rest, we were by nature objects of wrath" (Ephesians 2:1–3, NIV).

Let those verses speak to you. When you are trapped in slavery to prideful and self-centered actions, you're living as though you are still spiritually dead. Perhaps you have been numb to sinful ways.

Read the good news of the next verses:

"But because of his great love for us, God, who is rich in mercy, made us alive with Christ even when we were dead in transgressions—it is by grace you have been saved. And God raised us up with Christ and seated us with him in the heavenly realms in Christ Jesus, in order that in the coming ages he might show the incomparable riches of his grace, expressed in kindness to us in Christ Jesus. For it is by grace you have been saved, through faith—and this not from yourselves, it is the gift of God—not by works, so that no one can boast. For we are God's workmanship, created in Christ Jesus to do good works, which God prepared in advance for us to do" (Ephesians 2:4–10, NIV).

Allow God to speak to your heart right now. Trust in the One who created you and loves you deeply.

DAILY READING

Last week, you began addressing the reality of spiritual forces and battles. Having an eternal perspective is a large part of the PROVEN Model for living in purity and holiness. You're living in the midst of an ongoing battle between good and evil.[18] Your permanent home is not on earth but in heaven. This world is a war zone. As in all wars, there will be periods of great struggle and even injury, but we already know that God is the victor. Satan began as a created angel of God, and God cannot be defeated, especially by His own creation.

WEEK 1........ WEEK 2........ WEEK 3........ WEEK 4........ WEEK 5........ WEEK 6........ WEEK 7........ WEEK 8........ WEEK 9........ WEEK 10........ WEEK 11........ WEEK 12

DAY 1

As a child of God, you surely will taste of His victory and share in the fruit of His kingdom, but you are currently a part of this battle. Because we live in a war zone, it will be destructive to you if you cling to the notion that life in this world should be without difficulties. You will constantly blame God for these hardships rather than clinging to God to help you endure them. Choose to go to God for perseverance to endure hardships and other suffering within the Christian life (2 Timothy 2:3). The Lord uses your trials to make you fit for His kingdom. (James 1:2–4 (ESV) says, "Count it all joy, my brothers, when you meet trials of various kinds, ³for you know that the testing of your faith produces steadfastness. ⁴And let steadfastness have its full effect, that you may be perfect and complete, lacking in nothing.") Allow the Lord to lead the battle charge until the day of redemption, when you'll finally be at rest and apart from all evil. The Commander in Chief tells you that in this world, the only safe place for His servants is under His care and control. Meanwhile, the enemy awaits those who wander off and chart their own course.

God warns you in advance that you'll be tempted to leave His camp. Don't be deceived. Satan wants to rob you of peace. Therefore, stay on the Lord's path. Be mindful, however, of God's advance notice that you will experience suffering, even persecution (John 15:20). God uses these difficulties to fashion you into an even better servant, more equipped and prepared to do battle. Follow His instructions to network with other godly men and women, as iron sharpens iron (Proverbs 27:17). Think about it, who do you want beside you in times of war: someone not interested in conditioning, training, or following orders, or a fully trained, loyal, obedient, hard-working sister who is proficient in the weapons of war? Won't you join the spiritual sisterhood of Proven Women? Keep climbing up the holy mountain, encouraging one another along the way, but never allow the journey to distract you from Whom you are seeking and living for.

During battles and resulting victories, you'll gain perseverance and an unshakable faith in the Commander. When the next trials come, you'll realize and utilize the power of God as you gladly yield control to Him. In effect, you're stamped "tested and approved for use" by God, and you carry the attributes of a good servant: faithful, loyal, and obedient.

Never forget that God is your creator and that He designed you to live for and be in communion with Him. He has adopted you as His beloved daughter. If you refuse to accept your position in God's family, how will you fully live? How will you prevail against the evil one? It is pride that strives to accomplish that which you cannot and were not meant to do! Oh, how a proud heart refuses God and sees humility as weak! True humility turns to and relies upon the greatest Power in the universe. The Lord says that the lowly can move mountains because they look to the One who is able (Matthew 21:21).

WEEK 1........ WEEK 2........ WEEK 3........ WEEK 4........ WEEK 5........ WEEK 6........ WEEK 7........ WEEK 8........ WEEK 9........ WEEK 10........ WEEK 11 12

DAY 1

What are the key points of today's Daily Reading? Write them down.

_____

_____

_____

_____

Rely upon the power and strength of your Master, Jesus Christ, to overcome sin. Remember, when you fall in love with Jesus, you'll want to do His will. You'll want holiness more than you wanted pornography, greed, or other forms of self-will. Therefore, be passionate in your pursuit of God.

READ THE BIBLE

Be sure to read the Scriptures daily, and be ready to meet with God. Right now read and meditate on Colossians 1. What does this passage say about Christ?

_____

_____

_____

PRAY

God doesn't want you punching clocks, but He desires your first fruits. He wants you to talk with Him. Ask God to give you His perspective on prayer and to protect your time spent meeting alone with Him. Tell God about the things going on in your life, but don't forget to also pray for others.

WEEK 1........ WEEK 2........ WEEK 3........ WEEK 4........ WEEK 5........ WEEK 6........ WEEK 7........ WEEK 8........ WEEK 9........ WEEK 10.... **WEEK 11**....WEEK 12

DAY 1

Ask God to show you what a passionate pursuit of Him looks like. (Discuss this pursuit with your Proven Women leader and others next time you see them.)

- Draw near to God right now. According to James 4:8, He will draw near to you.

- Tell the Lord that you are renouncing all sin, but not just sin in general. Specifically tell Him the sins in your life—everything that separates you from intimacy with God and healthy relationships with others.

- Tell God that you're rejecting false intimacy (pornography, chat rooms, fantasy, or whatever it looks like for you) and pursuing open and honest relationships with Him and others.

- Keep praying for other Proven Men and Women.

- Pray for others. (List them.)

_____

_____

_____

_____

SPECIAL NOTE:

In Ephesians 2:10 (ESV), you are told: "For we are God's workmanship, created in Christ Jesus to do good works, which God prepared in advance for us to do." Do you see that the good works are not your own, but they are from God? God tells us that all of our "righteous acts are like filthy rags" (Isaiah 64:6, NIV). When you fall in love with Christ, you want what He wants. Only then are you able to do "good works" through Jesus, according to His purpose and plan (Ephesians 2:10; Philippians 2:13). In just the same way that you cannot earn God's love or salvation by your own good works (Ephesians 2:8–9), you cannot do good works to overcome sexual sins.

MEMORY VERSE

Ephesians 4:1–2(ESV): "I therefore, a prisoner for the Lord, urge you to walk in a manner worthy of the calling to which you have been called, with all humility and gentleness, with patience, bearing with one another in love."

WEEK 11 DAY 2 (TUESDAY)

KEY THOUGHT: God has given all of Himself to us.

DAILY READING

The first letter in a PROVEN life stands for **Passionately pursuing God** with your full heart by lifting praise, offering worship, and entering into relational prayer. Won't you turn to the Lord and break free from your old ways and prideful spirit that don't look outside of yourself? Falling in love with God is a matter of looking to and seeing God. God, and God alone, truly deserves praise. Declare the truth of His goodness and His love in Jesus' living, dying, resurrecting, and returning for us.

The by-product of a heart that freely worships God is a unity of spirit with Him. You actually grow closer to God, experiencing His character, during such times of praise. How remarkable! When you give God glory, your own heart expands. The Lord is released to fill even more of you. The more you humbly yield in passionate praise and pursuit of God, the more whole and complete you become. During times of open and vulnerable communication with God, old wounds are healed, and the fruit of the Holy Spirit abounds in your life. For instance, there will no longer be room in your heart for bitterness because when you relationally experience the Lord, you receive His joy, peace, and contentment. When your deepest relational need (intimacy with God) is met, you won't feel compelled to turn to false forms of intimacy or to medicate yourself with self-pity or chasing after the temporary pleasure or numbing aspects of illicit sexual activities.

WEEK 1 ..... WEEK 2 ..... WEEK 3 ..... WEEK 4 ..... WEEK 5 ..... WEEK 6 ..... WEEK 7 ..... WEEK 8 ..... WEEK 9 ..... WEEK 10 ..... **WEEK 11** ..... WEEK 12

DAY 2

Turn to Appendix D, which is an outline for using your heart, mind, and hands as a way of developing intimacy with God. Don't just read it to learn information, but determine to put these things into practice. Return to the study after dwelling on the outline.

HEARTWORK

The key to developing a heart and lifestyle of worship and praise is spending a great deal of time doing it. Don't cut corners here. Worshiping and praising God will transform you. Write Him a love note below:

_____

_____

_____

_____

READ THE BIBLE

Trust that the Bible is what God says it is, His Word. It is living and active. Read it to get to know God and not just learn about Him in your head. Read and meditate on Ephesians 2.

PRAY

It's time to adopt a new prayer life. God wants you to wrestle through issues with Him and to be passionate about the things you pray about. If you don't care about a response, why ask for it? If it is really important, however, then ask like it is. As your intimacy and dependence upon God grow, you'll pray more authentically and fervently. God is always listening when we pray with reverence.

Pray for your family and others. Be specific in your requests, asking for things in God's will and then being persistent. Also, thank Him now for the ways that He will answer your

WEEK 1........ WEEK 2........ WEEK 3........ WEEK 4........ WEEK 5........ WEEK 6........ WEEK 7........ WEEK 8........ WEEK 9........ WEEK 10.... WEEK 11 12

DAY 2

prayers in His perfect way and timing. Plan to spend five or ten minutes in prayer. If you make a list of names of people to pray for, you'll soon find that it won't be long enough.

_____

_____

_____

_____

_____

_____

_____

_____

_____

_____

_____

_____

MEMORY VERSE

Ephesians 4:1–2 (ESV): "I therefore, a prisoner for the Lord, urge you to walk in a manner worthy of the calling to which you have been called, with all humility and gentleness, with patience, bearing with one another in love."

WEEK 11 DAY 3 (WEDNESDAY)

KEY THOUGHT: Prayer is an intimate conversation of speaking and listening with the person who most loves you.

DAILY READING

Prayer invites God to act in and through your life. In fact, the entire power of God is available to His children during prayer. Have you learned how to pray? It may seem like a silly question to ask, but most people don't truly pray at all. Instead, they repeat words over and over again, string together eloquent-sounding phrases, or make long lists of things they want. Putting God's name at the beginning and end and saying "amen" doesn't turn these empty words into prayer. Prayer is simply talking to God, but you must come before God in reverence, realizing you are talking to your Creator. I think many times, we are not even engaging with God. We start talking without taking the time to center our mind on the fact that we are talking with our Beloved, Almighty, Creator, and Lord.

In his book, *The Screwtape Letters,*[20] C.S. Lewis talks about prayer. For those who do not know, this book is written as letters from one demon to his nephew, who is a lower demon and has been assigned to tempt a human. In one particular letter, the elder demon is teaching the lower demon how to keep people from praying. In this passage, the "Enemy" is referring to God. He writes, "Whenever they are attending to the Enemy Himself we are defeated, but there are ways of preventing them from doing so. The simplest is to turn their gaze away from Him towards themselves. Keep them watching their own minds and trying to produce *feelings* there by the action of their own wills. When they meant to ask Him for charity, let them, instead, start trying to manufacture charitable feelings for themselves and not notice that this is what they are doing. When they meant to pray for courage, let

WEEK 1........ WEEK 2........ WEEK 3........ WEEK 4........ WEEK 5........ WEEK 6........ WEEK 7........ WEEK 8........ WEEK 9........ WEEK 10........ WEEK 11 12

DAY 3

them really be trying to feel brave. When they say they are praying for forgiveness, let them really be trying to feel forgiven."

I know this really was eye opening for me when I read this. How many times do I think that I am praying when actually I am looking into myself and trying to transform myself for God? God is calling us to turn to Him with faith and expectation, to confess to Him where we are falling short and invite Him into our life to transform these areas.

It is never too late to learn to pray. Even the disciples, who had been walking with Jesus, asked to be taught how to pray (Luke 11:1). They certainly had heard Jesus pray many times before, so we can trust that they were not asking for specific words to repeat. Although meditating on the aspects of the prayer often referred to as "The Lord's Prayer" (Luke 11:2–4) can be a wonderful experience, you should guard against simply repeating these same words over and over. In Matthew 6, Jesus warns us about what prayer does not look like:

Matthew 6:5–15 (ESV)

"And when you pray, you must not be like the hypocrites. For they love to stand and pray in the synagogues and at the street corners, that they may be seen by others. Truly, I say to you, they have received their reward. [6]But when you pray, go into your room and shut the door and pray to your Father who is in secret. And your Father who sees in secret will reward you.

"[7]And when you pray, do not heap up empty phrases as the Gentiles do, for they think that they will be heard for their many words. [8]Do not be like them, for your Father knows what you need before you ask him. [9]Pray then like this:

> Our Father in heaven,
> hallowed be your name.
> [10]Your kingdom come,
> your will be done,
> on earth as it is in heaven.
> [11]Give us this day our daily bread,
> [12]and forgive us our debts,
> as we also have forgiven our debtors.
> [13]And lead us not into temptation,
> but deliver us from evil.

WEEK 1 .... WEEK 2 .... WEEK 3 .... WEEK 4 .... WEEK 5 .... WEEK 6 .... WEEK 7 .... WEEK 8 .... WEEK 9 .... WEEK 10 .... **WEEK 11** ....WEEK 12

DAY 3

"¹⁴For if you forgive others their trespasses, your heavenly Father will also forgive you, ¹⁵but if you do not forgive others their trespasses, neither will your Father forgive your trespasses."

The Lord tells you not to offer up empty words while praying. Don't just mindlessly say things, thinking that being long-winded and filling up time will fill a "prayer quota" (Matthew 6:7). The model Jesus taught was that in all things and at all times you are to communicate with your Heavenly Father. He starts out by reminding us to address the Father. The first few moments of prayer should be focusing our mind on Whom it is we are talking to. Once our mind is focused on God, we will come in reverence, humility, and authenticity. If we simply start talking, however, it is easy to mindless let words drift around our mind and call it prayer. Purpose to engage your heart and soul when you pray.

Turn to Appendix G, an outline of the purpose, practice, and power of prayer. Return here after you dwell on that outline. Keep asking God to teach you how to engage in real heart-felt, relational praying. Record your insights.

_____

_____

_____

Periodically, refer to the outline in Appendix G to realign your prayer life, keeping God in the center.

Recognize areas where your prayers were not prayers at all but were selfish requests, not based upon meeting with God. Right now, confess how you've merely asked God for things rather than seeking to know Him or to do His will.

HEARTWORK

E is for Eternal Perspective. Praying for others is a wonderful way of putting a Proven life into practice. Therefore, ask the Lord to instill in you a desire to pray for others like you really want God to bless them as dearly loved children.

WEEK 1 ...... WEEK 2 ...... WEEK 3 ...... WEEK 4 ...... WEEK 5 ...... WEEK 6 ...... WEEK 7 ...... WEEK 8 ...... WEEK 9 ...... WEEK 10 ...... **WEEK 11** ..... WEEK 12

DAY 3

READ THE BIBLE

Matthew 6:33 (ESV) "But seek first the kingdom of God and His righteousness, and all these things will be added to you." Mediate on this verse and write down some insights.

_____

_____

_____

_____

Read Ephesians 3.

PRAY

As you pray today, imagine yourself in a secret place where only God can see. Imagine it is just the two of you. Pray the Lord's Prayer with Him and then let Him guide you in that space.

Record your prayers below.

_____

_____

_____

_____

_____

_____

WEEK 1 .... WEEK 2 .... WEEK 3 .... WEEK 4 .... WEEK 5 .... WEEK 6 .... WEEK 7 .... WEEK 8 .... WEEK 9 .... WEEK 10 .... WEEK 11 .... WEEK 12

DAY 3

_____

_____

_____

_____

_____

_____

_____

_____

_____

_____

_____

SPECIAL NOTE:

The more you fix your eyes upon the Lord and live as a needy, dependent servant, the more you'll understand that God wants you to pray. You'll discover that God answers genuine prayers, where you communicate intimately with God to seek Him and His will. In short, relational prayers move God to action because they are based upon a PROVEN Model of living and communicating passionately, repentantly, openly, victoriously, eternally, and "networking" (together with Him).

MEMORY VERSE

Ephesians 4:1–2 (ESV): "I therefore, a prisoner for the Lord, urge you to walk in a manner worthy of the calling to which you have been called, with all humility and gentleness, with patience, bearing with one another in love."

WEEK 11 DAY 4 (THURSDAY)

KEY THOUGHT: God's own humility teaches us how to be humble.

DAILY READING

God asks you to wait upon and listen for Him. How can you hear a spirit Being who normally doesn't speak in words audible to your ears? Although this is a fair question, guard against doubting that God speaks to you.

First of all, don't be so proud to think that God must speak for your ears to hear. Is it not your heart that is the center of love? Is it not your heart that the Lord wants fully devoted to Him? Why not, then, expect the Lord to speak to your heart instead of to your ears? You may have heard others say they hear a still small voice in their hearts when God is speaking to them. The Lord wants you to hear Him this way as well. Is your heart soft and open to God? Are you being still, waiting, and expecting to hear from Him?

God also speaks to you while you are meditating upon His words in the Bible. At times when you read Scripture, your heart can melt as wax and even burn with unquenchable fire (Luke 24:32). Let your heart open up to God. It's time to put away pride and take on a humble heart that's fully dependent upon the Lord.

Do you want to see God? He's all around, and He reveals Himself to the humble, those who are thirsty for living water. Practice looking for Him. As you purpose to find God, you'll see the Lord's handiwork all around you. Ask God to open your eyes to the things He is doing. Look for and then thank the Lord throughout the day. You'll soon find that your praise can

WEEK 1........ WEEK 2........ WEEK 3........ WEEK 4........ WEEK 5........ WEEK 6........ WEEK 7........ WEEK 8........ WEEK 9........ WEEK 10........ WEEK 11 12

DAY 4

never cease. You could shout "Holy, holy, holy, Lord!" for millions of years and still not run out of reasons to praise Him for His flawless perfection in all that He is and does.

Turn to Appendix B and take time to read God's attributes, then return here.

Write out each attribute and express personal praise.

Attribute: _____
Praise:

_____

_____

Attribute: _____
Praise:

_____

_____

Attribute: _____
Praise:

_____

_____

Attribute: _____
Praise:

_____

_____

Attribute: _____
Praise:

_____

_____

WEEK 1 ...... WEEK 2 ...... WEEK 3 ...... WEEK 4 ...... WEEK 5 ...... WEEK 6 ...... WEEK 7 ...... WEEK 8 ...... WEEK 9 ...... WEEK 10 .... WEEK 11 ....12 WEEK

DAY 4

Do you see how humility toward God is not only appropriate but also fosters a reverence toward God? When we actually see God for who He is, it takes effort to suppress praise. As you stand in God's presence, shout out your praise! Allow your worship for God to passionately flow from your heart, lips, and hands.

HUMILITY

If you were on a swim team and Michael Phelps was also on that team, it wouldn't be weak to admit his strength or to select him to represent the team to swim against another team. You would clearly see the wisdom in this course of action. When it comes to spiritual matters, however, are you too proud to turn to God? Do you choose to fight Satan alone?

Humility appropriately recognizes your limitations. It also properly acknowledges good qualities in others and offers appropriate praises. We congratulate students on good grades, athletes on good performances, and chefs for good meals, yet we tend to withhold praise from God, who doesn't have a single flaw and performs works of might and wonder far beyond human abilities. It is time to re-evaluate the virtue of being humble before a mighty God. Allow this humility to bring about submission and obedience.

Humility is seeing yourself as your loving God sees you. Jot down notes describing how you've incorrectly viewed yourself (e.g., puffed up or self-righteous) and how you will now correctly see yourself through the lens of God (e.g., dearly loved, but a needy and dependent servant). Note, however, that humility is not about bashing yourself; it is all about being dependent upon God.

Jesus tells us this about being humble: "Take my yoke upon you and learn from me, for I am gentle and humble in heart, and you will find rest for your souls. For my yoke is easy and my burden light" (Matthew 11:29–30, NIV). Jesus Christ can tell you about humility because He set the perfect example for it. Jesus, who is God and created the world, chose to humble Himself by taking the form of a man so that you might live. Jesus didn't use His power to save Himself from persecution or His earthly body from death but was humble Himself to the point of being crucified as a sacrifice for you. Jesus endured scorn and ridicule and a death He didn't deserve, yet He didn't open His mouth in defense against false accusations (Acts 8:32). If He hadn't willingly been crucified for sins He didn't commit, you wouldn't have a Savior. Jesus humbly gave His life freely for you!

WEEK 1........ WEEK 2........ WEEK 3........ WEEK 4........ WEEK 5........ WEEK 6........ WEEK 7........ WEEK 8........ WEEK 9........WEEK 10 ....WEEK 11....WEEK 12

DAY 4

Read these verses on humility and record any insights:

"Humble yourselves, therefore, under God's mighty hand, that he may lift you up in due time" (1 Peter 5:6, NIV).

"Be completely humble and gentle; be patient, bearing with one another in love..." (Ephesians 4:2, NIV).

"Do everything without grumbling or arguing..." (Philippians 2:14, NIV).

"[4]Let each of you look not only to his own interests, but also to the interests of others. [5]Have this mind among yourselves, which is yours in Christ Jesus,[a] [6]who, though he was in the form of God, did not count equality with God a thing to be grasped,[b] [7]but emptied himself, by taking the form of a servant,[c] being born in the likeness of men. [8]And being found in human form, he humbled himself by becoming obedient to the point of death, even death on a cross" (Philippians 2:4–8, ESV).

"God opposes the proud but gives grace to the humble" (James 4:6, ESV).

Share your thoughts about God's humility.

_____

_____

The Lord doesn't sit in heaven waiting to whack anyone who asks for humility. True, sometimes God allows us to be knocked down a peg, and yes, it hurts at the moment; but this is not done out of vengeance or just to flatten us. Rather, God acts out of love, because "He guides the humble in what is right and teaches them His way..." (Psalm 25:9).

God seeks to build you up for use in His service. The Lord wants to perfect you. In fact, you're not usable for God's work when you're puffed up, running around, barking out orders as though you were the Commander in Chief, or developing your own plans apart from Him. Proven Women admit that God's ways are right, and they're glad that God humbles them. They continually ask for humility. We want God to lift us up more than we want to look good in the eyes of others. It's only when we are humble that God can work through us. Start viewing humility as a gift instead of a punishment. It's an opportunity for blessings!

WEEK 1........ WEEK 2........ WEEK 3........ WEEK 4........ WEEK 5........ WEEK 6........ WEEK 7........ WEEK 8........ WEEK 9........ WEEK 10........ **WEEK 11**.......WEEK 12

DAY 4

Here is another thought when it comes to humility. Sometimes people think that the opposite of pride is to have a low view of themselves. We hang our head and deny anything good about ourselves. We cannot take a compliment. We downplay success. But this is not true humility. Humility does not downplay things but gives credit where it is due. Someone once taught me that true humility includes gratitude. When someone compliments you, rather than shying away from the compliment, give God the credit in front of that person. When you see a victory in your life, don't gloat, but don't be in denial of the victory like it is no big deal. Praise God for the victory. God has given you talents, blessings, victories, and joys. Let's not boast. Let's not deny. Let's be grateful.

READ THE BIBLE

Is the Bible becoming your spiritual food as Christ said it should be (see Matthew 4:4)? Are you learning things about God and yourself through the readings? Spend some time reading Ephesians 4.

If you have time now or over the next several days, read through Psalm 27. Allow each verse to speak to your heart. Ask the Lord to open your heart to His love, perfection, and mercy. Commit every day to falling more deeply in love with God.

PRAY

Spend a few minutes right now asking God to humble you and give you a grateful spirit. Don't hold back. God created a way for you to relate to Him. Go to Him right now in relational prayer.

- Ask the Lord to fill you with His love.

- Express your love for God.

- Commit to being grateful and content.

- Listen for God. Ask Him to open your heart to Him; ask Him to reveal His will to you.

- Pray for others, including those who have hurt you.

WEEK 1........ WEEK 2........ WEEK 3........ WEEK 4........ WEEK 5........ WEEK 6........ WEEK 7........ WEEK 8........ WEEK 9........ WEEK 10 ....

WEEK 11

WEEK ..12

DAY 4

Record your prayers below.

_____

_____

_____

_____

_____

_____

_____

_____

_____

_____

_____

_____

_____

_____

_____

_____

MEMORY VERSE

Ephesians 4:1–2 (ESV): "I therefore, a prisoner for the Lord, urge you to walk in a manner worthy of the calling to which you have been called, with all humility and gentleness, with patience, bearing with one another in love."

WEEK 11 DAY 5 (FRIDAY)

KEY THOUGHT: Jesus calls us to follow Him away from our loneliness and into true peace.

DAILY READING

Do you view the command to pick up your cross daily and follow Christ as harsh? Perhaps you liken it to a contest to see who can withstand the most pain in trying to earn love. Jesus was not referring to physical pain but to dying to self in order to follow Him fully. This is a good thing when we realize that He is true life. Denying ourselves is denying the sinful works of the flesh that bring destruction to our lives. Allowing Christ to live through us brings about the fruit of the Spirit—love, joy, peace, patience, kindness, goodness, faithfulness, meekness, and self-control. He brings beauty where we bring division and harshness.

When Jesus says, "Take my yoke upon you," His desire is to lighten your load, not increase your burden (Matthew 11:30). To be honest, I didn't understand this verse when I was younger. Jesus calls us to come to Him when we are weary. We are to come to Him and take his yoke upon us because His burden is light. Before I understood grace, I didn't like this verse because I felt like His burden was what was exhausting me. I was trying so hard to live up to His expectations and make Him happy, and it was hard. I had no idea how His burden could be light. But someone finally taught me the truth behind this verse. A yoke is a contraption that links two animals together so that they can work together to shoulder a burden. Jesus wasn't asking me to take His burden on myself. He was asking me to yoke in with Him. When I do this, Jesus carries the entire burden on His shoulders while I walk alongside Him. But, this does require that I walk with Jesus. As soon as I walk away, the weight of the world is back on my shoulders.

WEEK 1 ..... WEEK 2 ..... WEEK 3 ..... WEEK 4 ..... WEEK 5 ..... WEEK 6 ..... WEEK 7 ..... WEEK 8 ..... WEEK 9 ..... WEEK 10 ..... WEEK 11 ..... WEEK 12

DAY 5

Jesus invites you to join your life with His. You take up the cross not by carrying it but by yielding to Jesus. You allow the Lord to supply the power. He provides the direction and carries the burden. You do, however, need to die to lust for the world and replace it with a longing for the Lord. Pray for this transformation of heart. You cannot replace these feelings on your own. You must stay in His camp to enjoy His protection and peace. Your will must bend to His, because only one can lead at a time. Start following the Lord and letting Him carry the load.

Chances are great that you have recently experienced, or are presently going through, a trial. List what you commonly do when facing a trial. For instance, do you rejoice, go numb, escape into fantasy, curse God, weep bitterly, engage in self-protection, or enlist others to defend you?

_____

_____

_____

_____

_____

_____

_____

You should expect trials, which have a divine purpose. Open your heart to what God says about trials: "Consider it pure joy, my brothers, whenever you face trials of many kinds, because you know that the testing of your faith develops perseverance. Perseverance must finish its work so that you may be mature and complete, not lacking anything. If any of you lacks wisdom, he should ask God, who gives generously to all without finding fault, and it will be given to him" (James 1:2–5, ESV).

It seems strange to expect joy during trials. This notion must truly come from God. However, be careful not to confuse joy with happiness. The world seeks happiness and quick fixes.

WEEK 1 .... WEEK 2 .... WEEK 3 .... WEEK 4 .... WEEK 5 .... WEEK 6 .... WEEK 7 .... WEEK 8 .... WEEK 9 .... WEEK 10 .... WEEK 11 .... WEEK 12

DAY 5

Joy, on the other hand, comes from an eternal perspective and from intimately experiencing God. Joy is not dependent upon circumstances, whether good or bad. Joy is finding contentment in all circumstances because you have yielded to the Lord and are no longer frantically trying to protect your so-called rights.

An example of joy not being dependent upon good circumstances includes the time when Jesus sent out some seventy people to do His work in nearby towns. He had given them power to perform miracles. An interesting interplay occurs when they return. Read carefully what transpires in Luke 10:17–20. The seventy return with joy and say to Jesus, "Lord, even the demons submit to us in your name." In response, Jesus says, "Do not rejoice that the spirits submit to you, but rejoice that your names are written in heaven." Contemplate this response, and then state why you think Christ spoke of this eternal perspective.

An example of joy not being rebuffed by bad circumstances is the life of Paul, who said while imprisoned and in chains, "I will continue to rejoice, for I know that through our prayers and the help given by the Spirit of Jesus Christ, what has happened to me will turn out for my deliverance" (Philippians 1:18–19, NIV). Paul also exhorted his readers (from his prison cell!): "Rejoice in the Lord always" (Philippians 4:4, NIV). Therefore, you can and should choose joy at all times in your life. You are responsible for your attitude and perspective. Rely on the Lord and keep an eternal focus. Choose to be joyful always. It's a decision you can make, provided you are acting in the strength of the Lord.

HEARTWORK

Chances are that you've had some moments of victory in your life, perhaps even months at a time, yet the same sin or a similar one usually makes its way back home. Why? It's never enough to empty yourself of temptation or evil. The Lord warns that a house swept clean is waiting, almost begging, to be filled with something (Matthew 12:43–45). If you throw out all pornography and make every effort to rid your life of things that were used in the rituals of sexual sins, you're an empty house. Unless you fill your heart, mind, and soul with the Lord, evil will return in even greater force than before. Therefore, fill your house daily with exalting Christ and loving others. Read the Bible to meet with God. The Bible is active and alive, so let it penetrate your soul. Honor God by treating your body as a temple where God resides. Prepare your mind by inviting and including the Lord in all you do, think, or say. Learn to pray continually by openly talking to God and dwelling upon Him throughout the day. Also, tell Him about everything in your life. In short, choose the one

WEEK 1........ WEEK 2........ WEEK 3........ WEEK 4........ WEEK 5....... WEEK 6........ WEEK 7........ WEEK 8........ WEEK 9........ WEEK 10 .... WEEK 11 12

DAY 5

master you will serve. Then live wholeheartedly for Him! Don't merely seek to rid yourself of temptation, but passionately pursue a real and active relationship with the living God.

READ THE BIBLE

Read Ephesians 5. Sing out to the Lord in your heart.

As part of a plan of praying continually, make time today or tonight to "pray-read" the names of God (Appendix A). Speak each of His names to Him in a loving and adoring manner. Give Him glory. Right now, make a decision to pursue a loving relationship with God the Father and Jesus His Son. Then put it into practice by spending time meeting with and experiencing God.

PRAY

Today, write out a prayer of praise. If you have a journal, then write it out there.

_____

_____

_____

_____

_____

_____

_____

TESTIMONY

When I was a little girl, I remember sweeping trash one night outside of my parent's convenient store. I couldn't have been more than nine years old. As I was minding my own business, my eye caught glimpse of a limo pulling in. The windows were tinted and I couldn't see anything inside, but I did see an image on a T.V. screen that I didn't fully understand. Out of curiosity, I took a step closer to the limo when all of a sudden the window cracked open and I heard a man's voice say, "get lost kid!"

I was humiliated and confused. What was I looking at? Why did I want more?

As I reflect back on this one story, I can't help but think of the ways that sin violates us. I'm not trying to claim that I was without sin, but at that moment, I remember that my innocence felt taken advantage of. My involuntary exposure to pornography led to a trail of curiosity, and eventually a portfolio of sin, but there was still something there that called out to give me a chance to escape.

Proven Women has helped to provide an escape from the sin I have been exposed to, and the sin I am guilty of. This community has given me a chance to face the skeletons in my closet, which I wished no one would ever see. I have found the freedom to do more than "get lost", but to be found! I have the courage to be known and the desire to let others know that they can be known too.

Passionate for God,
Repentant in spirit,
Open and honest,
Victorious in living,
Eternal in perspective, and
Networking with other ***PROVEN Women.***

PW

WEEK TWELVE

MEMORY VERSE

Ephesians 5:3 (ESV): "But sexual immorality and all impurity or covetousness must not even be named among you, as is proper among saints."

WEEK 12 DAY 1 (MONDAY)

KEY THOUGHT: Being a disciple of Jesus means always learning to love God and others.

DAILY READING

You're nearing the end of this Proven Women study. Do you see that your heart is changing? Keep asking the Lord to renew your mind and transform your will to be conformed to His.

The primary lesson for you this week is to be prepared to keep applying what you've learned in this study for the rest of your life (James 1:22). The second lesson is to be committed to networking with other Proven Men and Women in order to minister to others more effectively.

Do you have a burden for other people? As you begin taking the focus off yourself, you'll see great pain in the lives of others. You'll also start seeing people as dearly loved children of God and not as objects for your pleasure or your competition. The more you yield to God, the more you experience His divine nature, including His compassion.

Meditate upon the following passage: "Praise be to the God and Father of our Lord Jesus Christ, the Father of compassion and the God of all comfort, who comforts us in all our troubles, so that we can comfort those in any trouble with the comfort we ourselves have received from God. For just as the sufferings of Christ flow into our lives, so also through Christ our comfort overflows" (2 Corinthians 1:3–5, NIV).

WEEK 1........ WEEK 2........ WEEK 3........ WEEK 4........ WEEK 5........ WEEK 6........ WEEK 7........ WEEK 8........ WEEK 9........ WEEK 10 .... WEEK 11.....

WEEK 12

DAY 1

List what God does for you in times of trouble and state how He uses your troubles for good.

_____

_____

_____

Did you notice that as a Christian, you're not exempt from suffering? God warns you in advance that you'll suffer. God likens your difficulties to Christ's sufferings, which He says flow into your life. As the sufferings keep flowing into you, they need to be released or you'll grow bitter as you hold in all of your pain. God has a perfect plan for refreshing you by washing out your sufferings and any bitterness or anger as you extend comfort and compassion to others.

In one of the previous weeks, we talked about God being the God of comfort. Before we turn outwardly and comfort others, we need to sit and allow God and others to comfort us in our times of need. But as we find healing, there will come a time when God wants you to be that person who can help and comfort others. Eventually, God tells you to comfort others with the same comfort He granted to you. As you do, this extension of outward comfort to others continues to wash out the pain of your underlying trials and sufferings. If you don't extend yourself to other people, you bottle up the pain inside.

Consider the analogy of the Dead Sea. It's a tremendous body of water that has all of the elements for sustaining abundant life; yet it's dead because, unlike other seas, it's fed by many inlets but has no outlets feeding other waterways. By permitting incoming water and having no outflowing tributaries, the Dead Sea retains heavy quantities of salt and other impurities that kill life.

How about you? Do you merely want to hold inside of you all the blessings the Lord bestows upon you? If so, your refusal to look to the interests of others and extend heartfelt comfort and compassion is a restriction of the outflow, thus causing bitter waters and contaminants to remain inside your soul. Is any part of this true for you? State any prayers or commitments for releasing His blessing through your life into others. Talk to God right now.

WEEK 1........ WEEK 2........ WEEK 3........ WEEK 4........ WEEK 5........ WEEK 6........ WEEK 7........ WEEK 8........ WEEK 9........ WEEK 10........ WEEK 11........ **WEEK 12**

DAY 1

HELPING OTHERS

As a person is healed from a trouble, she generally longs to see others rescued from the same thing. For instance, when people first become Christians, they are excited to share their faith with others. They want their friends to know the great depth of God's love for them as well as the truth about the one and only way to Him: trusting in Jesus alone—not leaning on good deeds—for forgiveness of sin and reconciliation to God. Sadly, regardless of the level of your excitement, not everyone wants to hear about the Lord. What seems so clear to a believer remains hidden to non-Christians. For example, even though the Gospel of John states several times that a person must trust in Jesus alone by God's Spirit in order to be saved (John 3:3–16; 6:53; 11:25–27; 14:6), not all who read it choose to see it.

The same is true for those trapped in sexual sins. Now that you are finding freedom, you may want to help others find freedom. Some, however, aren't open to seeing their sin. They refuse to accept that the healing path requires total surrender over all aspects of their life to the Lord. They simply aren't willing to do whatever it takes to experience lasting freedom. Even reading this 12-week study won't change a person who doesn't want God to change her. Just as you can lead a horse to water but cannot make it drink, you can present the cool stream of living water to people trapped in sexual bondage, but you cannot force them to repent and turn to God.

HEARTWORK

Although your heart can be grieved over a dear friend who refuses God's mercy, grace, and healing, you shouldn't and cannot judge them. Don't forget that many of us have spent nearly a lifetime of self-centered living, including years of clinging to pornography, masturbation, lust, or fantasy. You must not force healing upon them. They need to be ready to repent and replace their selfish life with a Proven life and then make this decision of their own accord.

That doesn't mean there's nothing you can do for those who are still too proud and stubborn to yield to God. First and foremost, you can and should pray. As you're learning, only the Lord can change a heart. The good news is that prayer moves God to act. The perseverance you are developing through trials and by working through this Heartwork study will greatly benefit you now. It may take many hours, or even years, of praying to see fruit in another's life. Don't give up!

WEEK 1........ WEEK 2........ WEEK 3........ WEEK 4........ WEEK 5........ WEEK 6........ WEEK 7........ WEEK 8........ WEEK 9........ WEEK 10 .... WEEK 11..... **WEEK 12**

DAY 1

Second, continue living out a Proven life. Often, the only thing that others accept as proof of God's ability to change them is seeing another changed life. Let the light of God shine through you. As you yield control to God, you'll be changed from the inside out. Where you were once arrogant and sought praise, you're now becoming kind, gentle, compassionate, and caring. The change will be obvious to other proud men and women. They'll wonder what the source of the peace (and even joy) you have in your new position of humility is. And you'll be watched. After hearing your testimony, some will sit back and watch for several months before believing that your faith and new Proven life are real. Only when they are satisfied that you have changed and won't judge them will they take the risk of accepting help. Expect that many will still remain guarded as they share portions of their lives with you. They'll give some details and wait to test your reaction. The good news is that the unconditional love and non-judgmental heart that the Lord is forming in you can cut through some of the hardest defenses in those finally ready to do business with God.

Do you want to see others healed? As you tilt the mirror upward toward God and off of yourself, you'll want to love and serve others. The reflection they'll see is that of Christ, not you. The Lord wants to use you as His arms to hold and comfort the hurting. If you want to be used by God in the healing process in others' lives, pray specifically for the Lord to humble you and use you to work in other women. Your greatest need is not education or training, but to be filled by and to follow the leading of the Holy Spirit. To be used by God, you must know Him and live a life punctuated by prayer and praise. Therefore, make it your purpose to seek God with all of your heart, to yield total control, and to live by His Spirit. As you do, you're becoming more complete, stamped by God and ready to serve. What a privilege awaits!

N is for Networking with Other Proven Women. You have a role in networking with and encouraging others to become Proven. God will use your pain and struggles to help other women trapped in sexual bondage. Your life will be a shining example and a ray of hope. That's right! God will use your story to guide and encourage others just as He is using mine. Be sure that you're an encourager and a source of strength to others, rather than someone who complains, tears down, or destroys. Finally, stay connected with other Proven Women. Don't cut the cord and seek to strike out on your own. Remain part of the team. Be sure to encourage and strengthen other Proven Women; we all need continual encouragement.

WEEK 1........ WEEK 2........ WEEK 3........ WEEK 4........ WEEK 5........ WEEK 6........ WEEK 7........ WEEK 8........ WEEK 9........ WEEK 10....... WEEK 11......

WEEK 12

DAY 1

READ THE BIBLE

Read and listen for what God is saying to you. Then meditate upon what He reveals. Ask Him to talk to you. Read Ephesians 2 again. Be willing to slow down or stop when God presses something on your heart. It's communion with the Lord that counts, not the number of verses you read. Ask God to bring deep gratitude to your heart for the gospel as you read this chapter.

PRAY

Open your heart to the Lord. Keep communicating with Him for five to ten minutes.

- Ask God to make His will and plan for your life clear to you.

- Pray for His leading and direction.

- Commit to waiting upon the Lord.

- Keep this goal always before you: To make loving and pursuing God your number one priority for the rest of your life. Then you will recognize His voice and calling.

- Keep praying for others with a heart of compassion. (List them to help you remain focused.)

_____

_____

_____

SPECIAL NOTE:

You'll always make mistakes and offend people when you minister to others, but when you lead with your heart and minister in the Lord's strength, you'll be able to win many of your sisters. Set the example of saying, "I was wrong; please forgive me." Don't wait for a brother or sister to be more mature than you. Even if she was 90 percent at fault, always be the peacemaker and the one seeking reconciliation. "If it is possible, as far as it depends upon you, live at peace with everyone" (Romans 12:18, NIV).

MEMORY VERSE

Ephesians 5:3 (ESV): "But sexual immorality and all impurity or covetousness must not even be named among you, as is proper among saints."

WEEK 12 DAY 2 (TUESDAY)

KEY THOUGHT: Staying in relationship with God and others will continue to set us free.

Yesterday, you read the good news that God intends on using your victory through failures and struggles to help others (2 Corinthians 1:3–5). However, the Lord works through you only when you are living out a Proven life. This is because a proud person will stumble and lead others astray (Matthew 15:14). A humble, needy, and dependent servant, on the other hand, is the strongest woman on God's team. Today you'll learn more about your role in helping others.

DAILY READING

As you minister to others facing struggles with sexual temptations, be on guard against all forms of pride. Here are some common traps:

- Comparing yourself to others.

- Wanting to be seen as an expert.

- Seeking praise from others.

- Overlooking your own sins.

- Becoming so busy working for God that you stop meeting with Him.

Never forget that healing and spiritual maturity are lifetime processes. Your battle against sin is not over and will never end. Victory lasts only while you stay under God's wing, so expect a fight. Expect that as you hear the stories of others, you'll be exposed to sexual topics that can tempt you to fantasize and leave God's camp. Satan doesn't want you to be helping others he is trying to keep trapped in sin. The devil wants to distract you and

WEEK 1....... WEEK 2....... WEEK 3....... WEEK 4....... WEEK 5....... WEEK 6....... WEEK 7....... WEEK 8....... WEEK 9....... WEEK 10....... WEEK 11....... **WEEK 12**

DAY 2

make you fall. The Bible cautions us to be especially careful when seeking to restore a fallen sister because you might be tempted in the same way. (Galatians 6:1, ESV—"Brothers, if anyone is caught in any transgression, you who are spiritual should restore him in a spirit of gentleness. Keep watch on yourself, lest you too be tempted.")

If you get puffed up, God will allow you to deal with temptation in your own strength and stumble, even though He longs for you to turn to Him in humility. He won't rescue you if you wear a banner of pride; yet the Lord is faithful and true to forgive a repentant person. God wants you to be victorious. Therefore, don't throw in the towel if you have a setback. Rather, take on an eternal perspective that the goal is living intimately with God and receiving His righteousness. A setback should not deflate you but instead, motivate you further to sprint to God for help in becoming even more repentant, needy, and dependent upon the Lord. Consider these practical points for ministering to others:

HEARTWORK

1. Don't wait until you are perfect. Pride says you must be perfect in the eyes of others. Don't hold back from ministering to others or even leading a small group because you don't have formal training or a degree. The Holy Spirit is your best guide. If you're humble and demonstrate true love for others, you'll make a good and godly leader. Be willing to say that you're not an expert but rather a dependent servant of God looking to link up with other women who want to seek God with all of their hearts. Approaching others on equal footing can break down barriers for some. No one really wants to be lectured by someone who never struggles or who merely points out their flaws. It's unconditional love and kindness that lead people to repentance and draw them to the one place where healing occurs. Show that type of love to others, and they'll want the same Proven life that's being formed in you. (If you are thinking of hosting a small recovery group, obtain a copy of the Leader's Guide to this study, available through online bookstores or at *www.provenwomen.org*.)

2. Be open and honest, vulnerable and real. This example is so important for others to see and follow. Most people who struggle with sexual impurity are running from intimacy. They don't know how to be vulnerable. Most women who are wrestling with this issue are scared to death to open up because they believe they are the only woman struggling in this area. They need to hear from someone who is open and honest. This

WEEK WEEK WEEK WEEK WEEK WEEK WEEK WEEK WEEK WEEK WEEK WEEK
1........2........3........4........5........6........7........8........9........10........11..... 12

DAY 2

will encourage them to also be open and honest. Lack of vulnerability will thwart the healing process for both parties. In addition, love covers a multitude of sins (1 Peter 4:8). If you're speaking the truth in love (Ephesians 4:15) and others know you really want them to succeed, they can overlook some mistakes you'll make. At the same time, you should be repentant. For instance, if you use a shaming technique or judge the women in your group at any point, confess it and seek their forgiveness. Similarly, regularly confess to them your struggles, sins, and setbacks. Practice and model real repentance, such as being truly sorrowful for turning away from God and then racing back to Him.

3. Lead with your heart, not your head. Many seek to serve the Lord, but a woman of God is one who seeks Him with all of her heart. Your heart matters most to God. That's the place where He meets you. The same applies in times you're asked to speak or teach: Do so with your heart. Don't memorize speeches, but communicate from your heart. Teach others about the heart of God and how to possess a passionate, repentant, and open spirit. In all you do, do it out of a soft heart.

4. Practice and teach James 1:22 (NIV), which says, "Do not merely listen to the word, and so deceive yourselves. Do what it says." How often do we say to others: "I encourage you to read the Bible and pray"? And yet, how little do we do such things each day? Let's become doers of the Word. The Heartwork study is filled with many truths about the healing path, but it requires action in addition to desire. As for you, a fellow servant, you must act and carry out the commands of God as you encourage others to follow the same path. Never forget that head knowledge won't heal but will deceive. Love others well by practicing what you teach.

5. Teach others what it means to live a Proven life. We connect to God and receive Him into our lives through passionate praise and worship. A repentant spirit kills the pride that feeds on selfishness, which births sexual sin. Openness and honesty foster relationships that bring healing and replace the false intimacy we used as substitutes for the void in our lives. Victory is not won by a program but by yielding our life to a perfect and good God. Share the eternal perspective that we were created for a relationship with God and others. Make it your goal to point women to a real, deep, and intimate relationship with God. There's no other way to have continuous healing from the wounds of life or to be free to experience God. Knowing God, which is far different from knowing about Him, is life (John 17:3). Finally, for the rest of your life keep networking and connecting with other women.

WEEK 1........ WEEK 2........ WEEK 3........ WEEK 4........ WEEK 5........ WEEK 6........ WEEK 7........ WEEK 8........ WEEK 9........ WEEK 10........ WEEK 11.....

WEEK 12

DAY 2

6. Pray for others. This will be one of your most treasured duties, because only the Lord can change and heal a person. Therefore, spend time petitioning God on behalf of others. Be devoted to prayer! Along the same lines, be sure to communicate with these women during the week.

Be sure that when you talk to others, it's with a message that Jesus loves them unconditionally and is the only true source of healing. Explain to others that with Christ, hope is a promise and transformation is His delight. God will change anyone who yields to the Spirit of God and makes pursuing the Lord and His love her top priority in life. Make these things true in your life!

Ephesians 5:19–20 (NIV) teaches ways to be an encourager: "Speak to one another with psalms, hymns and spiritual songs. Sing and make music in your heart to the Lord, always giving thanks to God the Father for everything, in the name of our Lord Jesus Christ." If you're writing and singing psalms and hymns from your heart, and you're constantly giving thanks to God, you'll be a joyful person and a joy to be around. People will want to follow your example. Right now, commit to being an encourager and an encouragement. Your responsibilities include wearing compassion, kindness, humility, gentleness, and patience; to bear with and forgive one another; and to be self-controlled (Colossians 3:12–14; Ephesians 4:2.) Will you put on such things? Write out your commitment to pursuing God with all your heart and mind.

READ THE BIBLE

Read Ephesians 3. Take time to meditate and pray through the prayer that goes from verse 14 through the end of the chapter. Meditate on the truth that God can "do immeasurably more than all we ask or imagine" (verse 20). Ask God to expand your comprehension of His love.

PRAY

Engage in true relational prayers with your Lord.

- Ask God to open your heart to what love really is instead of false intimacy.

- Honestly evaluate your life in light of the Scriptures you read today.

- Confess ways you have not been patient or kind and how you have not protected others.

WEEK 1........ WEEK 2........ WEEK 3........ WEEK 4........ WEEK 5........ WEEK 6........ WEEK 7........ WEEK 8........ WEEK 9........ WEEK 10........ WEEK 11........ **WEEK 12**

DAY 2

Record your prayers below.

_____

_____

_____

_____

_____

_____

_____

_____

_____

_____

_____

_____

_____

_____

_____

_____

_____

_____

MEMORY VERSE

Ephesians 5:3 (ESV): "But sexual immorality and all impurity or covetousness must not even be named among you, as is proper among saints."

WEEK 12 DAY 3 (WEDNESDAY)

KEY THOUGHT: Discipleship is not a 12-Week study, it is a lifelong journey.

DAILY READING

Do you have a heart that is passionate for God? Right now, read "Developing a Heart of Worship" in Appendix D.

In the space below, prepare your own game plan for developing a heart of worship for God.

_____

_____

_____

_____

_____

HEARTWORK

ARE YOU LIVING A VICTORIOUS LIFE?

- If you're not walking in victory, what role model is there to follow?

WEEK 1 ...... WEEK 2 ...... WEEK 3 ...... WEEK 4 ...... WEEK 5 ...... WEEK 6 ...... WEEK 7 ...... WEEK 8 ...... WEEK 9 ...... WEEK 10 ...... WEEK 11 ...... **WEEK 12**

DAY 3

- The prayer of a righteous man is powerful and effective because it's heard by God (James 5:16).

- Seek God's righteousness by pursuing Him faithfully.

- To live by the Spirit is to walk in victory (Galatians 5:16). Don't walk, run to God! He never turns you away.

DO YOU HAVE AN ETERNAL PERSPECTIVE?

- Dwell on the fact that your home is in heaven. Put aside greed and the worries of this world.

- Do you truly know that God is good, and do you trust Him with all of your life?

- What is the primary purpose for your life? Have you shared with others your life goals?

- Are you investing your life in the lives of others, both in quality and quantity of time?

- Married women, are you the primary person responsible for nurturing your children? This includes loving them while helping them to discern right from wrong according to God's standards and teaching them about the knowledge and fear of God. Church youth groups support but don't replace the role and responsibility that you and your husband have to your children before God.

ARE YOU NETWORKING WITH OTHER PROVEN WOMEN?

- Are you investing your life in the lives of other women?

- Do you have close and intimate female friends?

- Are you vulnerable and even transparent with an accountability (network) partner?

This 12-week study is nearly over, so commit to repeating this Heartwork study or list your next study: _____

Will you commit to passing on a heart of worship to others, including your children? The second of the Ten Commandments states: "You shall not make for yourself an image in the form of anything in heaven above or on the earth beneath or in the waters below. ⁵You shall not bow down to them or worship them; for I, the Lord your God, am a jealous God, punishing the children for the sin of the parents to the third and fourth generation of those who hate me, ⁶but showing love to a thousand generations of those who love me and keep my commandments" (Exodus 20:4–6, NIV).

WEEK 1........ WEEK 2........ WEEK 3........ WEEK 4........ WEEK 5........ WEEK 6........ WEEK 7........ WEEK 8........ WEEK 9........ WEEK 10........ WEEK 11........ **WEEK 12**

DAY 3

God tells us that if we are idolaters, we will pass our sins down to our children and their children. Whether you are a mom or a future mom, ask God to help you protect their little minds from the things that ensnared you. If they walked in on you watching television, would it feed lust in their minds? Children pick up many habits from their parents. The good news is that if we turn to God, giving up our idols and loving the Lord with all of our hearts, God will show such great love and mercy to us that our children and their children will also be blessed.

READ THE BIBLE

Use the Bible as a way of getting to know and love God. Read Ephesians 4.

PRAY

Spend five or ten minutes talking to God. Ask Him to reveal any generational sins such as pride, greed, or lust. Ask Him to break them. Give total control to God and hold nothing back. Be committed to being stamped Proven.

- Pray for your children (or future children) and your spiritual children.

- Pray for your spouse (or future spouse).

- Pray for other Proven Women.

- Pray for your pastor.

- Pray for missionaries.

- Pray for others. (List them here.)

_____

_____

_____

WEEK 1........ WEEK 2........ WEEK 3........ WEEK 4........ WEEK 5........ WEEK 6........ WEEK 7........ WEEK 8........ WEEK 9........ WEEK 10........ WEEK 11..... WEEK 12

DAY 3

SPECIAL NOTE:

If you're a self-seeker, you'll pass down to your children and others the ways of the world and a life of discontentment. But if you die to yourself and are living by the Spirit, however, you'll pass on to them blessings upon blessings. It's really your choice. How selfish are you going to be? There are several things you can do for your children and others. First, live out the love of Christ. People, including children, know the difference between preaching and teaching. They know when you're real. How about it, are your faith and actions real?

Are you setting boundaries for your children or others you influence to keep them safe? These include:

- Knowing their friends.

- Installing internet blocks on all home computers and cell phones. Not allowing screens into the bedroom.

- Setting and enforcing curfews.

Be sure that you don't rely upon boundaries alone to protect your children or other people you influence. Just as setting boundaries doesn't turn away your own sensual desires, boundaries won't get rid of their sin nature either (Colossians 2:20–23). If you set rules such as no R-rated movies but then constantly slander other people in the home, what have you taught them? If you require them to go to church but you don't love God with all of your heart, won't they see church as something people just have to do?

Two of the best examples you can set for children are: (1) gently loving your children's father if he is in your life (if children know that their parents love each other, they feel safe, secure, and loved), and (2) showing sincere interest in their activities and achievements.

A few other ways of cultivating a heart of worship in your children (or spiritual children) include:

- Praying with them daily.

- Helping them select a daily devotional.

- Allowing them to see you in prayer and study.

WEEK 1........ WEEK 2........ WEEK 3........ WEEK 4........ WEEK 5........ WEEK 6........ WEEK 7........ WEEK 8........ WEEK 9........ WEEK 10........ WEEK 11..... WEEK 12

DAY 3

- Monitoring your inputs and theirs, including movies, TV, internet, books, magazines, and music.

- Attending church with your children. It's okay to make it a rule that your children will attend church, but also look for ways to make the experience real, meaningful, and enjoyable.

Part of training is explaining. Be ready to tell others why you do the above things. People need to understand the "why" before they can embrace these things themselves. Also, explain why we need to be humble, gentle, kind and patient. Write out your reasons to some of these items and then set aside "couch time" to discuss them as a family.

_____

_____

_____

_____

_____

_____

_____

_____

_____

_____

_____

MEMORY VERSE

Ephesians 5:3 (ESV): "But sexual immorality and all impurity or covetousness must not even be named among you, as is proper among saints."

WEEK 12 DAY 4 (THURSDAY)

KEY THOUGHT: Practicing purity means practicing wisdom in the way we live.

It's time to tear down and remove all idols in your life. With respect to the memory verse, what will you do to remove any hint of sexual immorality? For example, use an internet block, don't watch certain movies, stop coarse joking, and be wholly devoted to your husband if married. Removing hints of sexual sin also includes not being alone with men other than your spouse, not flirting, not taking second looks, not allowing yourself to enjoy the attention of the wrong men in your life. What other things will you remove or decide not to do to live as a pleasing sacrifice to the Lord? Don't be fooled. Where your mind or eyes wander reveals which master you're serving. List other ways to live in holiness and then make a game plan to carry out your goals.

DAILY READING

Let's review the big picture. Read Psalm 101 again. This starts out with worship and then warns against the things that will pull us away from worship.

What do you understand better now than you did twelve weeks ago?

_____

_____

_____

_____

WEEK 1........ WEEK 2........ WEEK 3........ WEEK 4........ WEEK 5........ WEEK 6........ WEEK 7........ WEEK 8........ WEEK 9........ WEEK 10........ WEEK 11........ **WEEK 12**

DAY 4

What will you do to remove any hints of the idol of greed from in your life? Greed could show up in your life in comparison to other women, fretting over finances and bills, fantasizing about becoming "the fairest of them all," or engaging in get-(rich, fit, or fixed) quick schemes. Choose to be content. Make this a firm decision.

We hope this series has consistently pointed you toward your real home in heaven and that you are experiencing new freedom. Always remember that healing is a work of God and that you must keep turning to and pursuing Him with all of your heart.

HEARTWORK

Make a covenant similar to this: Each new day the Lord gives me I will actively live out of His love for me instead of the lies of the world.

Remember the PROVEN acronym when you are no longer going through this workbook. Write out the importance of each of the things below in your own words.

Passionate for God

_____

_____

Repentant in spirit

_____

_____

Open and honest

_____

_____

WEEK 1........ WEEK 2........ WEEK 3........ WEEK 4........ WEEK 5........ WEEK 6........ WEEK 7........ WEEK 8........ WEEK 9........ WEEK 10 .... WEEK 11...... **WEEK 12**

DAY 4

Victorious in living

_____

_____

Eternal in perspective

_____

_____

Networked with other PROVEN WOMEN.

_____

_____

By living a Proven life, although you may be tempted daily, you'll be an approved workman who passes the test (2 Timothy 2:15). You can do this!

READ THE BIBLE

Read Ephesians 5. Hopefully you read this passage with new eyes as we have talked about God's design of marriage. Record any insights.

_____

_____

_____

_____

WEEK 1........ WEEK 2........ WEEK 3........ WEEK 4........ WEEK 5........ WEEK 6........ WEEK 7........ WEEK 8........ WEEK 9........ WEEK 10 .... WEEK 11 ....

WEEK 12

DAY 4

PRAY

Use Psalm 119:1–16 as a model. Talk to God about the new course of your life.

MEMORY VERSE

Ephesians 5:3 (ESV): "But sexual immorality and all impurity or covetousness must not even be named among you, as is proper among saints."

WEEK 12 DAY 5 (FRIDAY)

KEY THOUGHT: It is never about being perfect, it is always about being His.

Review all of your memory verses. Do you have all twelve memorized? If so, you'll be like the psalmist: "I have hidden your word in my heart that I might not sin against you" (Psalm 119:11). Keep referring to them so they become powerful reminders of truth. Write them out and post them around your house and in your car.

DAILY READING

One theme verse for Proven Ministries is 2 Timothy 2:15 (ESV): "Do your best to present yourself to God as one approved, a workman who does not need to be ashamed and who correctly handles the word of truth." You're now part of the Proven Ministries team, stamped approved by God. There's no need to be ashamed. You correctly handle the word of truth because you are living it out; you're doing what it says. God is becoming a real and intimate friend. You have been and are continuing to be transformed.

A gentle reminder: If you don't feel like a spiritual giant yet, that's okay. We are all a work in progress, and this growth will last for our entire lives. God is not concerned about how long your growth it is taking. He is concerned with whether or not you are turning to Him in your times of struggle. God wants you to love and worship Him. He desires to walk every step with you.

You can and need to count on God's promises. They must and will come to pass. Be still and rest in the Lord. Spiritual maturity is an ongoing and lifelong process. You will grow. Don't be impatient with yourself or with God. Keep staying the course. Victory is assured!

WEEK 1........ WEEK 2........ WEEK 3........ WEEK 4........ WEEK 5........ WEEK 6........ WEEK 7........ WEEK 8........ WEEK 9........ WEEK 10....... WEEK 11......

WEEK 12

DAY 5

If you experience a setback, don't quit. Instead, use it as a wake-up call that you always need God. This is a daily battle. But even when it doesn't seem like a battle, we are meant to daily walk with the Lord. **There is not a day in your life when you are not meant to rely on God.** We fall when we take the focus off of the Lord and put it back on ourselves or our circumstances.

Renew your heart and mind by going back to the source of life each time you fall. Don't get discouraged if it feels like a daily fight to remain in purity. God delights in your standing steadfast with Him. He isn't frustrated with you that this is still hard. Remember, God is interested in a relationship with you, not merely knowing that you don't commit or struggle with a particular sin. When you get complacent or live in your own strength, you're ripe for a fall; but don't throw in the towel. Accept discipline from the One who loves you and is seeking to draw you back (Hebrews 12:5–6). Keep growing in a deeper, dependent relationship with the Lord.

Recall two of the main reasons God created you: (1) to worship and glorify God, and (2) to be His child and friend (Matthew 4:10; James 2:23; John 1:12; and 1 John 3:1). Consider again how knowing these purposes for living gives you freedom and meaning in life. When you fight against this purpose, you fight against God. Always remember that the Lord wants you to turn to Him in love and fellowship and that He is patient and forgiving. The process of putting away idols and passionately seeking the Lord is what makes you whole and complete, bearing spiritual fruit instead of turning to selfish actions.

Don't ever lose sight of what it means to be PROVEN: **Passionately** pursuing God; **Repenting** when you fail; being **Open** and honest with your feelings and communication; walking in His **Victory**; keeping an **Eternal** perspective; and loving and serving, like **Networking** with others. This model is not just for those desiring sexual purity; it's what all of God's children are called to be. Live a Proven life. Test your life regularly against each letter of the PROVEN acronym, using it as a way to check the condition of your heart and as a reminder to embrace each of these elements.

HEARTWORK

Take a stand. Tell Satan, "No more ground!" Make an irrevocable commitment that pornography, masturbation, and sexual immorality of any kind are not an option in your life. Make absolute purity your spiritual act of worship (Romans 12:1–2).

WEEK 1........ WEEK 2........ WEEK 3........ WEEK 4........ WEEK 5........ WEEK 6........ WEEK 7........ WEEK 8........ WEEK 9........ WEEK 10 .... WEEK 11..... WEEK 12

DAY 5

Spend the last bit of time in this study worshiping God. Be in awe of Him. Read the names of God with passion and pleasure (see Appendix A) and get to know His perfect attributes (see Appendix B).

Use the space below to make a game plan, write a note to God, and chart a course for your life.

_____

_____

_____

_____

_____

_____

READ THE BIBLE

Read Ephesians 6. Remember, even though this study is ending today, God goes with you every single day into this spiritual battle. You have access to His armor every day. His Word is always at your fingertips, ready for you to read, study, mediate on, memorize, and apply.

PRAY

Thank God for the last twelve weeks getting to know Him and other women in your life. Thank Him for His kindness. Thank God for His companionship in your life and the lives of others.

_____

_____

_____

_____

WEEK 1........ WEEK 2........ WEEK 3........ WEEK 4........ WEEK 5........ WEEK 6........ WEEK 7........ WEEK 8........ WEEK 9........ WEEK 10 .... WEEK 11.....

WEEK 12

DAY 5

Final Remarks and Personal Salutation from the Founder of Proven Men Ministries, Ltd.

- Enjoy God, minister to your family, and do the things you've learned and will learn.

- Keep praying for and having fellowship with your brothers and sisters in Christ.

- Know that you're dearly loved and are God's most treasured possession!

- Keep finding meaningful and joyful ways to worship your precious Lord.

- Continue each day in study, in God's Word, and in prayer. Make sure you begin your next study immediately!

I have no greater joy than to hear that fellow Proven Men and Women are walking victoriously in the truth! Please make my joy complete by being like-minded, having the same love and passion for the Lord and each other, and becoming one in spirit and purpose. I look forward to reading letters and testimonies from you and witnessing the work of the Lord through your life and in the lives of those you touch.

Go forth! By presenting yourself to God as an approved workman, you will no longer need to be ashamed but will confidently handle the word of truth, which God entrusts to you, His friend (see 2 Timothy 2:15).

Keep referring to the PROVEN acronym to remind yourself how to live and Whom to live for!

Passionate for God.

Repentant in spirit.

Open and honest.

Victorious in living.

Eternal in perspective.

Networked with other PROVEN WOMEN.

 **SPECIAL NOTES**

Congratulations! You have finished the study. Our experience has been that lasting freedom (healing) comes when you regularly revisit this material and continue to do the important "Heartwork" the study helps to facilitate. Therefore, we encourage you to consider making a plan to walk through the study again alongside a different woman or group of women this time. If you have a person in mind, reach out today and ask them if they'd be interested in doing the study with you. Also, please consider joining our ministry support team by financially supporting our ministry with a generous tax-deductible donation. You can learn more about partnership opportunities at our website: *www.ProvenWomen.org.*

My Dear Sister,

As Proven Ministries continues to grow, we have been immensely blessed to hear of countless women who have discovered freedom and healing. This is no small feat, and such personal experiences of victory have the capability to inspire and offer hope to a great many. As God is the Master Storyteller, we believe that each child of His is made with a custom-tailored story in mind. There are no two alike, and with each story rests the potential for a triumphant testimony to be found. Such testimonies can be used to shine a light on all those who have been hiding in the dark for so long. I wanted to personally ask you if you would share your testimony with our team. Your testimony of how the Proven Women Devotional has supported your journey towards restoration and freedom could be used to inspire thousands. If you feel led to share your story to help others, please email your testimony to *info@provenwomen.org.*

CONGRATULATIONS!

Welcome to the Proven Team.

As a graduate we are excited to offer you a special gift
to honor your completion of the study.

This will also give you really cool perks throughout our ministry.

Please email, text, or call to receive your gift today.

info@provenwomen.org
803-900-3688

Appendix A: Names of God

GOD THE FATHER

Abba Father (Romans 8:15)

Ancient of Days (Daniel 7:9, 13)

Creator (Isaiah 27:11)

Father (Luke 11:2)

Father of the Heavenly Lights (James 1:17)

God Almighty (Genesis 17:1–2)

God Most High (Genesis 14:18–22)

God of Abraham, Isaac, and Jacob (Exodus 3:6)

God of Heaven and Earth (Ezra 1:2; 5:11)

God of Hope (Romans 15:13)

God Our Father (Ephesians 1:2)

Holy One (Isaiah 43:15)

Judge of the Earth (Psalm 94:2)

King (Isaiah 43:15)

King of Glory (Psalm 24:7–10)

King of Heaven (Daniel 4:37)

Living God (Romans 9:26)

Lord of All the Earth (Joshua 3:11)

Righteous Father (John 17:25)

The God of All Comfort (2 Corinthians 1:3)

The Great and Awesome God (Nehemiah 1:5)

The Lord Is My Banner (Exodus 17:15)

The Lord Our Maker (Psalm 95:6)

The Lord Who Heals (Exodus 15:26)

GOD THE SON

Advocate (Job 16:19; 1 John 2:1)

Alpha and Omega (Revelation 1:8)

Author and Perfecter (Hebrews 12:2)

Blessed and Only Ruler (Hebrews 2:10)

Bread of God (John 6:33)

Bread of Life (John 6:35)

Bridegroom (Matthew 25:1–10)

Chosen One (Isaiah 41:1)

Christ Jesus Our Lord (2 Timothy 1:2)

Cornerstone (1 Peter 2:6)

Deliverer (Romans 11:26)

Faithful and True (Revelation 19:11)

Foundation (1 Corinthians 3:11)

Fountain (Zechariah 13:1)

Friend (Matthew 11:19)

Gate (John 10:7–9)

Good Shepherd (John 10:11, 14)

High Priest (Hebrews 3:1)

Holy One (Acts 2:27)

Horn of Salvation (Luke 1:69)

I Am (John 8:58)

Immanuel (Matthew 1:23)

King of Kings (1 Timothy 6:14)

Lamb of God (John 1:36)

Light of the World (John 8:12)

Lord of Lords (1 Timothy 6:15)

Master (Matthew 23:8)

Mediator (1 Timothy 2:5)

Messiah (John 1:41)

Mighty God (Isaiah 9:6)

One and Only (John 1:14)

Our Righteousness (1 Corinthians 1:30)

Prince of Peace (Isaiah 9:6)

Redeemer (Isaiah 44:24)

Rock (1 Corinthians 10:4)

Ruler (Matthew 2:6)

Savior (Luke 2:11)

Son of Man (Matthew 8:20)

Sure Foundation (Isaiah 28:16)

Teacher (John 13:14)

The Almighty (Revelation 1:8)

The Beginning (Colossians 1:18)

The Way (John 14:6)

True God (1 John 5:20)
Truth (John 14:6)
Wonderful Counselor (Isaiah 9:6)
Word of God (Revelation 19:13)

GOD THE HOLY SPIRIT
Breath of the Almighty (Job 32:8)
Counselor (John 14:16)
Deposit (Ephesians 1:13–14)
Eternal Spirit (Hebrews 9:14)
Holy Spirit of God (Ephesians 4:30)
Living Water (John 7:38–39)
Promise of the Father (Acts 1:4)
Seal (Ephesians 4:30)

Spirit of Faith (1 Corinthians 12:9)
Spirit of Fire (Isaiah 4:4)
Spirit of God (Genesis 1:2)
Spirit of Judgment (Isaiah 4:4)
Spirit of Knowledge (Isaiah 11:2)
Spirit of Life (Romans 8:2)
Spirit of Power (Isaiah 11:2)
Spirit of Promise (Ephesians 1:13)
Spirit of Truth (John 14:17)
Spirit of Understanding (Isaiah 11:2)
Spirit of Wisdom (Isaiah 11:2)
Spirit Who Intercedes for Us (Romans 8:26–27)
Spirit Who Searches All Things (1 Corinthians 2:10)

APPENDIX B: ATTRIBUTES OF GOD

GOD IS:

Love (unfailing love)
(Exod 15:13; Psa 13:5– 6; 52:8; 1 John 4:7–16; Rom 8:38–39; Eph 3:17–19; 5:1–2)

Good
(2 Chron 7:3; Psa 119:68; 135:3; 145:9; Mark 10:18)

Faithful
(Deut 7:9; Psa 18:25; 33:4; 111:7; 145:13; 1 John 1:9; Heb 10:23; 1 Pet 4:19; 1 Cor 1:9; 1 Thes 5:24; 2 Thes 3:3)

Merciful
(Deut 4:31; Jer 3:12; 2 Sam 24:14; Neh 9:31; Dan 9:9; 2 Cor 4:1; Rom 11:31; 212:1; Eph 2:4; Luke 6:36)

Kind
(2 Sam 22:51; Isa 54:8; Jer 9:24; Psa 18:50; Luke 6:25; Rom 2:4; 11:22)

Patient (forbearing/long-suffering)
(Jer 15:15; Neh 9:17; Psa 145:8; 1 Tim 1:16; Rom 3:25; 2 Pet 3:15)

Compassionate
(Exod 22:27; 34:6; Neh 9:17; Psa 86:15; 103:8; 111:4; Joel 2:13)

Just
(Deut 32:4; Job 37:23; Psa 99 :4; Luke 18:7– 8; 2 Thes 1:5; Rev 16:7)

Righteous
(Isa 51:6; Jer 9:24; 23:6; Judges 5:11; Ezra 9:15; Neh 9:8; Psa 4:1; 7:9; 89:14; 97:12; 116:6; 119:137; 129:4; 145:17)

Jealous (jealous for our love)
(Exod 34:14; Deut 4:24; Zech 8:2; 2 Cor 11:2)

Gracious (grace)
(Josh 24:19; Isa 26:10; Neh 9:17; Exod 34:6–7; Psa 86:15; 108:8; 111:4; 116:5; 145:8; Titus 3:5–7; Eph 2:8)

Holy
(Isa 6:3; 57:15; Psa 30:4; 77:13; 99:3, 9; Matt 1:35; John 17:11; Rom 7:12; 1 Pet 1:15–16; Rev 4:8)

Wise (wisdom)
(Isa 28:29; Jer 10:12; 1 Cor 1:30; Col 2:2–3)

Truthful (veracity/truth)
(Num 23:19; Isa 45:19; Psa 31:5; John 3:33; 14:6)

Almighty
(Gen 17:1; 35:11; Psa 24:10; 46:7; 68:14; 80:7, 14; 84:1; 89:9; 2 Cor 6:18; James 5:4)

Pure
(2 Sam 22:27; Psa 18:26; 1 John 3:3)

Perfect/Blameless
(2 Sam 22:26, 31; Psa 18:25, 30; 19:7; Deut 32:4; Matt 5:48)

Gentle
(Matt 11:29; 21:5)

Forgiving
(Neh 9:17; Num 14:18; Psa 86:5; 99:8)

Wrathful (avenging evil)
(Nahum 1:2; Psa 7:11; Rom 1:18; 5:9; 9:22)

Independent (self-existing/self-sufficient)
(Psa 115:3; John 5:26; Rom 11:35–36)

Infinite (from everlasting to everlasting/beyond measure)
(Psa 33:11; 41:13; 90:1–2; Heb 1:8–12)

Eternal
(Gen 21:33; Neh 9 :5–6 ; Deut 33:27; Psa 93:2; John 8:58; Rev 1:8)

Supreme (pre-eminent)
(Exod 15:1, 11, 18; Psa 115:3; Col 1:15–19)

Incomprehensible (beyond full description or understanding)
(Job 36:26; Psa 104:1–4; Isa 36:26; 40:18–26; Rom 11:33–34; 1 Tim 6:15)

Majestic
(Exod 15:6 –7, 11; 1 Chron 29:11; Job 37:22; Psa 8:1, 9; 93:1; Jude 25)

Sovereign
(Isa 46:10; Dan 4:35; Psa 135:6; Eph1:11; Acts 4:24)

Immutable (unchanging)
(Malachi 3:6; Psa 102:27; James 1:17; Heb 6:17; 13:8)

Omnipotent (all-powerful/infinite power)
(Gen 18:14; 1 Sam 2:6 –7; Psa 18:13–15; Matt 19:26)

Omnipresent (everywhere)
(Jer 23:23–24; 2 Chron 2:6; Psa 139:7–16; Acts 17:27–28)

Omniscient (all-knowing/infinite knowledge)
(1 Kings 8:39; Psa 139:1– 6; Prov 3:19–20; 1 Cor 2:10)

Immortal (not created, but ever existing)
(Rom 1:23; 1 Tim 1:17; 6:15)

APPENDIX C: BOOK RECOMMENDATIONS

Life with a Capital L by Matt Heard (Multnomah, 2014)

False Intimacy: Understanding the Struggle of Sexual Addiction by Dr. Harry Schaumburg (NavPress, 1992)

Sexual Healing, God's Plan for the Sanctification of Broken Lives by Dr. David Kyle Foster (AbeBooks, 1995)

Lord, Is It Warfare? Teach Me to Stand by Kay Arthur (WaterBrook Press 2000)

APPENDIX D: DEVELOPING A HEART OF WORSHIP

The letter **P** in PROVEN stands for Passionate for God. Part of being passionate is having a heart of worship. What does this mean? It's when your desire to live for Christ becomes a consuming fire (see Hebrews 12:28–29).[1] Do you want to praise Jesus from deep within your heart and soul? Do you long to know God, to learn His names, and to see Him in His glory?

There are many ways to strengthen or deepen your passion for God, including improvements in your prayer life, singing and listening to Christ-centered songs, and writing your own psalms and letters to God. The key is to engage in purposeful worship of God and pursue intimacy with Him. This article suggests some ways to crank up the heat and allow God to fuel the flames. Use your freedom in Christ to develop other forms of thoughtful worship and praise. Be creative and make it exciting. Make a plan, or you won't do it.

Some suggestions for developing a greater heart of worship include:

Pray with passion. God is not a vending machine that gives you anything you want if you just ask. The Lord is a real being, and He wants a real relationship with you. Prayer is not about receiving things from God. It's all about communication with the living Lord. It's about striving toward becoming best friends. Honestly evaluate your prayer life. Is it your goal to become so close to God that you know His will and long to see it accomplished, or do you rush to ask Him to give you something?

If the only time you ever spoke to your neighbor was to borrow a tool, what kind of friendship would that be? God deserves better and wants more than a hurried "bless me" request. Besides, He is more interested in living the story with you. The more time you spend with God, the more you'll know His will—His good, pleasing, and perfect will (Romans 12:2). Then, when you do ask God to do something, it will be asking Him to do that which He already desires to accomplish. Prayer also includes listening and waiting. Don't be in such a rush to end prayer. Talk to the Lord as a personal being, sharing your struggles, fears, hopes, and dreams. Become friends.

A good way of keeping the focus off yourself (and, hence, not making selfish requests) is to replace asking for your own blessings with petitioning God on behalf of others, such as a co-worker, your pastor, or those you know are hurting or sick. *It's okay to ask God what He wants to accomplish through you and your prayers.* God doesn't hide Himself from those who earnestly seek Him and long to do His will. Again, guard against viewing God as a tool for bestowing blessings. Make your top priority getting to know God.

Tip: Read a book on prayer such as *The Circle Maker: Praying Circles Around Your Biggest Dreams and Greatest Fears* by Mark Batterson. Read it slowly; even just a few pages at a time. Ask your pastor for other books.

---

[1] "Therefore, since we are receiving a kingdom that cannot be shaken, let us be thankful, and so worship God acceptably with reverence and awe, for our 'God is a consuming fire.'"

Pray with others. Consider prayer walks in the woods with your wife, if you're married, or other Proven Women. Passionate praying builds strong bonds. Don't miss out.

Read the Bible daily. The Bible is God's very Word to you. It actually nourishes your soul just like food nourishes your body (Matthew 4:4).[2] The Word of God is living and active and penetrates a person's soul and spirit (Hebrews 4:12).[3] Therefore, do not neglect it (Psalm 119:6).[4]

Reading the Bible to find out about God is far different from reading it as part of your plan of pursuing the Lord to get to know Him. If your reading of the Bible has been dull or infrequent, change your heart and mind-set. Set your sights on reading to become intimate with God. Guaranteed—if you seek the Lord with all your heart, you'll fall in love with Him. He has no blemish or spot to turn your eyes away.

Consider beginning afresh by reading Psalm 119:1–40. Adopt this psalm as your own plea. Ask God to reveal Himself to you. Determine in your heart that you'll set out to enjoy God instead of reading the Bible to check off a list of things Christians are supposed to do. If you still struggle with desiring the things of God, spend time reading Psalm 51 and wrestling before the Lord until He grants you repentance and creates in you a clean and new heart that lives for Him. Don't take no for an answer.

When you read the Bible, read slowly, asking the Lord to open your eyes and heart to what He has to say to you. Don't race. Read until God shows you something new or exciting, then dwell on that point. Talk to God about it. Meditate on that new insight, and plan how it can be put into practice in your life. Get into a habit of making notes or circling words. Contemplate how to do what it says. You'll find that God has a lot to say if you'll listen and seek.

Study the Bible. This is slightly different from reading the Bible. By regularly studying passages, you should grow even deeper in your relationship with God. Consider a word study. For instance, use a Bible concordance and look up every verse containing a particular word, such as "perseverance," "suffering," "hope," or "grace." Choose a new word each time. Be sure to ask God to give you deeper understanding of these passages and to teach you what He wants you to learn about Him and about living a Proven life. Then do what the Lord reveals. Apply it in your daily life.

Write psalms to God. A special way of focusing on God and drawing closer to Him is by writing letters to God, which can be your own version of

---

2. "Man does not live on bread alone, but on every word that comes from the mouth of God."

3. "For the word of God is living and active. Sharper than any double-edged sword, it penetrates even to dividing soul and spirit, joints and marrow; it judges the thoughts and attitudes of the heart."

4. "Then I would not be put to shame when I consider all your commands."

a psalm. It's easier to do this than you think (see Appendix H). The Bible repeatedly tells you to sing psalms, and writing them is a form of singing them from your heart and soul (Colossians 3:16).[5] God will be pleased to read your heartfelt letters to Him. You'll also get to better know and appreciate the Lord!

Sing songs or hymns. Singing songs to the Lord isn't just for Sunday church services. Pouring out your heart in singing to God adds a different element of worship that can be deeply moving. Play worshipful songs in your car and at home and sing along. Don't be inhibited in praising the Lord. Ask God to tear down walls so that your heart is free to meet with and worship Him. It's okay to lift your hands in worship. Bust out of your constricted heart.

Tip: Consider strictly limiting or eliminating altogether secular music and television, because such songs and programs often contain values inconsistent with pursuing God with all of your heart and otherwise compete in terms of time and energy with your worship of God.

Meditate upon the names and attributes of God. You were created to worship God and to experience more and more of His nature. Meditating upon the beautiful names of God helps you get to know your dear Creator on a deeper level. Who doesn't like their name sweetly whispered by a loved one? Read God's names softly or aloud, but make it your goal to show reverence and invite Him into your heart as you communicate with Him in this intimate way. (See Appendix A for a list of God's names.) Similarly, meditating upon the attributes of God opens you up to His perfect nature and helps tear down walls that keep you trying to control life. The more you see God as good, the more you will allow Him into your life! (See Appendix B for a list of God's attributes.)

Condition your mind. Every man and woman daydreams and has a private thought life, but God tells you to take captive every idle thought and make it conform to Christ (2 Corinthians 10:5).[6] You're not to be conformed to this world (Romans 12:2)[7] or to love anything of this world (1 John 2:15).[8] Even fantasies about being a hero or winning the lottery can distract you from focusing your thoughts upon and trusting in God. Replace your former way of thinking with things that are true, noble, right, pure, lovely, admirable, excellent, or praiseworthy (Philippians 4:8).[9] Put a bouncer at the door to your

---

5. "Let the word of Christ dwell in you richly as you teach and admonish one another with all wisdom, and as you sing psalms, hymns and spiritual songs with gratitude in your hearts to God."

6. "We demolish arguments and every pretension that sets itself up against the knowledge of God, and we take captive every thought to make it obedient to Christ."

7. "Do not conform any longer to the pattern of this world, but be transformed by the renewing of your mind."

8. "Do not love the world or anything in the world. If anyone loves the world, the love of the Father is not in him."

9. "Finally, brothers, whatever is true, whatever is noble, whatever is right, whatever is pure, whatever is lovely, whatever is admirable—if anything is excellent or praiseworthy—think about such things."

mind. If you don't, then worldly lust will always be an occupant.

Include others. Each woman needs relationships. God created you to love Him, which is the greatest commandment, and to love others, the second greatest commandment (Matthew 22:37–39).[10] By developing and cultivating relationships with others who are actively seeking the Lord, you'll have friends you can talk to openly, sharing your struggles as well as engaging in praise and worship. Two Proven Women are as iron sharpening iron (Proverbs 27:17).[11] Therefore, link up with other Proven Women. Also, attend church to join with others in worship. Corporate worship that joins hearts and voices in hymns and praise to Jesus is uniquely different from how one person praises God alone at home. Don't miss out on it!

There are many ways to live for the Lord and worship and praise Him. God desires that they become your way of life, but you must plan for them. Go ahead and schedule each of these things into your daily life right now. Write out a daily timetable. Rise early each day to meet with God, and fix your gaze upon Him throughout the day. Eliminate things that compete or hinder your new lineup, or else you'll soon forget your promises and commitments and return to the former habits you had in living on the fringes of the Lord's courts instead of joining Him at His table.

---

10. "'Love the Lord your God with all your heart and with all your soul and with all your mind.' This is the first and greatest commandment. And the second is like it: 'Love your neighbor as yourself.'"
11. "As iron sharpens iron, so one man sharpens another."

APPENDIX E: THE ARMOR OF GOD (EPHESIANS 6:11–19)

❶ Helmet of Salvation

Sin starts in your heart but is carried out in your mind. If you don't take captive every idle thought and make it obedient to Christ (2 Corinthians 10:5), you're giving up valuable ground to the enemy. In fact, don't finish or enjoy evil thoughts, or they'll master you. Un-controlled thoughts become action, and actions become habits. Un-disciplined thinking keeps you in bondage to things like worry, greed, lust, doubts, and twisted doctrines. Therefore, immediately destroy all thoughts which are contrary to God's Word or your position in Christ. Slow down and listen to the quiet voice of your Commander in Chief through the earphone in your helmet and follow His orders. Read Philippians 4:8 and Colossians 3:12 for reminders of the types of things you are to dwell upon.

❷ Breastplate of Righteousness

You guard your heart, and do battle against the old sinful nature. You protect your heart from condemnation (which are lies) because you know and believe that God gave you His righteousness. By confessing your sins, repenting and remaining in God's camp, you won't give Satan an opportunity to take you captive or attack your vital organs.

❸ Shield of Faith

Satan's fiery darts of fear and doubt are quickly extinguished when you hold the shield of faith—soaked daily in the eternal water of life (God's Word). You believe and rest in God's specific truths. You never let your guard down but actively build up and rely upon your faith.

❹ Sword of the Spirit (Word of God)

Take the offensive in the battle. You won't find a better weapon for a spiritual fight than the Word of God (Hebrews 4:12). Use appropriate Scripture to submit to God and to resist the devil and he will flee (James 4:7). Grab hold of Scripture verses and fight back in the strength of the Lord, such as the twelve memory verses.

❺ Belt of Truth

Stand firm in the truth. Know it, believe it, embrace it, and use it! (Say to yourself: "I am saved from eternal condemnation, I do not doubt that God is good or that He is sovereign over my life, and I test all teachings against God's Word.")

❻ Prayer (Knees)

God answers real prayers. The condition of your heart and motives are key. For instance, you are to pray in the spirit at all times and especially for others (Ephesians 6:18), but, requests to God mixed with selfish motives are not prayers at all (James 4:3). God promises that when your prayers are in accordance with His will, the flood gates of heaven are opened (1 John 5:14). Therefore, the place of power is on your knees in submission to God in reverence and awe, seeking His perfect will.

❼ Gospel of Peace

You wear God's shoes and eagerly run toward peace. By being humble, and especially forgiving others (Hebrews 12:1–17), you live out peace with God and others and thereby outpace the adversary. You will remain in peak condition and do whatever it takes to live out peace. You will not keep accounts, withhold love, or harbor bitterness.

APPENDIX F: HOW DO I FEEL?

To be open and honest in relationships you must learn to recognize your feelings. Use this short list as an aid in identifying your feelings. Keep returning here frequently.

Happy?
ecstatic?
joyful?
thankful?
loved?
loving?
grateful?
included?
glad?

Sad?
disliked?
unloved?
grieving?
sorry?
regretful?
miserable?
remorseful?
distrusted?

Confident?
respected?
secure?
safe?
sure?
capable?
optimistic?
appreciated?
pleased?

Angry?
mad?
hateful?
bitter?
upset?
furious?
outraged?

Depressed?
insulted?
lonely?
bored?
withdrawn?
excluded?
incompetent?
neglected?
abandoned?

Stressed?
nervous?
tense?
negative?
exhausted?
debilitated?
weary?

Indifferent?
unconcerned?
weird?
strange?
foolish?

Afraid?
threatened?
insecure?
unsafe?
paranoid?

Discouraged?
frustrated?
exasperated?
overwhelmed?
defeated?
disappointed?

Hurt?
betrayed?
misled?
resentful?
cold?

Content?
peaceful?
gratified?

Anxious?
worried?
embarrassed?

Confused?
dismayed?
unsure?
perplexed?
shocked?

Jealous?
envious?

Greedy?
selfish?
arrogant?
smug?

APPENDIX G: THE PURPOSE, PRACTICE, AND POWER OF PRAYER OF PROVEN WOMEN

IN THE NAME OF JESUS

- Jesus will do what you ask in His name to bring glory to God the Father (John 14:13).

- You may ask Christ for anything in His name, and He will do it (John 14:14).

- Asking in Jesus' name is not merely saying the words, "In Jesus' name." It's similar to asking as though Jesus Himself were making the request.

RIGHT MOTIVES

- You don't receive because you ask with wrong motives (James 4:3).

- If you ask according to the will of God with faith, you shall receive it (1 John 5:14–15).

HUMILITY

- Abraham submitted to God while praying, even recognizing he was made from ashes. He didn't make selfish requests but prayed for others (Genesis 18:22–33).

REAL FAITH

- If you have faith and don't doubt, you can do all things (Matthew 21:21).

- If you believe, you'll receive what you ask for in prayer (Matthew 21:22).

- If you have faith, you'll do even greater things than what you have seen (John 14:12).

- Believe by calling on the Lord, because He answers His children (Psalm 17:6).

- Don't be anxious, but in all things, pray (Philippians 4:6–7).

JOINED TO THE LORD

- If you remain in Christ, and His Word in you, ask, and it will be given (John 15:7).

SINGLE-MINDED

- Be clear-minded and self-controlled so that you can pray (1 Peter 4:7–8).

- When you seek with all of your heart, you will find the Lord (Jeremiah 29:13).

GUIDED BY THE HOLY SPIRIT

- The Holy Spirit helps us pray (Romans 8:26).

- Pray in the Spirit (Ephesians 6:18; Jude 20).

EARNEST

- Elijah's earnest prayer stopped the rain for three years and then brought the rain (James 5:17–18).

- As Jesus prayed, His sweat was like drops of blood (Luke 22:44).

PERSISTENT

- Keep praying like the widow who continually went before the judge until he gave her what she wanted (Luke 18:1–5).

- Keep asking like the man with guests, who kept knocking at his neighbor's door at midnight until he received bread (Luke 11:5–9).

AT ALL TIMES AND IN ALL THINGS

- Pray continually (1 Thessalonians 5:17).

- Pray on all occasions with all kinds of prayers (Ephesians 6:18).

LOVE OTHERS AND PUT THEM FIRST

- You receive because you obey by loving God and others (1 John 3:21–23).

- Above all, love others (1 Peter 4:7–8).

FORGIVE OTHERS

- When you pray, forgive others so that your Father in heaven will forgive you (Mark 11:25).

- Pray for those who persecute you (Matthew 5:44).

PRAY FOR OTHERS

- It's a sin not to pray for others (1 Samuel 12:23).

- Join others in their struggle by praying for them (Romans 15:30).

- Stay alert and keep praying for others (Ephesians 1:15–19).

PRAY SELFLESSLY

- The Lord was displeased by the Pharisee who prayed about himself (Luke 18:11).

- Don't pray like hypocrites to be seen by men (Matthew 6:5).

SPECIFIC PRAYERS FOR OTHERS

- Ask God to give others the spirit of wisdom so they can know Him better (Ephesians 1:17–18).

- Ask God to strengthen others (Ephesians 3:16).

- Ask God to allow others to grasp the depth of His love for them (Ephesians 3:17–18).

- Ask God to help others be active in sharing their faith in the Lord (Philemon 6).

THE POWER OF PRAYER OF PROVEN WOMEN

- God tells you to pray, and He is pleased to meet with you and is moved by prayer.

- His church is to be a house of prayer (Matthew 21:13).

- If you're in trouble or sick, pray (James 5:13–14).

- The prayers of a righteous man are powerful and effective (James 5:16).

- The Lord hears the prayers of the righteous and delivers them from trouble (Psalm 34:15–17).

PROVEN WOMEN YIELD TO AND RELY UPON GOD

- Righteousness comes from God (Romans 3:22).

- God hears you not because of good things you've done but because of His mercy (Titus 3:5; Daniel 9:17–18).

- The righteous live by faith in God (Romans 1:17; Galatians 3:11).

- The righteous obey God (Romans 2:13).

- You can't become righteous by observing the law (Romans 3:20).

- Righteousness is by faith (Romans 3:22).

APPENDIX H: NETWORK PARTNERSHIPS, A KEY TO BREAKING FREE FROM THE GRIP OF PORNOGRAPHY

Fighting to overcome pornography or other sexually compulsive activities is one of the hardest struggles many women will face in life. At times, it can seem like you're the only one in the battle. There are many self-help books, but they never seem to bring lasting relief. You keep asking yourself, "Why doesn't it work for me? Why am I still in bondage to sin?"

The one thing missing from a self-directed healing path is a *Network Partner*. Just how important is this? Well, no serious athlete would compete without having a coach, no successful business lacks managers, and no lasting government exists without various forms of accountability. Why would a man plan to battle by himself the sin he has yet to overcome on his own after years of trying? Let's face it, we all need accountability. In fact, God designed you to be accountable to others, and lasting freedom requires walking the road to victory together with another woman.

What holds you back from living this out? Perhaps pangs of shame, guilt, and self-condemnation strike fear in your heart at the thought of openly sharing your failures and struggles. Maybe your pride and stubbornness won't let you admit you need help. Whatever your particular reason for shying away from accountability, one of the largest barriers to experiencing lasting freedom is a refusal to link up with another woman.

WHAT IS A "NETWORK PARTNER"?

The word accountability means "being obligated to account for your actions" or "being responsible to another." A *Network Partner* includes, but is more than confessing sins (James 5:16), submitting to others (Ephesians 5:21) and engaging in relationships. Although few Christian women quibble over whether they're accountable to God, often those trapped in bondage to pornography balk at God's proclamation that His children must also be accountable to and *networking* with others. The solution is not trying harder in your own power, but addressing the stubborn pride that keeps you from surrendering. In fact, this same pride feeds your indulgence in forbidden sensual pleasures.

BIBLICAL NETWORK PARTNERSHIPS

The Bible paints a vivid picture of the partnering relationship that develops through accountability among the brotherhood of believers. Consider the following ways the Lord says you are to be mutually accountable to others:

- Helping in time of need (Proverbs 17:17).
- Providing instruction (Romans 15:14).
- Comforting (2 Corinthians 1:3–5).
- Serving in love (Galatians 5:13).
- Gently restoring (Galatians 6:1).
- Carrying others' burdens (Galatians 6:2).

- Speaking the truth in love (Ephesians 4:15).

- Admonishing (Colossians 3:16).

- Building up (1 Thessalonians 5:11).

- Correcting (2 Timothy 4:2).

- Encouraging daily (Hebrews 3:13).

- Spurring on (Hebrews 10:24).

- Meeting together (Hebrews 10:25).

Clearly, Biblical *networking* is centered upon open and real relationships, and it requires you to concentrate on others instead of yourself, your rights, your expectations, and your circumstances. By removing yourself from the center, you not only become useful in the lives of others, but also gain an eternal perspective so necessary for living out a Proven life.

True Biblical *networking* positions you to engage in spiritually mature roles in aiding others, such as:

- Keeping confidences (Proverbs 16:28; 17:9).

- Warning to flee idolatry (1 Corinthians 10:14).

- Encouraging to purify self (2 Corinthians 12:21).

- Inspiring to stand firm (Philippians 4:1).

- Warning against being idle (1 Thessalonians 5:14).

- Urging to abstain from sin (1 Peter 2:11).

- Pointing toward heaven and staying pure (2 Peter 3:14).

- Reminding to love others (1 John 4:7).

A *Network Partner* is just that, a partner. Each are co-pilgrims, sharing similar goals and desiring the other to succeed. Both support, serve, and spur the other. As iron sharpens iron, so do two Proven Women sharpen each other (Proverbs 27:17).

PRACTICAL MATTERS FOR NETWORK PARTNERSHIPS

Are you ready to follow the Lord's teachings and ways by incorporating *networking* into your life? Below are some practical ways of beginning the process.

Choosing your *Network Partner.* Your Networking Partner should be someone with a similar goal of seeking after the Lord with all of her heart. She doesn't necessarily need to struggle with the same sin, but it's important that she has a soft heart and wants to grow closer to the Lord. Don't eliminate a woman merely because she isn't a spiritual giant. A heart that desires to grow will make her a great accountability partner.

She must be willing to commit to being *open and honest.* One of the biggest problems many women face is a reluctance to be vulnerable with others. Therefore, your *networking partner* must be willing to push through discomfort. Each of you needs to share intimate details regarding struggles, failures, hopes, dreams, and victories. This includes recognizing and then talking about feelings. Each must have the freedom and expectation to ask the other hard personal questions. Of course, confidences must be kept, because nothing breaks down a relationship faster than gossip (Proverbs 11:13; 16:28; 20:19).

Finally, your primary *networking partner* should not be your spouse or any other person of the opposite sex. There are many reasons, including that you need to develop other intimate relationships in order to foster a better relationship with your husband. In addition, it's damaging to a marriage to turn it into an accountability relationship, especially in the area of sexual sins. It often leads to a spouse engaging in a heightened role of looking for and finding faults in order to point out every sin committed. Moreover, it's not necessarily in the best interest of a spouse to know every minute detail of sexual sins, which can cause needless damage. For example, you should not confess to your spouse each and every lustful thought, which likely includes his friends. This will make him feel insecure, inadequate, and jealous. In short, you need a safe place to confess your sins in Godly accountability with other Proven Women.

Finding a Network Partner. Your church is one of the best places to look. There you can meet and develop relationships with women at a variety of women's functions, such as prayer meetings, Bible studies, breakfasts, and church-sponsored sports activities. You may also link up with women at church events such as coffee after church, corporate meetings such as prayer services, or a small group. You can also ask a pastor or other church leader for potential *networking partners*. Many churches have women's ministry leaders who you can talk to for help finding accountability.

These principles apply equally for teens looking for *networking partners*. Of course, the teen would contact the Youth Pastor and also look to youth ministries at church. In addition, there are some good outside Christian organizations to consider as potential places to look, such as Fellowship of Christian Athletes, Navigators, Youth for Christ, or Young Life.

If you're not regularly attending church, it may be time to start afresh (see Hebrews 10:25). There also are online accountability groups such as www.BeFreeinChrist.com. You can ask someone from a group such as this to work through the study with you, hold you accountable, or be a source of encouragement.

Finding a *Networking Partner* requires that you move outside of your comfort zone. It will even require that you take the initiative. It will be worth it because it will help you engage in open relationships and to *network* with other believers, which are essential components to living a Proven life. There is simply no replacement for personal interactions with others.

Deciding to take the risk. Right now, you may be facing a huge dilemma: "If I don't gain a *Networking Partner*, I won't experience lasting freedom and live a Proven life; but if I do share my struggle with others in the church, I may be judged or rejected." This fear is real. It's what keeps most Christian women planted in the pews. However, God demands that our sins be exposed to light to be eradicated, and accountability is a primary method. That doesn't mean there won't be pain associated with the process. In fact, if one *networking* relationship doesn't work, find another. Freedom is not a one-shot deal, but a new and lasting Proven lifestyle. Accept that God is sovereign and will provide you with all the strength you need in every circumstance.

Using the Proven Women study. The 12-week study was specifically designed for use with *networking partners* and can be a terrific way to initiate or strengthen accountability. First, each woman personally opens her heart to change while meeting with the Lord during the daily study. Second, the study incorporates times of prayer for your *networking partner*. Third, the study is geared toward weekly discussions. There's also a Leader's Guide to help you form support groups.

CONCLUSION

Many, if not most, women in the church face significant struggles with sexual purity, including pornography and masturbation. Most remain in bondage because they don't want to be the first to risk seeking out *networking partners*. Won't you break the mold, for your sake and the other women in your church who need it as much as you do? The prescription for lasting healing is incorporating all six letters of a Proven life, including *networking* with other Godly women. *Networking* is God's way of putting the final stamp upon you and freeing you from the false intimacy of pornography and masturbation. Don't stop short of God's promises and power by remaining isolated and closed. Choose today to take all steps necessary to link up with another woman in an *open and honest* networking partnership.

 **ENDNOTES**

1. Good Sex 2.0: What (Almost) Nobody Will Tell You About Sex-Session 4

2. Matt Heard, *Life with a Capital L*

3. Merriam-Webster Dictionary, "beauty"

4. Merriam-Webster Dictionary, "beauty"

5. Dr. Jeanne Brooks-Gunn, article, "The Developing Brain and Porn"

6. Dr. Jeanne Brooks-Gunn, article, "The Developing Brain and Porn"

7. Dr. David Kyle Foster, *Sexual Healing, God's Plan for the Sanctification of Broken Lives*, p. 194

8. Dr. David Kyle Foster, *Sexual Healing, God's Plan for the Sanctification of Broken Lives*, p. 191

9. Dr. Harry Schaumburg, *False Intimacy: Understanding the Struggle of Sexual Addiction*, p. 22

10. Dr. Harry Schaumburg, *False Intimacy: Understanding the Struggle of Sexual Addiction*, p. 31

11. Dr. Harry Schaumburg, *False Intimacy: Understanding the Struggle of Sexual Addiction*, p. 38

12. Dr. Harry Schaumburg, *False Intimacy: Understanding the Struggle of Sexual Addiction*, p. 72

13. Dr. Harry Schaumburg, *False Intimacy: Understanding the Struggle of Sexual Addiction*, p. 80

14. Dr. David Kyle Foster, *Sexual Healing, God's Plan for the Sanctification of Broken Lives*, p. 219

15. Dr. David Kyle Foster, *Sexual Healing, God's Plan for the Sanctification of Broken Lives*, p. 222

16. Dr. David Kyle Foster, *Sexual Healing, God's Plan for the Sanctification of Broken Lives*, p. 272

17. Dr. David Kyle Foster, *Sexual Healing, God's Plan for the Sanctification of Broken Lives*, p. 273

18. Kay Arthur, *Lord, Is It Warfare? Teach Me to Stand*

19. Dr. David Kyle Foster, *Sexual Healing, God's Plan for the Sanctification of Broken Lives*, p. 300

20. C. S. Lewis, *The Screwtape Letters*

Made in the USA
Columbia, SC
15 January 2020